RELIGIOUS COMMITMENT AND

This book is a balanced treatment of religion and politics in a pluralistic society. It describes the foundations of a free democracy, develops a theory of church-state separation, and integrates secular moral ideals with commitments of religious citizens. Just as there should be separation of church and state, there should be a balance between religious and secular arguments regarding law and public policy. To achieve this balance, Audi offers principles that accommodate religious reasons for action but rule out restricting freedom except on grounds of a kind that any rational citizen should accept. He shows how religious and secular moral considerations can be integrated in a world of religious pluralism and proposes ideals of civic virtue that express the mutual respect on which democracy depends. The book should engage readers interested in religion, journalism, or public affairs as well as readers in philosophy, law, political science, and related areas.

> One of the most important questions for the new century is how to balance the demands of politics and of religion. . . . *Religious Commitment and Secular Reason* is the best philosophical treatment to date. Any future discussion should take account of it.
>
> John Haldane, University of St. Andrews

> Audi has been one of the most thoughtful, provocative voices addressing this issue. . . . essential reading for all who would think clearly about religion in politics.
>
> Michael J. Perry, Wake Forest University

> Its analysis and argument should engage serious attention from political philosophers . . . religious scholars who make social and political policy recommendations . . . and denominational and other institutional leaders who make moral pronouncements.
>
> James M. Gustafson, Emory University

> . . . a helpful introduction to the current philosophical debate about religious argument in a liberal democracy, at the same time . . . a distinctive contribution to it . . . a fine text for introducing students to the topic.
>
> Charles Larmore, University of Chicago

Robert Audi is Charles J. Mach Distinguished Professor of Philosophy at the University of Nebraska, Lincoln. His books include *The Structure of Justification* (1993), *Moral Knowledge and Ethical Character* (1997), and (as editor) the widely acclaimed *Cambridge Dictionary of Philosophy*, now in its second edition.

RELIGIOUS COMMITMENT AND SECULAR REASON

ROBERT AUDI

University of Nebraska, Lincoln

PUBLISHED BY THE PRESS SYNDICATE OF THE UNIVERSITY OF CAMBRIDGE
The Pitt Building, Trumpington Street, Cambridge, United Kingdom

CAMBRIDGE UNIVERSITY PRESS
The Edinburgh Building, Cambridge CB2 2RU, UK http://www.cup.cam.ac.uk
40 West 20th Street, New York, NY 10011-4211, USA http://www.cup.org
10 Stamford Road, Oakleigh, Melbourne 3166, Australia
Ruiz de Alarcón 13, 28014 Madrid, Spain

First published 2000

Printed in the United States of America

Typeface Meridien 10/13 pt. *System* QuarkXPress™ 4.04 [AG]

A catalog record for this book is available from the British Library.

Library of Congress Cataloging in Publication Data

Audi, Robert
Religious commitment and secular reason / Robert Audi.
p. cm.
Includes index.
ISBN 0-521-77260-5 (hb) – ISBN 0-521-77570-1 (pbk.)
1. Religion and politics. 2. Citizenship – Moral and ethical aspects. I. Title.
BL65.P7 A84 2000
291.1′ – dc21
99-044606

ISBN 0 521 77260 5 hardback
ISBN 0 521 77570 1 paperback

To the Memory of My Father,
Who Was Fascinated by the Subject

CONTENTS

PREFACE

Religion and politics are perennial topics of concern and debate in any free society. Their interaction has recently become a major preoccupation in many parts of the world and especially in the United States. It is inevitable that reflective religious people should discuss religion and that thoughtful citizens should discuss politics. It is perhaps not inevitable, but it is altogether appropriate, for a liberal democracy – a free and democratic society – in which religion is a major cultural force to concern itself with the relation between religion and politics. This is particularly so where the religions represented in the society imply, or are readily seen to imply, a political philosophy or at least an ethic that bears directly on politics. All that certainly applies to Christianity, Judaism, and Islam, which are immensely important in the contemporary world and are the main religious perspectives of concern in this book.

My primary aim is to articulate a perspective on religion and politics that is appropriate for both citizens and institutions in a liberal democracy. I have in mind particularly, but by no means exclusively, religious citizens and governmental institutions. This task requires a position on separation of church and state. But even more urgently, it demands a good understanding of the proper balance between, on the one hand, religious commitments that bear on what sort of society we should have, and on the other hand, political and other secular considerations pertinent to the same range of objectives.

The broad area of my concern here is what might be called *the ethics of citizenship*. My main question in this domain is what ethical standards are best for religious citizens and for other citizens acting in ways that significantly affect religion. Citizens with roles in governmental or other influential institutions are commonly in the second category and often in the first as well. Parts of the book, however – such as the accounts of civic virtue and of grounds for governmental restrictions of liberty – bear on ethical questions of citizenship in non-religious matters.

I have written on this topic on a number of occasions in the past decade, but there are important aspects of the topic I have not previously addressed, and there is much that should be said to fill out and extend the position I have previously set out. My earlier work has not considered the normative grounding of a free and democratic society: roughly, how it can be justified as a political structure. A major basis for a good theory of the proper relation between religion and politics – applicable both to church-state separation and to the balance between religious and secular considerations in individual conduct – is an account of the ways in which a free democracy can be plausibly grounded. Chapter 1 provides a brief account of this sort. My earlier writings have also omitted consideration of a number of questions about the kinds of public discourse appropriate for religious citizens adhering to the principles I propose. This gap is filled mainly in Chapter 6. Given their much smaller scope, my previous essays do not discuss a number of other theorists addressing the same range of problems; in this respect, too, this book advances and clarifies my position, though even here I avoid lengthy discussions of the literature and often respond to critics, or refer to appropriate literature, in the notes that appear at the end.

As to clarification of the position I have so far set out on these matters, there have been many misinterpretations in the literature, and my experience in presenting my position to various audiences shows that it requires some reflection to get clearly in view. That understanding a complex theoretical perspective should require reflection is not unusual, but in this case there is the added problem that my position has been assimilated by some readers to other broadly liberal views – usually views less accommodating to religion – or, worse still, has been thought to have implications to which no major liberal theorist is committed.

The systematic articulation of my position that this book offers should do more than provide a wider basis for, and systematically set forth, my theory of church-state separation and of the proper balance between religious and political considerations. It should also state the theory in a way that makes it both more accessible and more plausible for general readers. Beyond that, it extends the theory in several directions, including the style and content of public discourse in which religious citizens may most appropriately bring their faith to bear. There are places where philosophers or legal or political theorists or clergy or students of religion will take a special interest; but even these more narrowly focused discussions are couched in as plain language as I could find, and the general movement of the book should be clear to readers with no special background in these fields.

This book has benefited greatly from the comments of friends, colleagues, critics, audiences I have addressed, students I have taught, and other writers on the topic, many (though unfortunately not all) of whom are referred to in the notes. My recent work has been supported by a generous fellowship from the Pew Foundation, by the University of Nebraska, particularly its Center for the Teaching and Study of Applied Ethics and its College of Arts and Sciences Initiative on Public Discourse and Human Values, and by Santa Clara University (where I have twice served terms as Distinguished Professor). Without the research opportunities they have provided, the book would have been at best delayed.

For permission to use, in revised form, material published in my essays, I am grateful to a number of editors and publishers. Although no chapter consists of a previously published work, and none of my previously published essays is reproduced either in its entirety or without revision of any parts of it that do appear, I have drawn substantially on my writings in the past decade. My first essay on this topic, "The Separation of Church and State and the Obligations of Citizenship" (*Philosophy & Public Affairs* 18, 3, 1989), provides background for some of Chapters 2 through 4 and contains some of the main principles defended there. "The Place of Religious Argument in a Free and Democratic Society" *(San Diego Law Review* 30, 4, 1993) is also a source of some of my ideas, particularly in Chapters 3 and 5. A wide-ranging essay called "Liberal Democracy and the Place of Religion in Politics," which appeared in *Religion in the Public Square: The Place of Religious Convictions in Political Debate* (Rowman and Littlefield, 1997), a book written jointly with Nicholas Wolterstorff as discussion partner, has provided material appearing in various places in Chapters 2 through 6. Chapter 6 incorporates parts of my essay "A Liberal Theory of Civic Virtue" *(Social Philosophy and Policy* 15, 1, 1998), and Chapter 7 draws on my "Preventing Abortion as a Test Case for the Justifiability of Violence" *(Journal of Ethics* 1, 2, 1997). Chapter 1 and the conclusion were written entirely for this book.

I cannot name all the people from whom I have learned something important on this general topic since beginning to address it publicly in the 1980s. But both from many conversations and from their work I have learned immensely from Kent Greenawalt, Michael Perry, and Nicholas Wolterstorff. Greenawalt's work was an early stimulus, and his books and many articles on the topic have been a lasting resource. Perry's writings have brought home new dimensions of the topic and posed challenges I am still addressing. Wolterstorff has provided both a contrasting perspective from which I continue to learn and insightful criticism that has led to many improvements. For detailed and helpful comments on and discussions of earlier versions of the entire manuscript I am grateful to Stephen Kershnar, Brian Lepard, and James B. Murphy. I have also benefited much from the comments of Larry Alexander, William Alston, Theodore Blumoff, Norman Dahl, Richard Duncan, Evan Fales, Richard Flathman, Jorge Garcia, Eugene Garver, Bernard Gert, James Gustafson, Stephen Kalish, Hugh LaFollette, Charles Larmore, Craig Lawson, Hugh McCann, Joseph Mendola, Allison Nespor, William Prior, Jack Sammons, Robert Schopp, Jeff Spinner-Halev, James Sterba, Eleonore Stump, Richard Swinburne, Mark Timmons, Mark van Roojen, William Wainwright, Linda Zagzebski, and especially Philip Quinn and Paul Weithman, who, in both their published criticism and their comments on work in progress, have indicated a number of places where my theory needed development or defense. Anonymous readers of this and other work of mine on the subject also deserve thanks, and I am grateful to Walter Havighurst for expert copy-editing and helpful queries. I only wish time had permitted doing justice to all the comments they and other readers of my work have given me, but I am confident that in numerous places they will see the effects of an effort to develop the needed responses.

PART ONE

THE FOUNDATIONS OF DEMOCRACY AND THE SEPARATION OF CHURCH AND STATE

CHAPTER ONE

THE PLURALITY OF PATHS TO LIBERAL DEMOCRACY

Democratic government is entirely dependent on the people it represents. Factions can cripple it. Indifference can undermine it. Fanatical consensus can pervert it into a tyranny of the majority. It thrives on the political commitment and mutual respect of its citizens, on fair competition among individuals and institutions, and on diversity in ideas, culture, and individual personalities. The present age is witnessing serious challenges to the historically strongest democracies and a multitude of forces that retard the development of new ones. There is political apathy among the citizens in many nations; self-serving governments are widespread; and in many other countries there is religious and political fanaticism. In and outside democratic nations, there is corruption among many who wield political power. In many parts of the world, there are structural injustices, both economic and political. A democratic society that does not effectively combat these evils – apathy, fanaticism, corruption, injustice, and other threats to democracy – is at best unstable.

This book addresses a clearly central aspect of the current challenge to democracy: the delicate problem of how a free and democratic society can achieve an appropriate harmony between religion and politics. As a source of human flourishing and as a stimulus to citizenship, religion has played a unique and powerful role in the development of democracy. Many religious traditions not only insist on preservation of liberty but also require their followers to be conscientious, constructive citizens. Religion can, however, be a divisive force in democratic politics. The impulse to pursue the Ultimate Good, particularly in an authoritative institutional context and with the support of others sharing the same religious outlook, can lead to a tendency, conscious or unconscious, to dominate others. A holy cause can sanctify extreme measures.

Is there a way to structure democracy in general, and in particular a way to shape the framework of moral principles appropriate to it, that leads to sociopolitical standards by which people of differing religious views – or none – can cooperate as citizens in an atmosphere of mutual respect? One thesis of this book is that there is. The task of this chapter is to lay a basis for showing this. Unlike some writers on the topic, I do not proceed by proposing a highly specific theory of the basis of democracy. I prefer to indicate a number of ways in which one might defend democracy – liberal democracy in particular – as the most desirable form of government in the modern world. We can then see how all of them bear on religion and politics. I begin with some broad features of liberal democracy.

LIBERAL DEMOCRACY

Liberal democracy is properly so called because of its two fundamental commitments: to the freedom of citizens and to their basic political equality, symbolized above all in the practice of according one person one vote. Kant put this dual commitment of liberal democracy even more strongly:

> [I]t is a fundamental principle of moral politics that in uniting itself into a nation a people ought to subscribe to freedom and equality as the sole constituents of its concept of right, and this is not a principle of prudence, but is founded on duty.[1]

Here we have not only the classical liberal stress on both freedom – in a very wide sense of the term – and equality, but also the affirmation that they exhaust the concept of right that is central for political philosophy. This affirmation goes beyond some liberal democratic positions in its emphasis on duty, as opposed to prudence, as a basis of democratic politics. In addition, it may have been influential in leading some liberal theorists to take only a "thin" theory of the good to be appropriate to the basic commitments of a liberal state. I find Kant's view by no means implausible, but do not unqualifiedly endorse it, and this book will be largely neutral concerning the difficult question (addressed in some detail in Chapter 3) of just how rich a conception of the good may be properly built into the constitutional framework of a liberal democracy.

One of the great challenges to both the theory and the practice of democracy is how to balance the competing forces that tend to arise from the pursuit of its two central ideals. The ideals of freedom and equality can produce conflicts in a democracy, and in practice they tend to pull a society in different directions.[2] Even given an idealized starting point in which all are equally influential in political matters, the exercise of liberty by the ingenious or naturally talented can create disproportionate political power. This outcome cannot be avoided without rigid controls that are inimical to the spirit of democracy. In any form, and regardless of how its ideals may be expressed in constitutional or other governing documents, a democracy respects the integrity, autonomy, and liberty of persons. The result will be that some citizens become economically more powerful, others better educated, and still others – whether from natural talent or economic power or educational advantage – highly proficient in persuading their fellow citizens to agree with them in political matters.

The promotion of liberty – indeed, even its protection – and the preservation of basic political equality may require extensive social programs. Democratic theorists differ on the appropriateness of such programs, for instance concerning welfare measures and other governmental services. This book takes no position on the justifiable limits here; its main points are compatible with either a liberal democracy that approaches a more or less "minimal state" or one that, like the United States and Western European democracies today, has a multitude of social programs.[3]

The centrality of the democratic respect for persons embodied in the ideals of liberty and equality accounts for why it is only *basic* equality of political power that is crucial. In practice, it is understood that some citizens are to have more political power than others. Legislators are elected with this clearly in mind; and they have far more non-basic political power than a representative citizen. Nonetheless, they have no additional votes in general elections; and although the special votes they cast in governing bodies extend to matters not directly before the citizenry, they are responsible to the electorate and serve ultimately at the pleasure of voters at large. It is, then, equal basic liberty that is crucial for democracy: in freedom of speech and protection from criminal penalties, for instance, citizens are to be equal. But even then, not every forum is appropriately available to every citizen. The legislative chamber must be restricted in some ways, and the requirements for maintaining a police force impose some limitations on the liberties of citizens and must extend a limited range of privileges to officers of the law.

I have spoken of democracy in general as respecting the autonomy and integrity of persons. It seems obvious that a liberal democracy must do this: if a vote is to represent the citizens' political will, it must be autonomous, which entails that it is not only uncoerced but free of the kind of manipulation that would prevent its appropriately representing the values of the voters; if freedom and political equality are to be preserved, this must be through the sorts of protections that maintain the integrity of persons.[4] I refer particularly to their bodily and psychological well-being, broadly construed. If we are thinking of democracy as developed in the United States or any other nation in which it may be conceived as a government of, by, and for the people, none of this should be controversial.

The 'for' here carries great weight. Conceiving a democracy as *for* the people suggests that in a certain way, a democracy – and certainly a liberal democracy – is *individualist.* It does not view the political structure of society as subordinated to the good of a sovereign, to the interests of a class of society, or even to the glory of God, though religious ideals and other normative standards may inspire it and may (as we shall see in Chapters 2–5) figure quite properly in major aspects of its development.

A liberal democracy does not even see the political structure of society as subordinated to the good of the "community" if this is an abstraction conceived as having ends that can be promoted without benefiting citizens in general. If, for instance, in the name of the community but at the expense of public health and basic education, one committed vast resources to building an army not required for defense, or to monuments not serving the aesthetic needs of the people, this would conflict with the ideals of liberal democracy. To be sure, there is more than one kind of conflict with those ideals. The deepest kind is *structural;* it pertains to the constitution of the state: roughly, to the operating rules, whether written in a constitution or not, that bind any government representing the state in question. A less deep kind of conflict occurs where a government adopts laws or policies that are not structurally prohibited yet, like building an army beyond defensive needs and at the expense of public health and basic education, tend to undermine the ideals of liberal democracy.

It is a special feature of liberal democracies that their structure provides sufficient freedom to allow policies that are significantly in tension with their underlying ideals. Overbuilding of an army, then, might be permissible by (reversible) democratic decision, but maintenance of an army larger than defense requires would probably be an inappropriate requirement to build into any constitution that meets liberal-democratic standards. The distinction is of course not sharp, and there are degrees of conflict in either case. Even where the distinction is clear, some citizens will be tempted to give maximal force to their preferences by building them into the constitutional structure. This is an additional reason, beyond the unclarity of the distinction, why, in the United States for instance, there is so much debate about whether certain policies should take the form of constitutional amendments. This book is concerned both with structural questions and with standards of conduct that apply where the laws or public policies under discussion are permissible under a sound liberal-democratic constitution.

The reference to a constitution may suggest that I am considering only a constitutional as opposed to proceduralist conception of democracy. I am assuming that a liberal-democratic society must have at least a set of unwritten structural standards for preserving liberty and basic political equality, but I do not assume that no proceduralist democracy can under any conditions achieve that end. Much of what I say, however, is most readily understood in relation to a constitutional democracy like that of the United States and other modern democracies, and it may often suggest the preferability of such a democracy over a procedural one, in which the majority rules by expressing its political will in voting, independently of constitutional restrictions on the outcome. Even on a proceduralist conception, however, there must be ground rules defining citizenship and voting. There will, then, be a de facto constitution even if it is alterable by simple majority vote. The points just made about political structure in a democracy as designed to be "for" the people can be applied either to the character of these ground rules or to a written constitution. I want to stress, however, that there is a spectrum of possible democratic structures running from the ideal of a pure proceduralism at one extreme to that of an unalterable constitution at the other.

Existing democracies have always fallen in between a pure procedural system and an unalterable constitutionalism,[5] and for good reason. If our only ground rules require just a simple majority vote on every issue that the people must decide (and identifying such issues is itself a challenge for a democracy), then we have at best a system that is both inefficient because decisions must wait upon wide dissemination of the issues and unstable because fundamental changes can be made as fast as a majority can be swayed to vote them in. This could be very fast indeed given our developing computer technology, which makes it possible to vote regularly from one's own home or from a private computer account.

To be sure, the better educated the citizenry, the less the danger posed by eliminating representative government as a filter between the people and social policy. But in the world as we know it, settling every legislative question by popular vote would not be our best policy. If, on the other hand, a constitution, however democratically adopted it may be, is entirely beyond amendment by the people, then we have a kind of tyranny by the first generation.

My concern, then, will be chiefly with democracies which have a constitutional structure that provides for its own revision. This is in part because my main focus is liberal democracies that in fact are so constituted and in part because it is useful to be able to distinguish between standards appropriate for constitutional adoption and those appropriate in other settings, such as crafting legislative policy or simply voting in ordinary elections. The main points that emerge about liberal democracy, however, will be applicable to it even in settings in which there is no strong constitutional framework.

OUTLINES OF A CASE FOR LIBERAL DEMOCRACY

A full-scale case for liberal democracy as a form of government would have to be both lengthy and comparative. My purposes in this book do not require direct comparison with other political structures, but indirect comparisons will be implicit at many points, particularly where we consider the implications of religious domination of a democracy, in which case the resulting society would be at best a non-liberal democracy.[6] There is also no need here to mount the kind of defense of liberal democracy that would be required if I were addressing readers for whom it is controversial whether we should have a democracy at all. It remains highly desirable, however, to see a number of ways in which a liberal democracy can be plausibly grounded. This is particularly so if one wants to argue, as I do, that certain principles applicable to religion and politics are justifiable from the point of view of *any* of the plausible groundings.

One might think that a plausible grounding of liberal democracy would have to be *moral*. Integrity and autonomy each seem to be moral ideals, and both suggest values that one might argue are best served in lives led under a liberal-democratic regime. I agree that a moral case for liberal democracy can be made plausible, but (as will be evident) I doubt that it is the only plausible kind of case to be made. Here and elsewhere in this book, moreover, I shall avoid assuming any sharp distinction between moral and non-moral values or standards. This is particularly appropriate to the first kind of grounding I want to consider, since it calls for a maximization of goodness conceived non-morally, but construes this very imperative as our basic moral requirement.

Utilitarianism

I refer, of course, to utilitarianism, and I propose to take John Stuart Mill's version in *Utilitarianism* (if indeed there is only one version there) as a basis of discussion. Since I am not endorsing the view in any form, I bypass consideration of the massive objections and replies to be found in the literature. I am assuming only that some version of the kind of view Mill presented is a serious contender that must be taken into account.

Before we explore the kind of grounding utilitarianism can provide for liberal democracy, we should distinguish two questions that can easily be run together in dealing with this issue. The first is the quasi-historical question of how, using whatever standard of good government is taken as basic, individuals who meet certain constraints – above all, being free, (fully) rational, and adequately informed – may be thought to have preferred liberal democracy over alternative forms of government.[7] The second is the structural question of how well liberal democracy, taken contemporaneously, say as embodied in a given nation as it is today, fulfills the standard. In part because of the influence of the social contract tradition, the former question has tended to dominate discussions of the grounding of liberal democracy. This is in some ways unfortunate, since the relevant contractual starting point is controversial and its conditions difficult to clarify and defend. In principle, however, the two approaches should yield the same answer: a free, rational, adequately informed person should not choose a system of government in the light of a standard unless that system can be expected to fulfill that standard under specifiable conditions; and such individuals should not approve of an actual system of government on the basis of a standard unless they can reasonably think they would have chosen it in the relevant way.

It is true, however, that showing individuals why, as free, rational, adequately informed prospective citizens, they would choose a system can serve both to *motivate* them to cooperate in it and to suggest a basis of their *political obligation,* by which I mean roughly their obligation to obey the law. Showing the latter basis has been of the first importance in political philosophy at least since Hobbes. I do not believe that a good case for liberal democracy as the best form of government must automatically provide an account of political obligation, though it must be consistent with the existence of such obligation and should indicate something about how such an account might proceed.[8] In any case, I do not address the problem of political obligation in any direct way in this book. We can understand both the major kinds of grounding of liberal democracy and their implications for standards bearing on religion and politics without associating them with any particular account of political obligation. Utilitarianism, for instance, can account for our having (prima facie) obligations to obey the law in a liberal democracy *if* it can account for the desirability of liberal democracy in the first place. Let us turn to that question.

Although the fine details of our formulation of utilitarianism should not be crucial here, we need something concrete to refer to, and the following act-utilitarian formulation roughly captures the central principle common at least to Bentham and Mill: an act is right if and only if it contributes at least as much to the proportion of (non-moral) good to evil (say, happiness to unhappiness, as Mill has it) in the relevant population (say, human beings) as any available alternative (where the proportion in question need not be strictly quantitative and the criteria for availability are non-moral[9]).

Before noting any of the well-known difficulties with this principle, I want to bring out what is plausible in it that makes it a useful starting point for a consideration of ways to ground liberal democracy. Above all, utilitarians would have us choose a system of government that does the most good for people. As Mill put it in *Representative Government,*

> We have now . . . obtained a foundation for a twofold division of merit which any set of political institutions can possess. It consists partly of the degree in which they promote the general mental advancement of the community, including under that phrase advancement in intellect, in virtue, and in practical activity and efficiency; and partly of the degree of perfection with which they organise the moral, intellectual, and active worth already existing . . . A government is to be judged by its action upon men, and by its action upon things; by what it makes of the citizens, and what it does with them; its tendency to improve or deteriorate the people themselves . . .[10]

On the face of it, this position is highly consonant with the idea of a democracy as *for* the people. Moreover, where the good is understood in terms of happiness or anything like it, we get an irreducibly *pluralistic* notion; for happiness can come from a variety of experiences and activities. This pluralism favors the liberality – especially the tolerance – of liberal democracy. No kind of happiness is ruled out as without value; hence there is a prima facie case for allowing any activity that leads to happiness. Moreover, no one's happiness is better than another's just because of whose it is; this goes with utilitarianism's treating everyone as a candidate to realize the good – or indeed to realize the bad, through causing oneself suffering – a kind of experience in which we seem more alike than in what makes us happy. This recognition of our equality insofar as we can experience happiness or suffering favors giving recognition, as a liberal democracy does, to the importance of the life of each and every citizen.

Less abstractly, utilitarians can plausibly argue that according every citizen a vote also helps to overcome alienation, which is a cause of unhappiness and political unrest, and to enhance cooperation, which is a source of progress in enhancing the good and in eliminating the evils of disease and scarcity. Clearly, how good a case can be made for a liberal democracy from utilitarian premises depends in part on our factual assumptions; but the liberal democracies of the world have done well enough materially relative to other kinds of society to give utilitarians prima facie evidence from which to argue that at least in relation to some of the major elements in happiness – particularly in the reduction of suffering – liberal democracy is the best candidate form of government to maximize the good.[11]

Difficulties remain, however. One problem is how to determine what population is relevant to our calculations. May a good utilitarian restrict consideration to a single nation, on the ground that a government will operate within its borders, or do all persons count equally? And how are we to count non-human animals? Worse still, can we, from utilitarian premises, do justice to questions of *distribution*, say by arguing, as surely Mill would, that what intuitively counts as unjust distribution will in the long run generate more suffering than happiness? And should the prevention and reduction of suffering not have priority over the production of happiness, in a way utilitarians cannot cogently account for? These and many other doubts about utilitarian distribution principles have been repeatedly expressed.[12]

To be sure, Mill might argue that suffering differs *qualitatively* from happiness in a way that gives it priority over happiness as a source of reasons for action, just as some pleasures, being higher than others, provide better reasons.[13] There are other ways to constrain utilitarianism to reduce or perhaps even avoid the difficulties just noted (and other difficulties). I cannot argue this, but I take it that by developing the points made here one can see how a liberal democracy can be supported from utilitarian assumptions and is probably the likeliest choice from that perspective, given what we now know about the conditions under which human society prospers in the ways that conduce to utility.

Instrumentalism

Utilitarianism presupposes some theory of the good. I have stressed the pluralism of a plausible utilitarianism, which enables it to avoid commitment to any narrow conception of the good. It may be argued, however, that a rational person need not recognize any *intrinsic* goods (things good in themselves, independently of their consequences), and that in any event it is best to ground liberal democracy from a perspective neutral with respect to the question of what, if anything, is intrinsically good. Might there be a point of view that any rational person may take, irrespective of any specific value commitments? It is natural to think so, and instrumentalism benefits from centering on what is often considered the least controversial standard of rationality. Let me explain.

A minimal condition for rationality, one might plausibly hold, is seeking means to one's own ends. For the tradition of Hume, instrumental rationality is indeed central for rational action: roughly, instrumentalists hold that an act is rational if, and only if, relative to the agent's beliefs it is at least as good as (as instrumental as) any available alternative in contributing to the desire satisfaction of the agent (one might specify that only rational beliefs count here, but that complication will not affect our discussion). The relevant desires are of course non-instrumental, such as the desire to enjoy a swim *for its own sake;* and an action contributes optimally to desire satisfaction when it contributes at least as much as any alternative to the quantity of such satisfaction. This is the sort of thing Hume had in mind in his famous affirmation of the instrumental role of reason: "reason is, and ought only to be the slave of the passions."[14] Applying this to the basis of political philosophy, he said that "sense of justice and injustice is not derived from nature but arises artificially" and that since the rules of justice serve our basic social ends, *"the rules of justice are establish'd by the artifice of men."*[15]

From an instrumentalist point of view, liberal democracy is attractive for some of the same reasons that make it attractive to utilitarianism. Being liberal, for instance, it leaves people free (within limits) to pursue what they want. On the assumption that what we naturally want *is* happiness, including the absence or elimination of suffering – an assumption that many accept in some form and that Mill took to represent a psychological law – it is not surprising that liberal democracy would appeal in similar ways to both traditions. To be sure, since instrumentalism does not take it as necessary that one have any desire for the things anyone *else* wants, the view does not fare as well as utilitarianism in justifying a social structure in which all have basic political equality. But if one assumes, as Hobbes and most later political theorists have, that people naturally have basic desires requiring peaceful coexistence with others, this disadvantage can be greatly reduced.

The contemporary philosopher who has done most to justify central principles for liberal democracy using largely (though by no means entirely) instrumentalist principles of rationality is John Rawls.[16] Embracing a contractarian approach constrained to eliminate biases, he argues that if, in specified conditions of ignorance of such biasing information as how wealthy they will be, rational persons choose a framework of social cooperation, it will be one in which the following two principles of justice are central. The first, which has priority and (in some version) is a standard basis for liberal democracy, requires allowing as much liberty to each of us as is consistent with a like liberty for others; the second principle requires that sociopolitical inequalities be justified by attaching to positions open to all by fair competition and by being such that their existence can be reasonably expected to benefit the worst off.[17] The idea, in part, is that even the worst off can endorse the existence of a system allowing such inequalities because they will be better off under it than under alternatives. Since, given the priority of the equal liberty principle, basic liberties are not negotiable, basic political liberty is protected, including one person, one vote, yet all are free within this structure to compete for a better position.

To be sure, as Rawls seems willing to grant, his starting position is not a *pure* instrumentalism. He makes the special assumption, for instance, that rational persons do not suffer from envy and hence are not willing to accept a system, such as a rigid egalitarian one, that gives them less of what they seek (such as wealth) than a Rawlsian system, simply in order to prevent others from having more of it.[18] I agree that envy as he describes it is not rational, but this assumption must be seen as a significant departure from a central feature of instrumentalism: its neutrality toward the ends we may have. The assumption rules out certain desires with significant political potential – including the not uncommon desire that certain others not have higher economic status than oneself – as incapable of supplying good reasons for action. Still, it is plausible to suppose that if he begs any questions here, they are not major, or are in any case not major questions we need pursue here.[19]

On the positive side, Rawls assumes (consistently with instrumentalism) that every rational person can be "presumed to want . . . rights and liberties, powers and opportunities, income and wealth."[20] This is not to say these things are intrinsically good. Intrinsic goodness is an inadmissible category for instrumentalism (and, on Rawls's neutralist understanding of it, perhaps for any basic standards of liberalism). But the assumption does give primary goods a functional equivalence to what is intrinsically good conceived as providing reasons for action; for what one (non-instrumentally) wants *is*, for instrumentalism, the basis of one's reasons for action.

It is left open to what *extent* each of these primary goods is wanted by rational persons, but they are nonetheless each assumed to be among the goals that partly determine what constitutes social justice. Now it is surely plausible to hold that from either a Humean instrumentalist point of view or the constrained instrumentalist point of view Rawls takes as a starting point, one would want the kind of freedom and equality that liberal democracy is committed to *if* one wants to coexist with others under a political system and cannot foresee what sort of position one would occupy. One would want freedom to pursue one's plans and enough political power to facilitate this. But, being unable to get more (basic) freedom and power than others have, and being unwilling to settle for less, one would want the kind of equality a liberal democracy guarantees.

It may be that we must qualify instrumentalism still further if Rawls's constrained instrumentalist case for his liberal framework is to succeed. I think, however, that his will remain a plausible approach and that it is striking for its rejection of any dependence on a specific conception of the good as a basis for framing a conception of social justice in a liberal democratic framework. There is a list of primary *goods,* but no conception of *the good,* and the primary goods are plural and capable of diverse interpretations and realizations. The refusal to presuppose a specific conception of the good (a position reiterated in Rawls's *Political Liberalism*) bears directly (as we shall see) on the principles the position implies for balancing religious and political considerations.

Kantianism

Given how strongly Kantian much of Rawls's position is, one might wonder why his approach to grounding core principles of liberal democracy should not be considered (as indeed it sometimes is) chiefly Kantian rather than taken to be the application of a constrained instrumentalism. In at least two important respects it is Kantian. First, we are to picture rational agents considering what principles they can endorse for all humanity, and we are to countenance only the principles of justice they select as universalizable in this way. Second, the principles that emerge fit well with an overall version of Kantian ethics, particularly in protecting the integrity and autonomy of persons by giving priority to the equal basic liberty principle. But (with the sorts of qualifications introduced above) these agents are to work from instrumentalist standards, whereas Kant was not an instrumentalist. Not only did he take good will to be an unconditional and presumably intrinsic good; his second main formulation of his central ethical principle, the categorical imperative, makes explicit use of the idea of persons as ends in themselves, in a sense implying that they have intrinsic value (worth) or, minimally, that something about their experiences or about conduct toward them (say, just conduct) does.[21] Certainly Rawls's version of basic principles of liberal democracy is meant to be of a kind that a Kantian would endorse; but Rawls apparently believes he is able to justify it from less controversial, morally neutral assumptions.

We should, then, consider what constitutes a Kantian approach to grounding liberal democracy, as opposed to a Kantian conception of the principles of justice that such a society – or any civilized society – should adopt. There is doubtless more than one approach one might call Kantian, but I think it is reasonable to take the most relevant part of Kant's position to be his comprehensive moral theory as expressed in his *Groundwork*. Indeed, his third main formulation of the categorical imperative – the kingdom of ends formulation, which says that a "rational being must always regard himself as making laws in a kingdom of ends"[22] – readily lends itself to application to the structure of society.

If, moreover, we also take as central Kant's intrinsic end formulation of the categorical imperative, which enjoins us always to "*treat humanity, whether in your own person or in the person of any other, never simply as a means, but always at the same time as an end*,"[23] then we find a basis for both the equal (and maximal) basic liberty and the basic political equality that are essential in liberal democracy. Limiting the liberty of others and treating them unequally (at least where this represents less good treatment than others receive) are both instances of failure to treat them as ends, except where this differential treatment is required by considerations of liberty and other basic values, in which case liberal democracy allows it. Indeed, Kantians take it that, as beings with dignity, we have a right not to be treated in these ways, and by developing this idea one may frame a *rights-based liberal theory*, on which citizens have rights against government, and against one another, that require preservation of both liberty and basic political equality.[24]

It must be granted that much work of interpretation is needed before one can find in Kantian ethics a detailed working out of a justification for liberal democracy. But, taken together, Kant's repeated emphasis on our autonomy, his insistence on treating ourselves no better than others (something that cannot be rationally universalized by Kantian lights), and his constant emphasis on the dignity of persons make it plausible to hold that only a liberal democracy can satisfy his ethical principles in the sociopolitical sphere.

From the point of view of using Kantian ethical theory to ground liberal democracy, it is risky to hold the theory to the rigors of some of Kant's examples, for instance to the apparently absolute prohibition of suicide and promise-breaking.[25] It is noteworthy, however, that where Kant does best in connecting his examples with his categorical imperative, he argues for a (prima facie) duty of beneficence of a kind that would conduce to citizenship in the context of interdependence that characterizes working democracies. It is clear that in addition to the negative moral requirements of non-interference and non-injury, his framework is meant to imply positive duties of cooperation of a kind essential in a well-functioning democracy. These duties require sharing not only policy decisions but the burdens of conducting communal life.

Virtue Ethics

Contemporary political philosophy is quite properly concerned with democratic government in huge and populous nations that must be ruled by an elaborate network of laws and social policies. This concern with rules and policies may make it easy to overlook a virtue-theoretic account of the basic standards underlying liberal democracy. But in principle one can frame such an account for a society of any scope, and the work of Elizabeth Anscombe, Philippa Foot, and, particularly in the past two decades, Alasdair MacIntyre has made virtue ethics an attractive option for many writers in ethics and political philosophy.[26] Plato and Aristotle, of course, were concerned with the virtues of statecraft and, more broadly, of citizenship; and their accounts of the just state can be adapted to apply to the present age. Let me briefly sketch how this might be done from a standpoint that draws selectively on Plato but also takes account of later developments in virtue ethics.

There is probably no richer paradigm of a virtue-theoretic approach to the theory of government than Plato's *Republic.* I believe that the *kind* of account he gives (a virtue-theoretic account in which the just state is appropriately parallel in governmental structure to the just individual) can be developed so that it leads to a liberal democracy rather than the oligarchy he favored. The ideal state is described as "wise, brave, temperate, and just" (Book 4, 427), and the "quality which makes it possible for the three . . . wisdom, courage, and temperance, to take their place in the commonwealth . . . would be justice" (Book 4, 433). Moreover, individual virtue is in a sense prior to virtue in the state: we are to understand justice at the level of the state in terms of justice in the individual. In general, "so far as the quality of justice is concerned, there will be no difference between a just man and a just society" (Book

4, 434), and "the same elements and characters that appear in the state must exist in every one of us; where else could they have come from? . . . states have . . . derived that character from their individual members" (Book 4, 435).[27] Proper civil government turns out to be virtuous self-government writ large.

A virtue-ethical grounding of a theory of government is also present in Aristotle, though his position is perhaps more complex than Plato's. In Aristotle's view that "the good is the same for a city as for an individual,"[28] however, he is in agreement with Plato. Virtue concepts remain basic for political theory as well as for individual conduct.

It is important to see that a virtue-theoretic approach to the foundations of the state can go a great distance toward liberal democracy. The broadest idea that makes this clear may be the conception of human nature as social and of good government as an exercise of civic virtue, conceived as the cluster of elements of character that conduce to a communal life in which people can achieve excellence. This ideal of good government can be plausibly argued to be best fulfilled in a liberal-democratic state (presumably republican in form). For such a state seems best fitted to encourage individual virtue in the sociopolitical realm; without freedom and political equality, citizens cannot exercise certain virtues at all and are severely limited in contributing to their common governance. Obedience will tend to overshadow autonomy.

The case I am outlining may be applicable even to much of the Platonic theory of the just state. One crucial element in civil government as Plato saw it can enable a theory like his to be used to undergird democracy as well as his own preferred form of government. He tells us that "real guardians" aim at "moulding our commonwealth with a view to the greatest happiness, not of one section of it, but of the whole" (Book 5, 465). Given the plurality and fluidity of the notion of happiness, this vision is adaptable to structuring the just state in a variety of ways, including some that yield a liberal democracy.

It has been widely argued that our concept of a virtue of character is dependent on prior notions of goodness, or of human flourishing, or of morally right action. For instance, many have thought that we can determine what constitutes good character only if we know what sorts of deeds people of good character tend to do.[29] There is no need to take a position on this matter here. The central point for our purposes is simply that the virtue-theoretic approach to establishing foundations for liberal democracy is historically significant and prima facie distinctive.

Suppose, however, that it is not independent of other kinds of normative theory. It might then be combined with one of the other ethical theories considered here, and I am confident that a consistent integration can be achieved in which the resulting view supports liberal democracy at least as well as either virtue ethics alone or the ethical theory on which it draws. Even apart from this, the notion of virtue is important in ethics and political philosophy (this will be especially apparent in Chapters 3 and 6). If a plausible notion of virtue in statecraft can even partially ground liberal democracy, that is significant.

Communitarianism

It should be plain that all the approaches to justifying liberal democracy so far considered accord a significant place to the social side of our nature. Utilitarians maintain that to maximize the good we must not only cooperate with others but also respect their rights, even when we have no ongoing relationship with them. Instrumentalists tend to hold a similar view concerning desire satisfaction: concentrate exclusively on your own and you will tend to get little of it. Kantians see us as properly aiming at coexistence in a kingdom of ends, and they insist, as do virtue theorists, on honesty with others and, within certain limits, beneficence toward them. It is not unnatural to go further and to maintain that human good itself is realizable only in a community. We might then see some form of liberal democracy as best constructed to foster human development, though if it is to be communitarian it must overcome the fragmentation that is a danger of excessive individualism.[30]

This communitarian conception of human flourishing may or may not be combined with the strong view that our very identity is social: that individuals are partly but essentially defined by their relations to others.[31] Whatever our biological independence of others, we are parents and children, teachers and students, buyers and sellers, and so forth. In what sense would the biological agent abstractable from all such relations in which I stand be me? And how can my life go well if those I care about suffer, and the institutions I believe in wither? If there is a sense in which I am not socially constituted, it is too thin to imply that my good is not in large part socially constituted.

Plato's *Republic* is a valuable source for communitarian ideas, as it is for virtue theory. In a vivid portrayal of an organic conception of the state, Socrates warns against disunity:

> And this disunion comes about when the words 'mine' and 'not mine,' 'another's' and 'not another's' are not applied to the same things throughout the community. The best ordered state will be the one in which the largest number of persons use these terms in the same sense, and which accordingly most resembles a single person. When one of us hurts his finger, the whole extent of those bodily connexions which are gathered up in the soul and unified by its ruling elements is made aware and it all shares as a whole in the pain of the suffering part . . . the best organised community . . . will recognize as a part of itself the individual citizen to whom good or evil happens, and will share as a whole in his joy or sorrow. (Book 5, 462)

Government as here portrayed has a unifying role, but is part of the body politic as a whole.

In addition to an individual's good being in part socially constituted, communitarianism reflects an emphasis on "the common good." Aquinas described law itself as "ordained toward the common good,"[32] and communitarian thinkers have criticized the political theory of Rawls and others as insufficiently providing for it.[33] It is quite possible, however, to grant that human good is fully realizable only in social settings, and even to hold that we would not be just the people we are if our social relations were dramatically different, without concluding that any value is realized by a community or social entity except through the happiness – or prosperity or flourishing or the like – of one or more individuals. Our modes of prosperity and even our very identity can be social without there being anything entirely social – such as the Community or the State conceived abstractly – to which we are in any way subordinate. Granted, I should do good deeds for the community; but if these do not benefit the poor or the elderly or children at play or any determinate individuals living now or in the future, I shall feel that my efforts were in vain.

The contrast I am drawing is between what we might call a *top-down approach* to political justification and a *bottom-up approach* to it. On the former, there is a general goal of good government, such as the welfare of the state or of the community as a whole, in terms of which one justifies laws and policies governing individuals. On the latter, properties of individuals, such as their well-being or flourishing or moral rights, are the standard by which government is judged good or bad. A communitarian rationale for liberal democracy (or any other form of government) readily lends itself to a top-down approach, though this is not strictly required by the ideal of communal welfare or, more broadly, communal flourishing, as the basic political standard.

Perhaps I have said nothing highly controversial about communitarianism. But if that is so, the implication may be that a communitarian approach to grounding liberal democracy is in need of supplementation either by a theory of the goods to be promoted – and evils to be avoided – by a form of government or at least by a theory of rational action. This is indeed how the approach is likely to be pursued by those of its proponents who adhere to some form of virtue ethics. Even if we count social goods as paramount, are there not individual goods to be weighed in deciding on a form of government? I can be in part socially constituted and still suffer in lonely silence or delight in a solitary afternoon of reading. Governmental powers should not make such solitary pleasures difficult for me. If my obligations to the Community are not constrained accordingly, I may find myself used simply as a means to Community goals in the abstract.

The tendency to use individuals as a means to the overall good of the relevant community may in the end be a liability of a utilitarian approach as well. But that approach – at least in the liberal tradition, and prominently in Mill – is individualist; individuals alone are the locus of value, and social obligations that help no determinate individuals are wasted. We know, of course, that in practice individual sacrifices in the name of the Community or the State or the Empire are meant to benefit individuals – if sometimes a very few. If communitarianism is not to be perverted into a rationale for subordinating some individuals to others, it must have a theory of value or rationality as a guide. Given that point, what is distinctive about it would seem to be the stress on the social elements in human life rather than a unique and independent approach to political justification.[34]

To say, however, that the most plausible form of communitarian approach to grounding democracy requires supplementation by another theory is not to say that it has no role at all or cannot enhance our understanding of what is desirable about democracy, including liberal democracy. Communitarian ideas can help us to see that basic equality in political power and in freedom of action need not make us selfishly pursue our private ends or conceive ourselves as atomic individuals for whom others are a means to our own ends. Far from it: the social conditions supported by a liberal state facilitate voluntary associations among people, free them to create institutions that embody deep-seated ideals they share, and provide a setting for mutual cooperation of the kind that makes ideals of community attractive. Combined, then, with values that communitarians tend to find compelling, a communitarian conception of the good society can justify a version of liberal democracy as the best among imperfect systems of government.

Theology

A theology can embody an ethic and a wide-ranging social-political philosophy. Christian theology (or at any rate Hebraic-Christian theology), which we may surely take as a paradigm, certainly does. In Aquinas and other systematic Christian thinkers we also find a theory of the grounding and legitimate powers of the state.[35] To consider any such theory in detail would require theological discussion as well as philosophical explication; here it will be enough simply to indicate in outline how many contemporary religious believers might view liberal democracy in relation to their faith.

One might think that for any religious believer to whom God is central and a text like the Bible is authoritative, the only acceptable way to judge a system of government is to compare it with the relevant religious ideals one frames from studying one's religious commitments. This is an approach taken by some believers. For them, liberal democracy may or may not be acceptable. But for a great many (particularly in the Christian and Jewish traditions), this approach is not required or is at least not exclusive. Consider a plausible alternative.

Suppose I am a serious but non-fundamentalist Christian (where by 'fundamentalist' I mean someone who takes an authoritative scripture, in this case the Bible, literally, at least so far as internal consistency permits).[36] I will be wary of any demands on me that seem to violate my religious commitments, but if I live in a moderately just society I need not for that reason screen every demand made on me by individuals I know or even by society. In addition, I may have the faith that God has created us so that what can be seen to be fully consonant with reason conceived non-religiously will also be consistent with God's commands (the basis of this faith is explored in detail in Chapter 5). I may then feel virtually as free as anyone else to view the basic questions of political theory from the point of view of some plausible general ethical perspective, such as Kantianism. Like many other secular – by which I mean roughly non-religious, not anti-religious – ethical positions, Kantianism encompasses the ethical principles (as opposed to the theological content) of the Ten Commandments.

It might be, however, that at some point I want to satisfy myself that the kind of government I support is fully consonant with my faith. It might occur to me that if God is the basic source of value in the universe and has infallibly commanded a certain kind of life, the state should not only not undermine such a life, it should promote it. Little reflection is needed to see that this promotional stance cannot be achieved without restricting major offices – perhaps the highest ones – to religiously committed leaders. It may then occur to me that even in my own tradition there is disagreement about important elements in Scripture. I will also be aware of other Christian traditions. Would it not invite strife in my own tradition, and certainly between it and other religious traditions, to restrict political offices? And if I take to heart the injunction, "Do unto others as you would have them do unto you," I may be at least reluctant – from a sense of fairness as well as from prudence – to support a government that does not provide for representation from entirely different religious traditions with as deeply felt a devotion to their ideals as I feel to mine. If, in addition, I have thought about how power can corrupt and about how different are the missions of clergy and government officials, I may prefer a form of government in which all are free to pursue their religious ideals under the spiritual guidance of their choice and the clergy are not faced with secular concerns that may dilute their spiritual commitments or obscure their religious vision. There are, then, internal as well as external reasons for religiously committed citizens to endorse a separation of church and state.

There are still other reasons for religious believers to favor a secular government of the kind endorsed by liberal democracy, and many religious believers today (like many believers and religious thinkers in the past) are committed to such government and confidently consider that commitment harmonious with their faith or even indirectly required by it. There remains a question concerning how neutral toward religion in general a liberal democracy should be. Here we find wide disagreement among the religious, as is evident from the recent history of legislation and court cases in the United States. That question will be considered in detail in the next chapter. It is enough here to have indicated how a religious starting point might lead one to want a liberal democracy as best for religious liberty, as desirable from the internal point of view of protecting religious institutions from becoming corrupted by politics or preoccupied with government, and as at least satisfactory in protecting other values a religious person might be expected to cherish.

Intuition and Common Sense

We have considered moral and non-moral approaches to grounding liberal democracy, as well as secular and religious approaches. But all of these approaches are theoretical in a sense in which not every moral approach need be, and intuitionism – as a common-sense moral pluralism – is not. Even in the form in which W. D. Ross articulated intuitionism in 1930, it provides a set of basic everyday moral principles that can be – and commonly are – used as guides to moral conduct. Rossian intuitionism affirms an irreducible plurality of basic moral principles, each principle centering on a different kind of ground, in the sense of a factor, such as an injustice occurring in one's community, implying a prima facie moral duty, say to change the distribution of economic opportunities. He proposed, as fundamental both in guiding daily moral practice and in articulating a sound ethical theory, a list of prima facie duties: duties of fidelity (promise-keeping, including honesty conceived as fidelity to one's word), reparation for one's wrongdoing, justice (particularly rectification of injustice), gratitude, beneficence, self-improvement, and non-injury.[37] If we consider just the position consisting of the principles calling for fulfillment of these duties, and leave aside the often associated controversial claim that they are self-evidently knowable, we have something one might consider not so much a theory as a kind of ethical commonsensism.

If we keep in mind that for at least some duties, there are correlative rights, we can find in intuitionism a basis for a version of a rights-based theory of the grounds of liberal democracy. There surely are moral rights not to be injured, not to be treated unjustly, and not to be lied to or cheated (the chief violations of the duty of fidelity). The existence of these rights might be held to be as intuitive as that of the prima facie duties Ross cited, and these rights are central for the liberty and basic political equality essential for liberal democracy. In explicating intuitionism, however, I prefer to concentrate on the principle version, as Ross did, rather than the rights version. But both have the advantage of offering standards that most reflective people, despite differences in their moral theories, find cogent as bases for civilized life.

Ross took each principle of prima facie duty to be in some sense intuitively (hence non-inferentially) known by those who appropriately understand it. In that way, the principles are not dependent on moral or political theories, such as the kinds described above. As to his calling the principles "self-evident" (in a special sense), we may set that notion aside in favor of the simpler idea of knowability without dependence on any special moral or political theory.[38] Given the wide scope and sociopolitical applicability of the principles, he would certainly hold that they are a good basis for judging whether a form of government is desirable. If a form of government permits officials to be unjust to citizens or to injure them, it is to that extent bad; if it encourages beneficence and self-improvement, it is to that extent good.

Given the stress on beneficence, intuitionism can use some of the same arguments that a utilitarian would take to support liberal democracy; given its stress on justice, it can use some that a Kantian would offer; and given the large role it accords to virtue, both in helping others and in self-improvement, it can use some that virtue ethics might offer. If, as is bound to be the case, a government is mixed, having some good and some bad points, intuitionists will consider its overall merits in the light of all the relevant facts available. There is no formula for a correct decision.[39] As these points indicate, intuitionism goes well with a bottom-up approach to grounding liberal democracy. Individuals and their mutual relations are taken as primary in moral and sociopolitical matters. Governmental and other institutions act through individuals and should serve their needs.

One might object that if the Rossian principles are in any sense self-evident or even highly intuitive, there should not be so much moral disagreement, including even disagreement on whether they themselves are true. Let me suggest that even if there should be persisting disagreement on the truth or status of the Rossian principles as general standards of conduct, there need not be disagreement, in particular cases of decision, about the basic moral force of the considerations they cite. For instance, whether or not we accept Ross's principles concerning promising and non-injury, we might, both in our abstract thinking and in regulating our conduct, take our having promised to do something as a basic moral reason to do it, or the fact that leaving a friend now would strand the friend to die in a house about to freeze from lack of fuel, as a basic reason not to do that. Such agreement *in* reasons for action – *operative agreement*, we might call it – does not require agreement *on* reasons, for instance on some principle expressing them, or on their force relative to other considerations. We can agree that a factor, such as avoidance of disappointing a friend, is a good reason for action even if neither of us can formulate, or we cannot both accept, a principle subsuming the case.

More commonly, we can agree on the positive or negative relevance of a reason, even if we differ on its force; this may occur where we can agree on a principle subsuming a case, say a case of injustice to be rectified, and the differing assessments of the force of the reason can lead to at least temporary disagreement on the final resolution of a moral issue, say on the appropriate kind of punishment. If, however, there is the kind of wide agreement in moral practice that I think there is among civilized people, then the most important kind of consensus needed for the theoretical success of intuitionism as a moral theory is in place. It can at least be argued that the truth and non-inferential justifiability of the relevant principles best explains the high degree of consensus among civilized people in wide segments of their everyday moral practice. Police brutality is universally abhorred; normal persons everywhere want freedom of movement and of speech; and a right to vote is usually wanted even by those who do not bother to exercise it.

As to the question whether there is any general theory available to help us in cases of conflicting intuitions, here I suggest that it may be possible to improve on Ross's view. Because he took the moral principles he considered basic to be self-evident and regarded the self-evident as, in turn, not admitting of proof, he neglected to explore the possibility of deriving those moral principles from, or integrating them in terms of, something more general. Although what is self-evident cannot be in *need* of justification by any such thing, it may yet admit of it.[40] Why not say, then, that we can *both* treat the Rossian principles (or similar ones) as a morally autonomous framework for judging a form of government and embed them in some way in a wider theory, such as Kant's?[41]

In some ways, this leaves the intuitionist approach sounding like an eclectic position that has no distinctive character. But that is not quite right: the idea that there are some wide-ranging moral principles intuitively knowable (or at least justifiedly believable on an intuitive basis) is defensible quite apart from any theory that unifies the several principles. Indeed, Ross and others would argue that unless there are some such principles, we have too little basis for accepting a more general theory in the first place. I consider this plausible: if we did not find some kinds of behavior prima facie obligatory or impermissible, we would have too few definite intuitions to warrant accepting a general moral theory. Would we even be inclined to construct, say, a utilitarian or Kantian theory – or a Universal Declaration of Human Rights – if we did not have intuitive paradigms of good and evil, right and wrong? I believe, then, that a carefully constructed intuitionist approach to political justification, with or without the help of a more general theory, is among the procedures we may reasonably use in attempting to ground liberal democracy. Any plausible intuitionist position will embody principles that tend to support according individuals the kind of extensive liberty and the basic political equality central for liberal democracy.

FREEDOM AND COERCION

Some of the plausible approaches to grounding liberal democracy are combinable, as are Kantianism and a kind of intuitionism;[42] others are incompatible, as in the case of Kantianism and utilitarianism. There is no need to discuss here all the possible combinations or alliances. The main point is that liberal democracy is supportable from a variety of plausible starting points. That some of them conflict may be an indication of the extent to which such democracy can provide a framework for day-to-day life on which people can agree in spite of some deeper differences in their ethics or theologies.

An important feature of all the plausible paths to grounding liberal democracy is that they support extensive freedom of action. For a truly liberal democracy, freedom is the default position: any behavior that there is not a compelling case to restrict is permissible. I believe that enough has been said about each of the groundings of liberal democracy just considered to make it plausible to take any of them to be capable of supporting this default position as an element in such democracy. To reiterate some main points: freedom tends to conduce to well-being and to enable people to satisfy their desires; it is essential for recognition of people as ends in themselves, for the realization of virtue, for building a sense of community, and for the protection of religious liberty; and intuitively moral principles and their correlative rights demand it. It will help here to consider one specific defense of the far-reaching freedom in question.

If any standard for what constitutes a compelling case for extensive freedom deserves to be called the classical one, it is John Stuart Mill's in *On Liberty.* The basic idea is that only self-protection warrants a society in restricting liberty; thus, for mentally competent adults, only probable harm to others is an adequate ground for coercion. As Mill famously put it,

> The object of this Essay is to assert one very simple principle, as entitled to govern absolutely the dealings of society with the individual in the way of compulsion and control . . . That principle is, that the sole end for which mankind are warranted, individually or collectively, in interfering with the liberty of action of any of their number, is self-protection . . . to prevent harm to others.[43]

A great deal must be said to interpret this, but what is of special relevance here is how harm (and consequently protecting anyone from it) is to be understood. Let us consider this from the point of view of the approaches we have explored to grounding liberal democracy. All of them would allow harm of sufficient probability and magnitude a role in limiting freedom; the question is how harm might be understood. One case is of course bodily harm, but that is less problematic than nonphysical harms.

Any truly liberal democracy will tend to take forcible restrictions of freedom on the part of normal (e.g. sane and rational) adults to be a harm, at least in the sense of a prima facie wrong to the restricted individuals and in need of justification. I am harmed if prevented, on penalty of imprisonment, from speaking in public on a political issue. Thus, someone who would silence me may, by Mill's principle, be prevented from doing so. More positively, since freedom of expression is a liberty all of us can have, it is guaranteed by a liberal democracy as essential to respecting autonomy. By contrast, I might also be held to be harmed if taught to believe in evolution instead of a competing religious account of human genesis. Why should a liberal state refuse to intervene here?

Recall the major routes to grounding liberal democracy that we have considered as perhaps the most plausible of the fundamental paths to its justification. The utilitarian appeal, like the basic Kantian and intuitionist appeal, is not to any theologically defined good; the basic instrumentalist appeal is not to any kind of intrinsic goodness at all; and the communitarian appeal takes its account (or conception) of the good from some more basic theory of grounds for liberal democracy or of reasons for action in general. If any approach to grounding democracy is to allow coercion on the basis of a religiously grounded conception of harm, it would seem to be a theological approach. Some theological approaches will do this. If, however, I have been right about the representative non-fundamentalist approach I sketched, it is not clear that the result here would be any different from what one would expect on the basis of a secular grounding of the sort we find in, say, a Kantian or even a broadly instrumentalist grounding such as Rawls's.

Let me develop this point, since it is central for this book as a whole. Suppose I were to endorse a democratic system in which the majority religion (mine, say) may coerce those who satisfy its criteria for religiously harming it. Must I not in fairness be ready to have some other religious denomination do the same to me if – as can happen in a democracy – it becomes a majority? This consideration should at least give me pause. If I recall that most religious harms, such as restricting religious freedom or inculcating an alien religion, *also* satisfy non-religious criteria warranting coercive prevention, I may be even more likely to adopt a secular standard for grounds of legal coercion, since they will seem to suffice for religious protection without exposing me to coercion by other religious groups. Religious liberty, for instance, can be preserved under a general protection of freedom, which will not in turn expose one to coercion by another religion. I may also have learned from the history of religion that clergy who must govern are liable to corruption by politics or the power and wealth that political activity may bring.

If, moreover, one believes that God has so constructed the world that proper standards for freedom and coercion are discoverable by an adequately conscientious application of secular reason (a matter discussed in detail in Chapter 5), one may be reluctant to adopt a standard for coercion that is not defensible by such reasoning. A good secular standard will protect religious liberty, though not for specifically religious reasons; and if it restricts religious practices, this is only where they call for behavior, such as suicide or human sacrifice, that most religions proscribe.[44]

If liberal democracy may be plausibly grounded both from a secular point of view and also from the point of view of a (non-fundamentalist) religious believer, this is surely in part because the normative standards that support it are both permissive regarding what sorts of lives citizens may lead and protective of their free choices. Granted, no democracy can prevent a majority's instituting laws that undermine the liberty of all or some of the people; the point is that the best rationales for a liberal democracy forbid restricting freedom except where it is required to prevent serious harm or to preserve equal basic liberty or equal basic political power. To be sure, these are wide-ranging ideals, and they are not easily separated from ideals concerning socioeconomic opportunities or from standards of material well-being. Poverty and ignorance impair the exercise of liberty and tend to reduce one's political power and even one's autonomy. Still, all of the plausible ways of grounding liberal democracy considered here (and so far as I can tell all of the plausible ways there are) require that coercion be backed by arguments of a kind that citizens can endorse regardless of which of these ways – or combinations of them – they might favor as expressing the basis on which they want to live as citizens.

The rest of this book will address a major dimension of what a good set of liberal-democratic standards for freedom and coercion should be and to what extent it may be acceptable to religious believers who disapprove of some of the conduct it protects. In doing this, we can also explore further how the various paths to liberal democracy may be charted in more detail or may come together or diverge. The result, I hope, will be a better understanding of both democracy and the role of religion in democratic politics.

CHAPTER TWO

THE SEPARATION OF CHURCH AND STATE

Liberal democracies are free societies and are above all committed to preserving basic liberty and basic equality of political power. There are many conceptions of liberal democracy. We have seen the possibility of a spectrum ranging from pure proceduralist conceptions to strong constitutional frameworks. At one end, perhaps unoccupied by any major historical figure in the liberal tradition, are minimalist, procedural conceptions that simply provide for a framework in which democracy can operate; they impose no constraints on the social goals appropriate to a free and democratic society.[1] At the other end are rich substantive conceptions that build in such goals as human flourishing and respect for persons. On any of these conceptions, and certainly on any plausible constitutionalist view, freedom of religion will be a central value to be preserved.

Constitutional democracies are the main concern of this book. It is not necessary to present a full-scale account of a constitutional liberal democracy, but I will proceed on the working hypothesis that a major basis for determining how much substance may be built into the constitutional structure of a liberal democracy is what might be called a *fidelity to essential premises standard:* a liberal political theory meant to guide such a democracy should incorporate in its vision of a just society enough to fulfill the theory's essential underlying ideals – and include nothing inconsistent with them. We have seen reasons to hold that realizing this vision precludes governmental preference for any particular religion. Preservation of the ideals of equal basic liberty and political power seem to require separation of church and state. The appropriate character of that separation is a matter of continuing controversy. My hope is to contribute something toward its resolution. We might begin with an outline of a separation of church and state that seems plausible from the point of view of the groundings of liberal democracy described in Chapter 1.

THREE CENTRAL PRINCIPLES OF CHURCH-STATE SEPARATION

Historically, the idea that there should be a separation between "the church" – a term I use generally to refer to religious institutions of any character – and the state concerns chiefly those two entities conceived institutionally: as large-scale social unities rather than merely as collections of loosely affiliated people acting as individuals. Some of the issues raised by institutional separation have counterparts in the lives of individuals and will be discussed in detail in Chapter 4. My initial concern, however, is the large-scale separation viewed mainly as constraining governments in relation to the religious institutions under their jurisdiction.

If we think of the theory of separation of church and state as applied to governmental institutions in relation to religious ones, we find at least three basic principles in any full-blooded liberal version of the separation view.[2] These are bound together most prominently by the ideal of religious liberty as a central element in a free society. But, for the kinds of reasons set out in Chapter 1, other ideals, such as those of the equal basic rights of persons regardless of their religious affiliation, of unfettered democratic participation, of social pluralism, and, more generally, of human flourishing, support and can also unify the various elements in the institutional theory of separation of church and state.

The first separation principle – which I shall call the *libertarian principle* – says that the state must permit the practice of any religion, though within certain limits. This is a principle of *tolerance*. It does not imply approval of any particular religion; it simply recognizes the importance to citizens of their freedom to practice their religion and, on the negative side, the inappropriateness of interference with that freedom by governmental institutions. The same kind of basis that grounds this recognition, however, provides a rationale for restricting religious practices in special cases, as where human sacrifice is required by a religion or its practices pose threats to public health, say by prohibiting inoculations necessary to prevent epidemics. It should go without saying that the boundaries of legitimate state power are unclear in such matters. In a liberal democracy, however, the burden of proof is on the state wherever it would restrict religious liberty. This point derives from the commitment to freedom as a fundamental value in liberal democracy.

The second principle – the *equalitarian principle* – says that the state may not give preference to one religion over another. This is a principle of *impartiality.* The principle not only rules out an established church – whose existence might be plausibly argued to be compatible with the libertarian principle – but also precludes such practices as legally requiring a certain religious affiliation as a condition for public office. There are, to be sure, kinds and degrees of establishment, and some kinds may have minimal impact or may be accompanied by compensations for the privileges they extend to the established church. Still, other things equal, the greater the degree of establishment in a society, the less it counts as a liberal democracy.[3]

The third principle – which I shall call the *neutrality principle* – is less commonly affirmed, but also belongs to any full-blooded liberal democratic account of separation of church and state. It says that the state should neither favor nor disfavor religion (or the religious) *as such,* that is, give positive or negative preference to institutions or persons simply because they are religious. As the reference to both positive and negative preference indicates, this principle requires neutrality not only among religions, but also between the religious and the non-religious. It may be regarded as an extension of the religious impartiality affirmed by the equalitarian principle, but is perhaps best conceived as a principle of that precludes governmental *favoritism.*

Why should a free and democratic society endorse these three principles? In different terms, why should it accept the rather far-reaching liberalism they imply, rather than some weaker form of liberal democratic theory? This is a large question, and I shall cite only quite general supporting grounds. I take the principles in turn.

The Libertarian Principle

It seems beyond dispute that both from the moral point of view and from the perspective of political structure, a society without religious liberty is simply not adequately free. Moreover, freedom is required for democracy, at least in any sense of 'democracy' relevant here – a sense in which such a form of government is of, for, and by the people. Thus, if one's ideal is a free and democratic society, one wants a social (presumably constitutional) framework to guarantee at least the following three kinds of religious liberty: first, freedom of religious belief, understood to prohibit the state or anyone else from forcibly inculcating religious beliefs in the general population, whether by early education of children or by forcing adults to submit to brainwashing or other cognitive manipulation;[4] second, freedom of worship, involving, minimally, a right of peaceable religious assembly, as well as a right to offer prayers by oneself, orally as well as silently, and with appropriate rituals; and third, freedom to engage in (and to teach one's children if one has any) the practices and rituals of one's religion, provided these practices do not violate certain basic moral rights. Clearly, then, a free and democratic society should adopt the libertarian principle. A society without the freedom it guarantees would be intolerant and would offer inadequate protection against governmental coercion. That protection is surely one of the underlying grounds of church-state separation in the U.S. Constitution and in other foundational documents elsewhere in the world, and it has figured in American judicial history; but I cannot here explore that history or even the relevant literature on Constitutional interpretation.[5]

Insofar as the notion of the religious is unclear, the scope of principles of separation of church and state will be correspondingly so. I cannot here define 'religious', but it must for our purposes be taken sufficiently narrowly to permit a distinction between the moral and the religious, so that, for instance, not just any seriously held moral belief counts as religious. A liberal democracy may properly appeal to moral considerations, both at the constitutional level and in making and interpreting laws and policies within a constitutional framework. Consider, for example, the appeal to a notion of justice in establishing criminal penalties and to obligations of beneficence in determining provisions of the welfare system. In distinguishing the religious from the moral and from other non-religious notions, the issues that most concern us are those in which some theistic religion figures. Non-theistic religions (if indeed there are such in any full-blooded sense of 'religion') pose – other things equal – far less serious church-state problems. This is in good part (though not entirely) because theistic religions tend to be in certain ways authoritarian. My main focus will be on religious elements conceived as pertaining to theistic religions.

It may help in understanding what constitutes a religion to keep in mind nine important features, each of which is relevant, though not strictly necessary, to a social institution's constituting a religion:

1. Belief in one or more supernatural beings.
2. A distinction between sacred and profane objects.
3. Ritual acts focused on those objects.
4. A moral code believed to be sanctioned by the god(s).
5. Religious feelings (awe, mystery, etc.) that tend to be aroused by the sacred objects and during rituals.
6. Prayer and other communicative forms of conduct concerning the god(s).
7. A world view according adherents a significant place in the universe.
8. A more or less comprehensive organization of one's life based on the world view.
9. A social organization bound together by (1)–(8).[6]

The richest paradigms of religion, such as Christianity, Judaism, and Islam, exhibit all of these features and because of that – as well as in virtue of their place in the contemporary world – are especially good cases to consider in relation to separation of church and state. They are also good cases in that they take God to be omniscient, omnipotent, and omnibenevolent, and hence, in their different ways, claim a special authority in the lives of their adherents. It is these three that I shall mainly have in mind in what follows, but nearly all of the points made about the relation between the religious and the political are meant to apply, to some extent, to any religion.

The Equalitarian Principle

The case for the equalitarian principle is more complicated than the case for the libertarian principle. The (or a) central premise of the former case is that if the state prefers one or more religions, its people might well find it hard to practice another, or would at least feel pressure to adopt or give preferential treatment to the (or a) religion favored by the state. The degree of pressure would tend to be proportional to the strength of governmental preference. That preference might be great enough to require a certain religious affiliation for holding a government job, or as minor as the state's inviting clergy from only one religion to officiate at small, local ceremonies.

Any governmental religious preference for a particular religion, however, creates some tendency for greater power to accrue to those identified with the preferred religion, particularly if it is that of the majority of the citizenry. Even if the existence of certain disproportionate powers does not necessarily (or at least does not directly) restrict anyone's liberty, concentration of power in a religious group as such easily impairs democracy, in which citizens should have equal opportunities to exercise political power on a fair basis. It may also threaten religious freedom in particular. Moreover, where a state establishes or prefers a given religion, we may anticipate (though it is perhaps not inevitable) that certain laws will significantly reflect the world view associated with that religion. These are among the reasons why a free and democratic society should adopt the equalitarian principle.

Even where the libertarian principle is respected, the equalitarian principle is needed to protect citizens against governmental discrimination, whether against religions that are not established or preferred or against the non-religious. Such discrimination can be serious even where it is not represented by legal restrictions of those not preferred under the non-equalitarian policies in question. Opportunity can be drastically limited even where one is not strictly unfree to seek its benefits. Granted, liberal democracies accept differences in opportunity that stem from differences in effort and even in natural endowment;[7] but limitations in opportunity that derive from one's lacking a preferred religious affiliation are not acceptable in such a society. This is understandable, moreover, from both secular and religious perspectives: these limitations violate standards of basic liberty and basic equality, and even a religious majority can see that they pave the way for its own disadvantage should another religious group become dominant.

Given how many democratic nations have an established church, one may wonder whether the equalitarian principle is meant to imply that they do not deserve the name 'democracy' or are at best not *liberal* democracies. There is nothing in the notion of democracy simpliciter that absolutely requires a democracy to abide by the principle. Even the libertarian principle is implicit in that notion only on two (highly plausible) assumptions: first, that sufficient liberty for the people to govern implies religious liberty, and second (and perhaps controversially), that this level of liberty requires adherence to the principle rather than a weaker alternative. Mere democracy, however, is not my concern and is of far less interest than liberal democracy, which is my central focus.

It is liberal democracy, with its stress on freedom as well as basic political equality, that is the avowed goal of the leading democracies of the world. For liberal democracy, the equalitarian principle should be instituted in the ideal case. Perhaps, however, the imperative expressed by this 'should' can be overridden. If, for special reasons, such as a deep attachment to a tradition, the principle is not instituted, there should be safeguards against abuses of the religious preference involved. If, for instance, the English can show that the effects that retaining their established church has on liberty are slight and that eliminating it would have highly detrimental results of certain kinds, then the principle does not imply that Britain is not a liberal democracy. It does imply that the ideal of liberal democracy has not been fully reached, that protections of liberty and basic political equality must be maintained in relation to the established church, and that a rationale is needed to justify its continuance insofar as a liberal democracy is the nation's political ideal.

The Neutrality Principle

To see the rationale for the neutrality principle, recall first of all that religious liberty, broadly conceived, includes the freedom to suspend judgment on or even categorically reject religious views. If the state shows preference for religious institutions as such (or for the practice of religion in general), there may well be pressure to adopt a religion, and quite possibly discrimination against those who do not. To be sure, some kinds of state preference for religious people or institutions as such are consistent with religious liberty; hence, the neutrality principle cannot be simply derived from the libertarian principle. Nor can it be derived from the equalitarian principle, which is consistent with preferring the religious over the non-religious. The latter calls for state *neutrality among religions;* the former calls for state *neutrality toward religion.*[8] More must be said about the liberal-democratic rationale for the latter standard.

There are many domains of possible state preference for the religious as such. Mandatory prayer sessions in public schools, a privileged status for religious exemptions from combat duty, and religious eligibility requirements for adopting children are examples. Other possibilities are tax deductions given to people sending their children to church-supported schools but not to people sending them to secular private schools, preference for religious citizens (other things equal) in filling government posts ordinarily earned by competition on the basis of merit alone, and statutory roles for religious institutions or their representatives in government, as in the case of the Archbishop of Canterbury in England.[9]

Preferences of the sort indicated may tend toward political domination by the religious, even if in principle the pressures created by those preferences could be prevented from causing it. Thus, even if there is protection both from religious tyranny and from discriminatory exclusions of some disfavored groups on religious grounds, governmental preference of the religious as such is likely to give them advantages that threaten a proper democratic distribution of political power. It can also reduce the level of free *exercise* of liberty, as opposed to its mere legal *scope*. The more difficult it is to exercise a liberty – as where non-religious people must make themselves conspicuous by abstaining from reciting the Pledge of Allegiance to the U.S. flag – the less we tend to do it.[10] A good democratic government – one that is truly at work for the people – not only protects the exercise of the liberties it recognizes; it does what it reasonably can to facilitate their exercise. A liberty that is too costly to exercise is like a food one cannot afford. Even when one would like to have it and would flourish by consuming it, in practice one can do so only with outside help.

My emphasis so far in arguing for the neutrality principle has been mainly considerations of liberty, though these are not entirely separable from considerations of equality. In any case, a further ground for the neutrality principle is the ideal of equal treatment not solely among the religious but among citizens in general, an ideal that, like liberty, I am taking as basic for a free and democratic society. Governmental preference for the religious as such is intrinsically unequal treatment of the religious and non-religious, however minor the resulting material differences may be.

There are, however, further reasons for a liberal democracy to adopt the neutrality principle even if such a society need not be committed to protecting the freedom not to be religious and can, at least at the constitutional level, accord the same rights to the religious and the non-religious alike. (These reasons may of course also provide support for the equalitarian principle.) Once the state favors the religious over the non-religious, at least three problems arise, any of which can lead to erosion of freedom and democracy.

The first problem that arises in a democracy which does not abide by the neutrality principle is that where there is a majority affiliation, the views and even the interests of this group are likely to dominate legislation and policy affecting religion, sometimes to the detriment of religious minorities, for instance in the treatment of religious schools and the celebration of major events, such as inaugurations and holidays. Here it must be remembered that even if the equalitarian principle is being observed, religious groups may be represented, on a fair basis, in influential social roles. On the normal democratic assumption that representation should be proportionate, one could thus expect a majority religious group to dominate in the wide range of public activities and programs that benefit religious practice, say in research support, public service that counts as an alternative to military conscription, exemptions from taxation on tuition or other expenses, and so forth.[11]

The second problem is that religious disagreements are likely to polarize government, especially regarding law and policy concerning religion, say requirements for conscientious objector status or, at the institutional level, for tax exemption. Each religious group will tend to have its own conception not only of what constitutes a religion in the first place but also of what criteria a religious group must fulfill to receive exemptions or other benefits. Granted that secular disputes can also polarize, other things equal they have less tendency to do this or at least to produce irreconcilable differences. If ideological disputes, say between communism and fascism, seem exceptions to this point, that may be in part because of how much an ideology can have in common with a religion. Indeed, there may be no sharp distinction between certain kinds of deeply internalized ideology and certain kinds of religion. (The more like a religion an ideology is, of course, the less other things are equal and the better the case for treating it like a religion in relation to the three separation principles.)[12] Secular disputes, as compared with religious ones, also tend to be resolvable without either side's making as deep concessions.

The third problem is that if a government prefers the religious over the non-religious, it will tend, through the pronouncements and social policies that express that preference, to influence churches, and, in deciding what to promote in the religious sphere, to begin to set criteria for what counts as being religious in the sense that qualifies institutions for preference. Once there are benefits to be had, there will be stretching to meet the criteria for getting them. This is a likely way to much "entanglement" of the government in religious affairs and, perhaps equally serious, of religious institutions in governmental affairs even where governmental regulation of churches is not at issue.[13]

It might be argued that the only reason to avoid reducing the exercise, as opposed to the scope, of freedom in a democratic society is a commitment to fostering pluralism, which is an optional goal for such a society. It is true that pluralism is not a constitutive aim of liberal democracy even if, as a matter of contingent fact, pluralism fosters freedom and democracy. But the distinction between reducing the scope and reducing the exercise of freedom is not sharp: apart from a courageous few, making the exercise of a freedom costly shades into narrowing its scope. Some American citizens, for example, may at least not feel free to abstain from reciting the Pledge of Allegiance where it is called for in a setting in which, as parents, they are not anonymous, such as a high school convocation; and by and large only courageous schoolchildren would absent themselves from voluntary religious assemblies in a school where a vast majority attend them.

Quite independently of a commitment to fostering pluralism, a liberal democracy should avoid reducing the exercise of freedom. Diminutions in the exercise of freedom tend to lessen creativity both in the lives of individuals and in the solution of social problems. If that exercise is made too costly, a society with high ideals of freedom and a commitment to extensive legal protections of it may still be *effectively* quite lacking in freedom among the people.

To be sure, there are justifiable exceptions to the requirement of equal freedom for all citizens, as where certain government officials have, as such, privileges both in economic power and in the scope of their liberty. But equality in the sense that concerns us is not equivalent to *uniformity*. Veterans may have some privileges others lack, partly on the ground that the military would not be treated equally if asked to take risks or make sacrifices without special compensation, such as they might expect from comparably risky work in civilian life. Cases like this, in which a standard of fairness is a basis for interpreting a governmental obligation of neutrality, show something so far not explicit: the neutrality in question is not moral but, in a broad sense, political.

On balance, then, the neutrality principle seems required to guarantee protection from governmental favoritism, in the sense implicit in preferential treatment of the religious over the non-religious. Even if this treatment does not involve discrimination in favor of one religious group, non-religious citizens will tend to *feel* it as discrimination and not as a legitimate expression of the will of a democratic majority. Freedom and democracy are best served by principles that keep the state from restricting *or* influencing religious institutions as such any more than is required for enacting laws and policies that are justified on non-religious grounds.[14]

CHURCH-STATE SEPARATION VIEWED FROM A RELIGIOUS STANDPOINT

My concern so far has been with governmental activities as they affect religion and, even more, with standards of sociopolitical conduct appropriate to conscientious citizens in a free and democratic society. But a full-blooded liberal theory of institutional separation of the religious and the political has another component, also based on ideals underlying liberal democracy. For many of the same reasons why the state should not interfere in religion, churches should not interfere in government. The point is not legal or even constitutional. I am not suggesting, for example, that church donations to political candidates must be illegal in a liberal democracy – though presumably they should be *if* churches have tax-exempt status. My point is that protection of religious liberty, and certainly of governmental neutrality toward religious institutions, is better served if, normally, churches as such abstain from political action.

Why is it not enough of a constraint to endorse an ideal for liberal democracy that calls on churches in such a society to balance religious and secular considerations (especially moral ones) in deciding their position on sociopolitical matters? Why should we go beyond this to the suggested proposal for political neutrality on the part of churches? This is an important question on which political theorists disagree among themselves, with only some of them taking the suggested step toward neutrality. The matter deserves reflection.

Ecclesiastical Neutrality

One possible ground for the neutrality proposal is that in their official institutional actions churches are commonly understood to be acting as religious institutions whose major concerns and bases of action are always religious and thus best not pursued in politics. The suggested argument has some force, but we must not give it undue weight. The common understanding in question has limited force when it does apply, and, in any case, it does not always apply. It is simply not true that religious institutions can properly have, or act upon, only religious reasons. For at least a great many churches, it can be quite proper both to take a moral position as such and to consider a moral conclusion as such to be sufficient for a political position.

To be sure, a church could be committed to taking no moral positions simply as such but *only* those it sees as theologically grounded. This, however, is by no means inevitable and seems inappropriate to at least much of the Hebraic-Christian tradition. By contrast, a church's requiring its public policy stances to be consistent with religious standards is a quite different matter and a far weaker constraint. I think it turns out, then, that we need a more fine-grained understanding of the proper role of churches in a free and democratic society than we can achieve either by construing them as governed in every detail by theological or religious considerations or by simply asking what would constitute good institutional citizenship on their part.

Let me tentatively suggest, as a partial solution to the problem of how best to conceive the role of churches in democratic politics, a *principle of ecclesiastical political neutrality:* in a free and democratic society, churches committed to being institutional citizens in such a society have a prima facie obligation to abstain from supporting candidates for public office or pressing for laws or public policies that restrict human conduct, particularly religious or other basic liberties.[15] This principle applies not only to religious institutions as social entities but to their official representatives acting as such.[16] Even for churches not committed to citizenship in a liberal democracy, a case can be made that it would be good for them to recognize such an obligation of neutrality, but here I restrict attention to churches having that commitment. My concern is with the usual case in which a church has extensive community involvement and a serious concern for the welfare of the people of the country (or countries) in which its congregation resides. A number of other comments (far more than I can make here) are also required.

First, I do not take the neutrality obligation to be likely to prevail under just any social conditions, and it obviously does not apply to laws protecting the basic freedoms necessary in a liberal democracy. Second, under conditions of tyranny, freedom and democracy might be restorable only if churches *do* support candidates for (public) office. A clear threat of such tyranny, as in pre-Nazi Germany, may also warrant such support. Third, I do not take the obligation in question to be specifically religious or theological, since it need not be grounded in religious or theological elements, and indeed not every religious tradition must contain elements that would sustain it. Whether the obligation has a sufficient moral basis depends in part on whether there are (as Chapter 1 suggests there are) sufficient moral grounds for liberal democracy as the best form of government.[17] But even apart from how this question is resolved, there are considerations of good institutional citizenship and of prudence that support the principle of ecclesiastical political neutrality for churches living under conditions of freedom and democracy.

The Political and the Moral

The ecclesiastical neutrality principle will be too strong if we construe 'political' in the broad sense of 'contested in the arena of politics' – call this the *polemical sense* – or in the sense it has in 'political philosophy', wherein it means roughly 'concerning the appropriate or the basic structure of civil society' (a very wide concept is needed here, encompassing both conceptual and normative notions). Call the latter the *philosophical sense*. The term 'political' must be taken rather narrowly, so that moral issues are not construed as necessarily political, even if they enter into distinctly political debates, but not so narrowly that pressing for restrictive laws or public policies[18] – such as policies requiring periods of prayer or meditation in public schools – does not count as political.

In the paradigm cases of the narrowly political, the notion of the political is *indexical*, in the sense of having essential reference to particular individuals. Thus, I take a question to be political in this narrow sense when it essentially concerns *who* among existing people (or their descendants or heirs) will (or should) govern, for instance who will win an election or secure an appointment in government or, more broadly, a position of authority in an institution, such as a political party or a university or a large business, that has power over people. A paradigm of a political preference in this sense is favoring a particular candidate for office. By contrast, a question of what structure a government should have is political in the wider, philosophical sense. Take, for instance, the question whether the United States should move toward a parliamentary system. To be sure, pursuing a question that is political in the wider sense can be motivated by what is political in the narrow, indexical sense (and conversely): it can be a disguised way of getting people to agree to a set of arrangements because it favors one's own party or candidates. But the distinction remains viable in principle and is important in practice.

The difference between the political in the narrow sense and the moral can be masked by the application of a single term, such as 'the abortion issue', to both moral questions about its ethical permissibility and political questions about the degree of legal protection it should have and whose policies will be enacted. Paradigms of political questions in the narrow sense are what specific persons or what particular party will or should hold governmental power. Somewhat less clear cases of the political – at least they are not necessarily political in the narrow sense – are what policies should govern relations, including immigration, with specific foreign countries (for here determinate individuals and their rights are directly at stake). We might speak here of what is political in *the social policy sense.*

When we come to what specific structure should be enacted for taxation, welfare, criminal justice, health care, and military systems, we have issues that can be treated as political in the broad, philosophical sense, for instance where general criteria in these domains are at issue from the point of view of social justice. But social justice can also be construed as political in a narrower sense depending on how clearly the adoption of a policy in such domains would give governmental power to specific individuals. There are many other political questions. Some of these have major moral dimensions, and we cannot hope to make a plausible distinction between the moral and the political that is sharp enough to put every sociopolitical question clearly on one side or the other.

The separation of church and state does not require, nor do any sound principles demand, that churches should not publicly take moral positions, even if there is political controversy about them. Publicly taking moral positions is indeed a positive religious obligation in many religions. There are, to be sure, different ways of supporting moral positions. Some are closer than others to political statements, as where government officials of only one party are cited as immoral despite the prominence of comparable offenders who are officials in another party. Clergy should in general seek to avoid even the appearance of partisanship. These matters call for discretion and do not admit of codification.[19]

Internal and External Political Activities

In applying the ecclesiastical neutrality principle, it is important to distinguish – as with other politically significant institutions, such as universities – between *internal* and *external* political activities and, in both cases, between *official* and *unofficial* political statements and positions. Internal activities are directed toward members, external activities toward an external group, such as society as a whole (these are the pure cases; there are myriad mixtures raising special problems that I cannot take up here). The principle of ecclesiastical political neutrality applies differently to the external than to the internal activities. A church's publicly promoting political candidates is, prima facie, poor institutional citizenship; its doing so internally need not be, though it may tend to corrupt the church's spiritual mission or may put undue pressure on its members, or both. Insofar as good citizenship is a matter of private conduct that directly affects public behavior such as voting, a church's engaging in politics internally, as distinct from generally educating parishioners morally and sociopolitically, can be poor institutional citizenship.[20]

It matters considerably whether a church's political activity is official or unofficial, say carried on in private conversations as opposed to a letter to parishioners. Here again the internal-external distinction is relevant. Public support by clergy of a candidate for office may, especially when represented as an official church position, exert pressure on church members, on ordinary citizens, on candidates for public office (who may, e.g., curry favor or solicit opposing clerical statements), or on government officials (who may, for instance, think they are hearing, in the voice of one or more clergy, the wishes or views of the members of the relevant religious group).

The principle of ecclesiastical political neutrality would not undermine churches' encouraging their members' *participation* in politics.

Churches' doing this is not narrowly political, and the participation may be argued to be a moral obligation of citizenship and as such properly supportable by churches. Nor does the principle unduly restrict the manner of political participation by religious citizens, including clergy, or imply that they should not consider such participation an aspect of their religious commitments. A minister or rabbi could, under this principle, both publicly oppose nuclear dumping in the oceans and, during religious services, preach against political apathy. Civic indolence may be criticized both as a failure to fulfill a religious obligation to improve the world and as a moral vice in citizens. Taking political positions from the pulpit (and in other institutional ways), however, would be (prima facie) objectionable under the principle.

Some public activities commonly conceived as those of a church do not count as official. Thus, a church-sponsored group, such as one opposing an unjust war, or a service committee that, in its humane activities, defies government policy, is not necessarily an official representative of the church's position. Neither affiliation nor sponsorship entails endorsement, much less an official role in representing an institution as such. Even then, affiliated church groups may distinguish their moral from their political aims, and prudence often dictates explicitly doing so. Their activities will often be met with a presumption that their views represent their church, and that presumption will tend to prevail if advocacy is not prominently said to express the group's own autonomous views.

It must be granted that there are moral statements which, combined with certain obvious facts about politicians, government officials, or foreign powers, imply condemnation or approval of them. But there is a crucial difference between affirming moral truths which, *with* certain facts, imply political judgments, and on the other hand, making political judgments themselves. Politically relevant matters of fact, such as the effects of a social policy, or the likelihood of AIDS patients infecting their caregivers, or the costs of nursing home care for Alzheimer's disease, may be controversial. This point should make it natural, and may create some obligation, for parishioners and many others to explore the relevant facts before drawing political conclusions to which they are relevant. Such explorations may produce unexpected results and, sometimes, final views that reflect independence of judgment or departures from orthodoxy. The study of facts can change people's judgments and even their values, and it is a salutary activity even where it does not.

Ecclesiastical political neutrality, by contrast with political involvement by churches, makes more room for the exercise of reflective and independent citizenship.

When the suggested distinction between the moral and the (narrowly) political is observed, the political bearing of factual issues is left to the individual judgment of those in the congregation or audience. That judgment constitutes an important filter between clerical deliverances and political action. Even people who accept the moral judgments expressed by their church, find it obvious how the facts are relevant to those judgments, and draw an obviously implied political conclusion will have traversed a certain inferential distance. Doing so is an exercise of autonomy.[21]

I am not in the least suggesting that the principle of ecclesiastical political neutrality should be written into law; but if it is not conscientiously observed, then candidates for public office may be unduly influenced to serve the special, even the distinctively religious, interests of certain churches, particularly if there is a majority church. Furthermore, the polarities afflicting relations between certain religious groups are more likely to surface in government decision making, where the public interest should be the overriding concern.

Admittedly, some polarization may arise from *any* public political disagreement, particularly when institutions themselves square off. But whereas in a free and democratic society, political controversy is inevitable, religious polarization is not. Moreover, some clergy represent themselves as having, or in any case are generally taken to have, special insight into matters of human conduct; this (among other factors) increases the chance of sociopolitical polarization if religious institutions as such enter into politics and (certain kinds of) public policy debate. The possibility of polarization remains even if those institutions do this only or chiefly within their own congregations.

The risks of polarization are matched by a different kind of liability that goes with political activity by clergy. I refer to their moral authority, both in and outside their congregations. This is not to deny that it is possible to bring moral authority into politics, and indeed I have stressed that moral leadership by the clergy can greatly help in this. But moral leadership is easily clouded by political activities. The support of specific candidates or even parties tends to erode moral authority.

Granted, for clergy who address contemporary issues, the ecclesiastical neutrality principle is not easy to observe. However hard clergy may try to avoid using religious authority in a political fashion, religiously motivated moral concerns may easily shade into political ones. Certainly an admirable moral sermon on, for example, the duties of charity, could have obvious implications for legislative decisions on welfare policy. Here it will be important just how obvious those implications are and whether they are affirmed; intonation and context are crucial too. But if, in borderline cases, the moral and political intermingle, there is still a generally plain difference between, say, giving a moral sermon about the quality of contemporary movies and endorsing candidates, political parties, or politically contested public policy positions.[22]

Clerical Leadership in Civic Life

One might object to the ecclesiastical neutrality principle that the clergy are obligated to help bring into being a morally acceptable democracy and thus to promote, for example, economic justice, which might in turn require criticizing the federal government's policy on minimum wages.[23] Two distinctions are essential to appraising this objection. The first is between the obligations of clergy as citizens and their distinctively clerical obligations. The second is between the obligation to promote these ideals *in general,* especially as broadly moral, and the obligation to promote them *politically,* through specific parties or policies.

I heartily acknowledge obligations of citizenship – and freedom of political action – on the part of clergy. But I take it that argument is needed to show that the clergy *as such* are obligated to promote democracy, particularly if the promotion is to be political, for instance by helping to elect a preferred party (among those committed to democracy in general). Moral principle is one thing, political strategy quite another. I have argued that clergy committed to freedom and democracy are prima facie obligated not to promote candidates for office or specific laws or public policies that restrict human conduct. I agree that they should oppose, for instance, economic injustice; but proposing a specific wage structure or a detailed strategy of disarmament is quite another matter.

Similarly, powerful opposition to racial injustice is to be expected of, for example, clergy in the Hebraic-Christian tradition, and it may be quite specific in terms of real or imaginary examples of wrongdoing held up as abominable. Martin Luther King, Jr., combined religious and moral criticism of the system he sought to reform, but his most important criticism was not political in the narrow sense, and his overall civil rights mission did not require him to be political in that sense. Support of one political party's particular way of dealing with a problem, as opposed to a competing strategy proposed by another party, is quite different from moral criticism; the former is one kind of thing the ecclesiastical neutrality principle is intended to restrict. It may as a matter of contingent fact turn out that what a reformer calls for on moral grounds is supported by only one party; but there remains an important difference between calling for the reform and supporting the party as such.

It is – or in any case should be – through the moral and spiritual power of churches that they improve society rather than through their direct exercises of political power; and I fear that churches' regularly exercising political power might produce religious fractures and quite possibly religious domination. Such domination, particularly in certain sectors of civic life, would wrongly limit the freedom of the religious and the non-religious alike. If there is a Protestant or Catholic or Jewish or Moslem position on a political issue, candidates may not only bend over backward to win church endorsement on that issue, but also covet it in other areas. To some extent this already occurs in, for example, the United States; and if there is little enough disagreement, or ingenious enough compromise, or a wise enough clergy, or a sufficiently educated citizenry, democracy may still thrive. But it is more likely to thrive if the clergy judiciously abide by a reasonable standard of political neutrality.

To say that churches have a prima facie obligation to be politically neutral in the ways I have described, and that their support of a free and democratic society should not be political in the narrow sense, is not to deny that from the point of view of liberal-democratic theory – even if not invariably of theology – religious institutions can have an important role in such a society. They can and should function as a spiritual and moral counterpoise to the power of the state. They should also provide a major alternative to secular institutions in the competition for the allegiance of the people. Churches should be independent, then, of both the state and other institutions in matters of value, vigilant toward the abuse of power, and supportive of individuality among citizens. Their positive role is not limited to their own members; it extends to other segments of the population. Fulfilling this constructive function in a democracy does not require their entering politics and is supported better by their spiritual and moral leadership than by any narrowly political activities.

The principle of ecclesiastical political neutrality must not be thought to be supported only by considerations of religious liberty and democratic ideals. It may also protect the integrity of religious institutions themselves. Politics and public policy are a complex and absorbing business, and to acquire the knowledge of them requisite to speak with the authority properly befitting a corporate church voice (or even an influential clerical voice) can easily reduce the time and commitment needed for spiritual and moral matters. It is one thing to criticize economic injustice in a general way; it is quite another to make a responsible judgment that the minimum wage should be raised or, say, increased to $7.65. The ecclesiastical neutrality principle can thus help to prevent dilution of the clergy's religious function. As Moses gave the commandments of the Lord, the first is "You shall have no other Gods before me" (Exodus 20:3 and Deuteronomy 5:7); and Jesus taught that one cannot serve God and mammon (Matthew 6:24). Politics should be a worthier pursuit than money and other false gods, but we must still ask how well one can serve God and the state.

A church can, to be sure, have a research arm. But its staff must still be selected and supervised. That is no trivial exercise. Moreover, either the clergy sets the agenda for the research staff or it risks forfeiting control. In either case those who provide information on, say, the social or educational needs of a people, can become, especially for politically active churches, the tail that wags the dog. Similar considerations apply to churches' support of political action committees.

There are external as well as internal factors that support the ecclesiastical neutrality principle. Interdenominational strife and other conflicts among religious institutions have already been suggested. Quite apart from that, political action by churches exposes them to retaliation of a kind that they might be able to avoid. One might argue, for instance, that without a significant degree of political neutrality, churches would at best have had more difficulty than they in fact did in surviving under communism in Europe. It might also be argued that their moral and spiritual force had more to do with bringing repressive regimes down than any specifically political agenda or activity that they engaged in or might have undertaken.

APPLICATIONS OF CHURCH-STATE SEPARATION: PUBLIC OBSERVANCES, EDUCATIONAL POLICY, AND TAX EXEMPTION

The kind of separation of church and state appropriate to a liberal democracy and consonant with the three separation principles I have proposed can be clarified further by considering some of their applications. The libertarian, equalitarian, and neutrality principles each have a degree of ineliminable vagueness, and there is also the problem of how, in applying them, competing values should be weighted. These difficulties can be reduced by examining the principles in practice.

Religious Observances in Public Schools

Consider the hotly contested issue of prayer in public schools. Mandatory periods of prayer, such as daily assemblies addressed by clergy or others offering prayers, would violate the libertarian principle if that is understood, as it should be, to protect freedom *not* to practice a religion. Moreover, if, as may well be so, it is impossible to frame prayers equally acceptable to all faiths, then mandatory oral or written prayers in public schools would also be likely to violate the equalitarian principle. Some religious interests are likely to prevail over others, especially where there is a majority affiliation. One natural course would be to displease as few as possible by reflecting those majority preferences least offensive to any significant minority attending. Still, majority preferences would tend to be offensive to certain religious minorities. One might try for a lowest common denominator. But what offends none may also please none and may as a result generate an unhealthy competition to rectify the problem.

What, then, of voluntary periods for silent prayer? This is a difficult case.[24] Here the non-religious are left free not to participate. Moreover, since there is no oral prayer, presumably none of the religious need be offended – though someone might object to being invited to pray without the chance to hear or speak certain crucial words. On the other hand, given the conformism of many schoolchildren, might there not be pressure on many of the non-religious to join, or pressure on some of the religious to boycott as a gesture of support for non-religious friends who do not join? People being as they are, even voluntary silent prayer periods might diminish religious toleration and, ultimately, religious liberty.

A quite different point is that even if no particular religious outlook colors a prayer, in requiring or even sponsoring the offering of that prayer, the state is still, at least by proxy, establishing a religious practice.[25] The voluntariness of a practice must not be thought to imply that it is not officially established; nor would its non-denominational character show that it does not implicitly endorse a religion, in the sense of that phrase crucial for liberal democracy. The institutional and content requirements for a religion can be met by agents of government even without their preferring any standing church. A religion need not be inaugurated by a prophet, and it can be constructed by eclectic compilation, as well as from scripture or tradition. Thus, the neutrality principle is favored by the anti-establishment premises of the separation doctrine, and not only by libertarian or pluralistic considerations, or by equal treatment of churches. A government could establish a religion even without giving preference to any existing church and hence without violating the equalitarian principle. Establishing a religion requires neither coercion nor an antecedently existing institution as a candidate for establishment.

In a different vein, voluntary periods of prayer in public schools are by no means clearly in the interest of the religious. Here we can see one reason why religious as well as non-religious citizens may want to avoid governmental entanglement with religion regardless of good intentions on all sides. By confronting religious children with non-believers, the practice may easily give those children the impression – alien to most faiths – that religious conviction is only a matter of personal preference. Moreover, the division between those who go to prayer and those who do not may be dangerously polarizing.

It might seem that we could solve the problem by setting aside a period of time each day or week described as devoted to prayer *or* meditation. For everyone should appreciate the secular values of meditation, and there is no strong case on grounds of separation of church and state to resist such a practice. But the description 'prayer or meditation' would at best reduce the polarization, particularly if, as is likely, students generally recognize that it is mainly for encouraging or facilitating prayer that the relevant periods are set aside. A time reserved simply for meditation might avoid these difficulties; but if it could be described in a way that makes that likely, it might also have less appeal to those who hope that it will promote religious practice. For them, moreover, there would be an incentive to see it used properly. That would tend to polarize, for instance when, as seems inevitable, children ask of others, "What were you thinking about?"

Permitting voluntary periods for prayer or meditation might, then, seem after all to violate the neutrality principle, since the effect of such a policy might well be to promote the practice of religion. That is doubtful, however, unless it can be shown that such policies are intrinsically promotional toward religion. This is at best unlikely to be demonstrable; for one thing, in a society dominated by secularism, these policies could plainly have the opposite effect, in part because the religious might not wish to worship with secular meditators and might even feel discriminated against as engaging in unpopular activity. For another, accommodating the felt needs of the people for free time to think what they will or pursue any activity they take to be essential in their lives is a legitimate ground for governmental support, regardless of their special preferences for the use of the time or space provided. These points imply nothing about the wisdom of such governmental actions, but I cannot see a good case that they constitute more than a prima facie difficulty under the neutrality principle.

The singing of Christmas carols and perhaps certain hymns in public schools may easily be assimilated to that of prayer, but it is quite different. For one thing, what is said in prayer is affirmed, and it tends to express, and to be taken to express, one's beliefs. It is at least in some sense *confessional.* But what one sings in carols, and even hymns, one need not be affirming; nor need it be taken to express what one believes, any more than a student asked to recite a poem celebrating spring must be thought to accept its sentiments. These performances may be at least mainly aesthetic.

Despite these points, it must be granted that singing religious carols or devotional hymns is difficult to assimilate into mere musical training or into simple celebration of the Christmas season conceived as a time of merriment and gift-giving. There is a continuum from presenting songs and other works as simply of aesthetic or academic interest to treating them as sacred. Some students, however, might feel alienated from the activity if it is even religiously tinged. Hence, despite the importance of the distinction between confessional and aesthetic self-expression, care must be taken by public schools having Christmas carols and hymns during school hours; doing so can easily infringe the equalitarian principle and may also constitute a failure in governmental neutrality. Adding non-Christian songs tends to help, though the problem of finding a balanced mix remains. Finding this mix has led to what has been called the "two reindeer rule," in reference to the need for reindeer as secular symbols to provide a creche on public property with an appropriate mix of secular elements. Suppose one finds such a mix. Does one still violate the neutrality principle? This depends on the details; for instance, at least some of the songs, like the essentially secular "Rudolph the Red-Nosed Reindeer" and "White Christmas," seem to blend into the cultural meaning of the holiday season. It matters greatly, of course, not only what songs are selected, but in what context they are introduced and sung.

Governmental Aid to Sectarian Schools

Another major problem area is that of governmental aid to church-affiliated schools. Again, my concern is to clarify the three principles, not to settle specific issues about their scope.[26] Conceptually, one can distinguish aid that furthers the schools' sectarian purposes from aid that serves their secular educational ends. The latter kind of aid need not violate separation of church and state, provided non-religious private schools receive comparable support. But in practice it may be impossible to prevent aid to a sectarian school from furthering its overall aims and thereby its religious purposes. This can be so even in a school that admits students not committed to its faith and makes religious instruction optional for them.

An important option here is to give aid directly to students, perhaps approximately what they would receive if attending a public school. But since this aid might relieve the schools' general budgets, it might again help to advance sectarian purposes. A further distinction, then, is between aid to students that relieves them of ordinary payments to the school and aid that is special, as where mentally or emotionally disadvantaged students are given instruction that would be an extra cost even in a public school. Here it is arguable that to require such aid to be used on public premises or administered only by employees of public institutions imposes an unreasonable burden on the student.

There is, however, a wider issue: any aid to religiously affiliated schools helps them compete with secular institutions – private as well as public – and thereby arguably favors the religious; yet providing *no* aid for such education (beyond tax exemption for the schools in question) makes the exercise of religious liberty more expensive for citizens committed to attending sectarian schools but also required to pay taxes to support public schools. Moreover, aid to private schools whether secular or religious, designated for non-religious educational purposes, is arguably a kind of equal treatment before the law that represents the appropriate liberal-democratic neutrality. It is hardly surprising that aid to private schools and to students who attend them continues to be hotly contested, and that the principles I propose yield no simple resolution.[27]

Tax Exemption for Religious Institutions

The question of support for sectarian schools raises the issue of how the tax-exempt status of churches squares with the separation of church and state. Prima facie, it is preferential treatment of religious institutions. But churches are non-profit, charitable institutions, and these points seem to justify their exemption. To be sure, if there are criteria for non-religious, non-profit charitable organizations which churches do not have to meet, then there is prima facie preference. I cannot pursue any specific criteria for exemption; my point is just that as long as churches have significant charitable and philanthropic functions, their tax-exempt status does not by itself entail preferential treatment of religious institutions as such.

It may be, however, that the libertarian principle should also come in here; it might warrant tax exemption for churches even if charity and philanthropy are not a major part of their function. Consider the power to tax, with all its regulative and investigatory tentacles. It is the power to restrict, pressure, sometimes control, and sometimes choke to death. If we are to preserve religious liberty, and particularly to prevent the government from treating some religions better than others, it may be best not to give the state this power over churches, at least over their non-profit functions (any activities they may conduct for profit, as opposed to charitable or religious activity, presumably should be taxable).

If this is so, however, what justifies taxing businesses? The short answer is that they are run for profit. A long answer might begin by pointing out that, even if they were not, one's relation to one's business is quite different from one's relation to one's religion (though there are also issues I cannot address here, concerning whether taxation is a legitimate requisition of private property). One can go from one business to another and retain one's basic ideals, capacities, and identity as a person. But losing one's religion is (or certainly can be) far more profound. Even the capitalistic right to own a business at all is of lesser status in a free and democratic society than the right to practice one's religion.

The Problem of Criteria for a Religious Institution

So far in this section, I have largely neglected the problem of how to tell what constitutes a religious institution or a religion. The problem is important not only because a proper separation of church and state cannot be adequately described apart from a reasonably clear conception of religion, but also because too wide a conception of religion may produce excessive separation and too narrow a conception may cause insufficient separation. Must a religion be, from the point of view of the state, at least, theistic, as many adherents of the main religions of the Western world tend to think? And what about purported religions that are, say, both pagan and enjoin immoral practices, such as human sacrifice?

As suggested earlier in this chapter, we are unlikely to find any simple, uncontroversial definition of 'religion'.[28] This is a difficult and enduring problem, but it need not be crippling, either conceptually or legally. For there is a long list of uncontroversial cases, including most of those that raise the gravest cultural and legal issues; and there are some clearly relevant features – including devotion to a deity, rites and practices related to a deity, a theological conception of the meaning or value of human life, attitudes of reverence, and a central place in the life of the people in question – such that possession of a great majority of these features is normally both necessary and sufficient for the presence of a religion.

As these points indicate, although a good detailed definition of 'religion' is an immense task, it is not needed for case-by-case application of the three principles of separation. For that, and especially for the first two principles, a broad conception should be one's guide: in a liberal democracy it is generally better to extend a liberty to someone using 'religion' loosely than to deny it because of a too restrictive definition. Error on the inclusive side is at least limited by the point that separation of church and state does not protect violations of basic human rights, even if, like other doctrines meant mainly to preserve liberty, it does protect speech and ritual in which those violations are advocated. Suppose, indeed, that no precise, sound definition of 'religion' can be framed. It remains true that in the light of the three proposed principles of separation, resolving specific church-state issues is usually possible given the intuitions we have about what constitutes a religion, provided these intuitions are tempered by an understanding of the uncontroversial cases, both of religion and of its separation from the state.

Two negative points can also help. First, as suggested earlier in distinguishing a religion from an ethic, a moral outlook on life, even reverently held, is not sufficient for its possessor's being religious in the sense relevant to separation of church and state. Second, one does not have a religion simply because *some* coherent set of ideals is central in one's life. Even holding a world view "religiously" does not imply that it is itself a religion, or that one is a religious person. (The moral and existential-centrality notions of religion I am rejecting here, which are often uncritically accepted, also seem defective in other ways, but there is no need to discuss them further now.)

To be sure, there are some who speak of "civil religion" or even "secular religion" and take it that there is such a thing at least in the United States – a set of ideals Americans believe in that are revered and, in content, comprehensive enough to guide much of daily life, though they need not be theistic.[29] If there is a sense of 'religion' – as opposed to a suggestive metaphorical use of the term – in which a religion can be not only non-theistic but secular, it is not a major concern in this book. If, on the other hand, invocations or manifestations of civil religion imply a commitment to or endorsement of religion in the main sense (and particularly theistic religion), then the separation principles clearly apply to them.[30]

I believe, then, that we need not violate the separation doctrine in the very act of interpreting it, particularly if we observe certain distinctions. The most important cases in practice, moreover, are those involving churches whose religious character is not in question. There have, to be sure, been both debatable cases and arrant pretensions, as where year-round residents of a New York resort town, tired of paying high property taxes to compensate for churches' having bought up the old hotels, became "ordained," with a parsonage cropping up for every household. Though a legal failure, the venture did illustrate the important point that an elastic doctrine can be stretched from both ends.

Reviewing some of the larger points that have emerged in this chapter, we should first keep in mind that discussion of the separation of church and state should be viewed from both directions: from the point of view of the state as maintaining an adequate distance from, and independence of, the church, and conversely. Liberal democracy requires an appropriate separation in both directions, though the most important structural requirements of such separation consist in standards addressed to the state. These are above all the libertarian, equalitarian, and neutrality principles. The same standards of liberty that protect individuals, however, apply to non-governmental institutions. The separation of church and state that should be practiced by the former, then – expressed in part in the principle of ecclesiastical political neutrality – is a matter chiefly of the requirements of good citizenship, institutional and individual, rather than of constitutional or legal structure. It remains true that the same ideals of liberty and basic political equality that seem to demand the other three principles strongly support that principle. The principle is perhaps equally supported by internal considerations of the religious integrity of churches. But political neutrality does not entail moral neutrality, and the exercise of the former tends to support both the religious mission and the moral authority of religious institutions.

CHAPTER THREE

CHURCH-STATE SEPARATION AND THE JUSTIFICATION OF GOVERNMENTAL POWER

For liberal democracies, the overall purpose of government is to serve the people. This requires the protection of liberty and the maintenance of basic political equality, and those ideals in turn are the most important single ground for separation of church and state. It is particularly when the activities of government are coercive – as they generally are in the establishment of laws and public policies – that separation of church and state is important. It is also important in everyday governmental discussions and deliberations that do not lead to law or public policy yet are, for instance, interpretive or merely exploratory. But there is a special need for separation of church and state in the justification of governmental coercion. I have in mind chiefly the kinds of coercion achievable by legal penalties, but the coercion of public opinion and the threat of social ostracism also belong under a similar heading. Some of the reasons for this special need are evident from the case made in Chapter 2 for the libertarian, equalitarian, and neutrality principles. But far more should be said about the permissible grounds of coercion; and if a separation of church and state is required for coercion, we should also explore the role that religious arguments may nonetheless properly play in a liberal democracy. These two tasks are the main concern of this chapter. I begin with the larger question whether *any* large-scale conception of the good, secular or religious, is an appropriate commitment of a liberal democracy.

LIBERAL DEMOCRACY AND CONCEPTIONS OF THE GOOD

There is a wide range of views regarding the extent to which a liberal democracy may be committed to a large-scale conception of the good for human beings (John Rawls and others use 'comprehensive conception of the good', and that term will also serve provided it is not taken to rule out views that do not apply to every dimension of life but do posit a sufficiently definite notion of the good to bear substantially on the proper function of a liberal-democratic government). One view is that no such conception is an appropriate commitment of liberal democracy and a religiously based conception of the good is simply a special case of a comprehensive conception of the good. Rawls has recently gone so far as to say that "Moral doctrines are on a level with religion."[1]

A less restrictive position is that some presuppositions about the good may be commitments of a liberal democracy, but religious conceptions are not among them. Those who hold this view may or may not regard religious conceptions as significantly different from other particular conceptions of the good that are not appropriate commitments of a liberal democracy. The less restrictive view seems preferable in the light of both the nature of liberal democracy and the most plausible ways of grounding it. Let us explore the question with an eye toward the role a conception of the good may play in determining the requirements for governmental coercion.

The Supposed Value-Neutrality of Liberal Democracy

It is true that there are theories, and general conceptions, of the good for human beings that are not an appropriate basis for the underlying structure of law in a liberal democracy. There are also corrupt conceptions of the good, such as those a tyranny might devise for its self-perpetuation, that are not even an appropriate basis of a single piece of legislation on a minor segment of public life. But the almost unrestricted exclusion of conceptions of the good favored by some neutralists seems excessive. To be sure, if one thinks of morality as an institution directed essentially toward preventing or reducing evils,[2] it is natural to suppose that the law should share this goal. Such a view of morality may be one (or even the main) route to the libertarian version of liberalism. But there is no sharp distinction, and perhaps no workable one of any kind, between preventing harm and promoting some good. Consider education. Compulsory education is essential to prevent the harms attendant upon ignorance. Can we, however, reasonably design a required curriculum with no presuppositions as to what counts as good human functioning, what skills are needed for good citizenship, and what is worth knowing for its own sake? Surely not.

Neutralists differ considerably regarding just how definite a conception of the good a liberal democracy may assume. Some take the view that government should promote human well-being, but they characterize this goal in terms that are, as regards intrinsic goodness, value-neutral. This approach is represented by Rawls's appeal to "primary goods," such as respect and economic security, which he takes every rational person to want but does not consider to be intrinsically good.[3] Using this kind of strategy, welfare liberalism can claim to be at least as neutralist toward intrinsic goodness as libertarianism. In my view, that claim is at best a surface truth. Primary goods are functional equivalents of intrinsic goods, and in their name the state can do much the same things it can do in the name of intrinsic goods. Considerations of economic security, for instance, can lead to adopting high tax rates, and considerations of respect for persons can produce far-reaching equal opportunity legislation. Here coercion is justified on grounds taken to have the same kind of force that intrinsic goods are commonly felt to have.

Suppose, moreover, that we do not assume that certain things are intrinsically good and, with Humean instrumentalism, we tie the goods suitable as a basis for structuring a welfare state to human nature – at least in the sense that we assume there are some things every rational person naturally wants. Social justice will then be at the mercy of the contingencies of desire. Given how our desires can be influenced by fashion, circumstance, and demagoguery, and given the growing specter of a technology that can alter our very genes, one wants moral and political theories that, in an overall way, at least, can provide a way to judge human desires independently of what they happen to be at the time policy decisions must be made. This by no means implies that what we naturally want – or at least what we want when unmanipulated and adequately informed – is not important for sociopolitical decisions, but I do not believe that we can properly guide such decisions by presupposing the authority of the basic desires of people at any given time and place.[4]

To be sure, any plausible theory of the basis of liberal democracy will (as we have seen) affirm at least two values as essential constituents in such a society: liberty and basic political equality. Even if one insists that the state should be neutral on every *other* value and particularly toward overall conceptions of the good, one will need some kind of account of the kinds of harms or evils that warrant such restrictions of liberty as are necessary and, in order to determine eligibility for voting, a theory of what constitutes competence to vote. Here it is plain that some things will be functionally intrinsic evils. I suspect that some will also be functionally intrinsic goods. Recall compulsory education, which is a requirement for assuring competence to vote, at least at the legislative level. One may certainly seek to design a political structure in which the state is as nearly neutral as possible about the good, but there are drastic limits to how far this can go.[5]

We need at least two distinctions here: a distinction between neutrality in matters of taste and plan of life and neutrality in matters of basic value and basic moral standards, which accommodate a wide range of tastes and plans of life; and a second distinction between structural neutrality – roughly, neutrality at the constitutional level – and policy neutrality. A liberal *state* need not be neutral about freedom, justice – distributive as well as retributive – education, and health care. It should be neutral (within the limits of protection of the population) about the aesthetic preferences of citizens in their own dwellings, their choice of friends, their vacation preferences. A liberal-democratic *government,* however, need not be neutral in matters left open by a sound structure, such as the architectural style of government buildings or even proportion of funds allocated to education as opposed to upkeep of national parks. Here majority preference has largely unlimited dominion.

There is one further pair of distinctions we need. The first is between disagreement in theory and disagreement in practice; the second is a related distinction between disagreement *on* reasons and disagreement *in* reasons. Consider these in turn.

It is too often assumed that where people cannot agree on theories of the good they cannot in practice agree on what in particular *is* good. But surely this is a mistake. Even a Kantian and a utilitarian can agree that (for example) the danger of epidemic justifies compulsory inoculation when there is a safe, reliable vaccine. In part, neutralists may be thinking of the point that a liberal state should not presuppose any specific ethical theory. One can accept that and still maintain that a liberal-democratic state may be committed to certain human goods as goals of social policy and that among these are preservation of liberty and basic political equality, high-quality education, and enhancement of material opportunities for citizens.

Even apart from holding different theories (or any general theories), people may disagree on the second-order question whether a kind of consideration is a reason, or a good one, even if, in the first-order matter of *giving* reasons or making judgments or inferences, they take much the same factors as reasons and even accord them similar weight. Consider the idea that there is prima facie moral reason to do good deeds. Stated in the abstract, this idea is likely to be initially puzzling and probably controversial. But the same people who differ on its truth may agree, with respect to a wide range of acts done to help others, that they are good deeds and that their being so was a reason (justification, ground, warrant) for doing them. Someone who does not recognize that helping an old person who has slipped on ice is generally a good (minimally decent, appropriate, important) thing to do is (thankfully) hard to find. And if, in explaining my reaching my appointment a minute late, I cited as my reason that I wanted to help in such an urgent matter, it would be a rare person who would deny that I had a good reason. Agreement in reasons may be imperfect; but that would also hold for factual notions, such as the stability of a bridge or the effectiveness of a vaccine, and it is not a ground for special skepticism about reasons for action.

Overall, then, I do not see that the strong neutrality thesis – the view that a liberal democracy cannot presuppose any large-scale view of the good – is sustainable. Even the value commitments needed for determining the *scope* of liberty and the proper means of maintaining basic political equality seem to require recognition of some definite human goods as well as the evils that a liberal democratic government should seek to prevent. There are many ways in which such a government should be neutral, but the strong neutrality thesis goes beyond them. Let me suggest another way to see this and related points.

Fidelity to the Essential Premises of Liberal Democracy

It seems reasonable for a liberal democracy to build into its structure as much in the way of substantive promotion of the good as is implied in the essential premises underlying the liberal political theory by which it lives. The essential premises are not necessarily those actually appealed to by proponents, but those that must be *common* to all the sets of grounds sufficient to justify the sociopolitical vision. The essential premises are defined, then, as those minimally required for justification, not those historically used for the purpose. (I assume here that a liberal democracy as a form of government can be justified.) Normally, these two categories, the justificatory and the historical, substantially overlap. If they did not, the fidelity to essential premises idea would be less interesting. Still, there could be a divergence: the historical inspiration for a liberal democracy could in principle lack justificatory force; and the minimally justifying grounds could, in some historical circumstances, lack persuasive power.

To illustrate the fidelity to premises idea, suppose that justification of a liberal political theory as a basis for governing a society requires at least this: ideals of free democracy, in a sense implying one person, one vote; autonomy, in the sense of self-determination in a context of extensive liberty; respect for persons, implying at least equal treatment before the law and a legal system nurturing self-respect; and material well-being (including psychological well-being). In that case, proponents of the liberal theory in question might reasonably require that a society take positive steps to protect and promote these ideals. Such an approach would warrant something at least close to the five ideas of the good that Rawls finds in justice as fairness[6] (and probably more), but my purposes in this chapter do not require endorsing any specific list of goods as essential aims in a liberal democracy. The list just given, however, expresses a plausible core.

It is easy to go too far, however, especially in interpreting psychological well-being. Someone might, for instance, require religious observances by all citizens as part of a realization of our psychological and social good. This pattern is not entailed by the relevant notion of psychological well-being; and if it were, that notion would be at odds with the neutrality principle. Still, one can go beyond the minimal premises needed for guiding the achievement of justice alone without becoming committed to a theory of the good that is unduly restrictive. Compulsory education illustrates this point. One could take it to be a good, and certainly to be crucial for avoiding myriad evils, quite apart from a theory, as opposed to an intuitively plausible standard, of the good.

Suppose, by contrast, that a liberal democracy chooses to justify its liberal theory solely on certain pragmatic grounds that may be considered less controversial than the kinds just specified. From an instrumentalist standpoint, for instance, one might appeal to the goal of maximizing preference satisfaction within a framework of social harmony and political liberties. This approach will countenance only a thinner notion of the good than I prefer, though (as argued in Chapter 1) it could still be seen to be committed to separation of church and state. Suppose, however, that a morally inspired liberal political theory is justified, for example one that stresses the responsibility of government to facilitate human flourishing. A richer notion of the good might then be objectively warranted, say one that emphasizes enhancing the people's autonomy and ability to actualize their human capacities, whereas a wholly pragmatically founded society, being unable to countenance the grounds of the morally inspired theory, would not be justified, in practice, in building these social goals into its structure. It could support the same goals provided a majority wanted this, but could not have a deeper constitutional commitment to them.

A SURROGACY CONCEPTION OF JUSTIFIED COERCION

Even within a fidelity to essential premises conception of liberal democracy, there is an important distinction between grounds appropriate for a liberal society in justifying promotion of the goods it may endorse and grounds appropriate to justifying coercion. Here again I appeal to a general principle as a constraint. It seems to me that once autonomy is taken sufficiently seriously – as it will be not only by liberal political theorists in any of the seven traditions considered in Chapter 1, but also by any sound moral theory – the way is open to view the justification of coercion in a framework that gives high priority to respect for the self-determination of persons. A liberal democracy embodies, after all, a government both for and by the people; the justification of coercion, then, should be warrantable as something they would approve under appropriate conditions for selecting the kind of civic life of freedom and equality to which they are committed. For purposes of social-political philosophy, I suggest it is fruitful to work from a surrogacy conception of justified coercion, especially for cases of governmental coercion. Insofar as this conception is sound, it supports both the ideals of liberty and equality central for liberal democracy and its separation of church and state.

On this surrogacy view (which I merely sketch here), coercing a person, for a particular reason, to perform an action, in a given set of circumstances, is fully justified only if at least the following three conditions hold in the circumstances (perhaps with further qualification they, or some extension of them, are also sufficient for justified coercion). (a)

Someone else (most often, fellow citizens in the cases that concern us) has a (moral) right, in the circumstances, to have this action performed by the person – certainly a feature of most cases in which a liberal democracy can reasonably coerce its citizens – or at least the person morally ought to perform the action in the circumstances, for example to abstain from stealing from others. (b) If fully rational (hence willing to imagine a reversal of positions or roles between oneself and others) and adequately informed about the situation, the person would see that (a) holds and would, for the reason in question, say from a sense of how theft creates mistrust and chaos, or for some essentially related reason, perform the action, or at least tend to do so.[7] (c) The action in question is both an "important" kind of conduct (as opposed to breaking a casual promise to meet for lunch at the usual place) and one that may be reasonably believed to affect someone else (and perhaps not of a highly personal kind at all).[8] Thus, it is permissible, on grounds of the general welfare, to coerce people to pay taxes only if they ought to do so in the circumstances, can see this, and would (if fully rational and adequately informed) be appropriately motivated by seeing it; whereas it is not permissible to coerce someone to give up, say, smoking, provided it does not significantly affect others.[9]

It is not self-evident, to be sure, that each citizen in a democracy like that of the United States today or similarly democratic nations has a right (for instance) to other citizens' paying their taxes, or even that there ought to be taxes levied on everyone above a certain financial threshold, but this is at least arguable. It should also be noted that even if a sociopolitical system is not maximally just or for some other reason should be replaced by a better one, it does not follow that the only coercive legislation justified in that system is a kind that *would* be justified under a relevant superior system. Above all, whether we are legislators or ordinary citizens, there are things we morally ought to do in some circumstances that we ought not to do in others; and a moral obligation to do something is consistent with a moral justification or even obligation to change the circumstances that call for it. We can be morally obligated to obey a law that we are also morally obligated to try to change; and, as some cases of civil disobedience illustrate, we can be morally obligated to accept punishment under a law even if we are not thus obligated to obey it.

As these examples suggest, the greater the coercion to be justified (say, in terms of how much liberty it undermines) the more important the behavior in question must be; and parentalism, for normal adults, is ruled out. On the view I propose, then, we may coerce people to do only – but not all – things that they would autonomously do if adequately informed and fully rational.[10] The view explains why justified coercion is not *resented* by people when they later adequately understand its rationale, why some coercion is consonant with liberal-democratic ideals of autonomy, and why the kind that is can be supported by citizens *independently* of what they happen to approve of politically (at least in the narrow sense), religiously, or, to a large extent, even morally. I certainly do not claim that the proposed surrogacy conception makes it easy to determine just when governmental coercion is warranted; but it would be naive to think that any sound standard for determining this would in general make that easy.

If the perspective on liberal democracy I have sketched is correct, then it should be clear to understand why in such a society the use of secular reasons must have a major role in sociopolitical decisions (secular reasons need not, of course, be anti-religious and will be characterized in some detail in Chapter 4). Indeed, if there is a secular reason which is esoteric in a sense implying that a normal rational person cannot understand it, then a stronger requirement is needed; one might thus speak of public reason, as Rawls and others do.[11] The secularity requirement seems to apply especially to decisions that authorize social coercion, whether through law or even through restrictive social policies not backed by legal sanctions. If I am coerced on grounds that cannot motivate me, as a rational informed person, to do the thing in question, I cannot come to identify with the deed and will tend to resent having to do it. Even if the deed in fact *is* my obligation, where only esoteric knowledge – say, through revelation that only initiated people experience – can show that it is, I will tend to resent the coercion. This kind of basis of coercion breeds alienation.

It is part of the underlying rationale of liberal democracy that we not have to feel this kind of resentment – that we give up autonomy only where, no matter what our specific preferences or our particular world view, we can be expected, given adequate rationality and sufficient information, to see that we would have (or would at least tend to have) so acted on our own. At least in the vast majority of cases where there are adequate reasons for the relevant kind of coercion, these reasons are suitably accessible (say, with some explanation and perhaps some instruction) to normal rational persons. If there are exceptions, then we must add to the requirement of secularity that the reasons be appropriately accessible.

It may be objected that a rational person should want to be coerced by the *truth,* that is, coerced to do something one would voluntarily do assuming one is rational and believes the truth in question.[12] Suppose I am about to imbibe a fatal drink and refuse to believe that it is poisoned. Here I would certainly want to be saved from death even if I had to be prevented by force. Granted. But here it is easy to run a test and convince me of my error. Laws and social policies are not so easily shown to benefit us or to be otherwise acceptable. More important, if their basis is religious, some people may be constitutionally incapable of accepting it even if they are rational *and* the grounding premises are true. Commitment to liberal democracy is in part a commitment to avoiding the kind of alienating coercion this would constitute.

It may not be self-evident that this liberal commitment to the avoidance of alienating coercion is preferable to being saved from evil by coercion on the basis of certain truths one is missing; but it is far from self-evident that coercion in the name of truth will save its beneficiaries any more often than pursuing truth under liberal-democratic arrangements. Nor is it self-evident that the promised salvation is always preferable to living autonomously with all the risks that implies.

One might think that the importance of secular reasons is *derivative* from that of public reasons, that is (roughly), reasons the relevant public understands. But this is not so. For one thing, as I have been arguing, a liberal democracy must make special efforts to prevent religious domination of one group by another, and this would apply even if public reasons for such domination could be found. This, in turn, is supported by at least three points. One is that the authority structure common in many religions can make a desire to dominate other groups natural and can provide a rationale for it. What could be more important or beneficial to others than saving their souls? Another point is that the dictates of a religion often extend to the religious as well as secular conduct of persons, so that if domination occurs it undermines even religious freedom. To save their souls people must not only cease evil deeds but also worship appropriately. It is in part to prevent compulsion to worship – and especially to do so in some prescribed way – that religious freedom is a kind quite properly given high priority by a liberal democracy; and if religious considerations threaten it more than non-public influences in general, this provides additional reason for a liberal democracy to constrain the role of those considerations.

A third ground for denying that the importance of specifically secular reason is derivative from that of public reason is connected with the authority that religious principles, directives, and traditions are commonly felt to have. Where religious convictions are a basis of a disagreement, it is, other things equal, less likely that the disputants can achieve resolution or even peacefully agree to disagree. If God's will is felt to be clear, there is likely to seem to be only one way to view the issue. This can apply as much to prima facie non-religious problems such as health care as it does to specifically religious practices.

Granted, a non-religious source of conviction can also be felt to be infallible, and it may also be non-public. But not every non-public source of views and preferences poses the authority problem raised by many religions, or the special threat to religious freedom that can arise from certain kinds of unconstrained religious convictions. Particularly when people believe that extreme measures, such as bravely fighting a holy war, carry an eternal reward, they tend to be ready to take them. Being ready to die, they may find it much easier to kill.

THE POSITIVE ROLE OF RELIGIOUS ARGUMENTS IN A LIBERAL DEMOCRACY

It is important that my defense of separation of church and state not be taken to imply that religious arguments can make no positive contribution in the life of a liberal democracy. That is far from true.[13] It will help first to say something about what constitutes a religious argument and then to note some of the kinds of roles religious arguments can play. It will then be clear that separation of church and state does not require eliminating religious considerations or religious language from public life.

What is a religious, as opposed to a secular, argument? Reference is often made to religious arguments as if the notion were well understood, but I doubt that it is generally well understood, especially apart from the examples people commonly have in mind in using it, such as arguments from one of the Ten Commandments to a conclusion about how we should act. The question of what constitutes a religious argument turns out to be particularly difficult once we realize that an argument can be religious in a sense important for church-state issues even when it does not explicitly appeal to any religious notion or doctrine. There are several criteria, each indicating a different way in which an argument can be religious.

The Content Criterion for a Religious Argument

On the content criterion, a religious argument is one with essential religious content (as opposed to, say, merely quoted religious statements). Paradigmatically, this would be theistic content, say a reference to a divine command to have no graven images. But there are other cases, such as appeals to scripture, or to a religious leader, as a guide in human life. Full clarification of the concept of religious content would require nothing less than an analysis of the notion of a religion. For our purposes, it should be sufficient to think in terms of theistic, especially monotheistic, religions like Christianity, Judaism, and Islam, which are highly representative of the faiths posing challenges to a liberal democracy that seeks to give proper weight, in civic and political life, to religious considerations.

We would also do well to construe the relevant kind of religious content as *substantive,* for instance as expressing divine commands. We are not concerned with noncommittal or accidental religious content, as where a speaker refers, without endorsement, to someone else's statement of a religious doctrine.[14] A more difficult example would be one in which legislators or other public officials argue for a position on the ground that the vast majority of their constituents, for deep religious reasons, favor it. There are at least two cases here: one in which the reference to the religious convictions of constituents is simply added information, perhaps to indicate the depth of the people's convictions; and one in which the convictions' *being* religious is given justificatory weight in the argument. In the latter but not the former case religious content figures essentially in the legislators' argument, though even here we have only a *second-order* religious argument: roughly, one in which a positive evaluation of a set of religious reasons, but no religious reason itself, is given a justificatory role.

Even in the former case, where religious reasons are simply taken as evidence of deep conviction, a church-state issue arises, and in a way that might lead some people to call the argument religious. Granting that one's constituents' favoring something on religious reasons is not itself a religious as opposed to (say) sociological fact, still, giving it weight as deeply felt *because* of those reasons does raise questions about the appropriate role of religious considerations in a liberal democracy. Would one, for instance, have taken political or ethical or aesthetic reasons as seriously, and, if not, would that be justifiable solely on social-psychological grounds concerning what does or does not indicate depth of conviction? If it would be so justifiable, then the special consideration given to the religious reasons might accord with the neutrality principle proposed in Chapter 2. This book is concerned to help us deal with such issues, whatever kind of argument may raise them. Contentually religious arguments are the primary kind that people think of as religious and may be the sort that most often raises church-state issues; but they are not the only kind. We must consider other kinds if we are to develop an adequate theory of the relation between religious considerations and the sociopolitical domain.

The Evidential Criterion for a Religious Argument

On a second criterion of religious argument, an argument is religious not because of what it says but (roughly speaking) because of how it must be justified. Specifically, I propose to call an argument *evidentially (epistemically) religious* provided that (a) its premises, or (b) its conclusion, or (c) both, or indeed (d) its premises' *warranting* its conclusion, cannot be known, or at least cannot be justifiably accepted, apart from reliance on religious considerations, for instance scripture or revelation or clerical authority.

Most evidentially religious arguments will also be theistic in content; but not all arguments with theistic or religious content need be evidentially religious. Consider a poor argument for a sound, purely moral conclusion, say that one should try to render aid to neighbors in need. Let the premise be an approving attribution of a moral view to the Bible, for example the statement that according to Moses, God prohibited bearing false witness against one's neighbors. This is not a statement of a moral view or otherwise evidentially sufficient for the conclusion, which concerns a different though related topic: rendering aid to neighbors in need. Thus, this argument would not meet the proposed evidential criterion, since the (limited) knowledge and justification one might try to find for endorsing it is non-religious. (1) The argument's premise, being only an attribution of a moral view and not itself a moral statement, does not warrant its conclusion, which is a moral statement; and the premise cannot be, even on a religious basis, known or justifiedly believed to warrant it.[15] (2) The truth of the premise *can* be known on textual as opposed to religious grounds. (3) The conclusion itself *could* (on the non-skeptical assumptions I am making) also be known or justifiably believed on secular moral grounds.

A major reason for singling out evidentially religious arguments is that it seems possible for an argument to be evidentially religious without having *any* religious content. It is hard to find uncontroversial examples, but even a controversial one will bring out what an evidentially religious argument is. Consider a version of the widely cited genetic argument for the personhood of the zygote: the argument that since all the normal human genetic information is present in the zygote and will (normally) result in a clear case of a person at the end of a natural process (pregnancy), the zygote itself *is* a person (in this context, roughly a human being in the sense implying the full complement of moral rights). Now it might be contended that if this conclusion can be known or justifiably believed through these premises, it is on a religious basis, for example on the basis of justification for believing that God ensouls members of the human species (in the widest sense of this phrase) at the first moment when their genetic shape is determined, that is, at conception. A plausible counter to taking the genetic argument to be evidentially religious is that one could have a purely *metaphysical* argument for ensoulment at this stage, or at any rate for personhood thereat.[16] (The status of the genetic argument is considered in more detail in Chapter 7).

A related source of examples is natural law arguments. Consider the argument (which I do not claim is widely endorsed at present) that since the natural end, or a primary natural end, of intercourse is procreation, and contraception thwarts that end, contraception is wrong. It is not evident that the key, first premise can be known or justifiedly believed apart from theistic grounds. But even supposing that, given a statistical or other objective standard of what is natural, it can be, it is arguable that the premises cannot be justifiedly taken to *warrant* the conclusion except on assumptions such as that patterns in the natural order reveal divine intentions regarding how human life should be conducted. Unless thwarting a natural end of an act is contrary to divine intention, why should it be morally wrong? It is this sort of dependency on religious considerations that seems to many to underlie the major natural law arguments for moral conclusions and hence to undermine their ostensibly naturalistic, or at least ostensibly non-theistic, character.

The notion of proper function can also be invoked here, as where one might argue that since the proper function of the feet is to aid walking, to bind a child's feet to keep them small (as has been done in some cultures) is wrong. This argument has a certain plausibility. Still, the notion of what is proper may be brought to nature as well as derived from it; arguably, if we did not have a disposition to consider walking in a certain way desirable, the argument would have no force for us. The problem is how to decide proper function independently of a non-natural standard, whether theological or moral. From the point of view of this book, if the problem is soluble even to the extent that no theological standard need be invoked, then natural law considerations are not ruled out by considerations of separation of church and state.[17]

The Motivational Criterion for a Religious Argument

A third criterion is motivational: an argument, as articulated by a person in a context, may be said to be (motivationally) religious, in that context, provided an essential part of the person's motivation for presenting it is to accomplish a religious purpose, for instance to elicit obedience to God's will or to fulfill a religious obligation to one's church. There may be more than one such purpose, and the purposes may be causally or evidentially independent, as where each derives from respect for an independent religious source.

This criterion is different in kind from the first two. To see this, notice that 'argument' has two main uses: to designate a linguistic process, roughly the offering of one or more propositions as reasons for another proposition; and to refer to an abstract product of such a process, roughly the essential content put forward in arguing. The motivational criterion applies to an argument as linguistically presented, not to an argument construed as an abstract structure of propositions. Such a linguistic criterion is proponent-relative and contextual. Thus, strictly speaking, the motivational criterion applies primarily to reasoning *processes* and only derivatively to arguments as the abstract structures realized in those processes; but since arguments do their chief work when expressed, and since in many of its uses the term 'argument' designates those processes, it is appropriate to treat the motivational criterion as applicable to them.

The content of a motivationally religious argument need not be religious. If the genetic argument is (in some instances) motivationally religious, it illustrates this. Certain natural law arguments might also be instances. And if some of them need not be evidentially religious, they could still be motivationally religious; this could hold even if they are neither evidentially nor contentually religious.

The Historical Criterion for a Religious Argument

An argument can also be religious by a fourth, historical criterion, one that, like the motivational standard, is linguistic. Consider the argument that since taking an "innocent human life" is wrong or, especially, violates the dignity of the human person, physician-assisted suicide is wrong. Here we have an argument that seems to many to be persuasive in its own right, yet there is no question that on many occasions of its use the argument traces to, and derives some of its persuasive power from, such religious ideas as that God giveth life, and only God should take it (at least apart from self-defense and punishment). The idea is roughly this: an argument, as used on a particular occasion, is religious in the historical sense provided that, as used on that occasion, it genetically traces, explicitly or implicitly, by some mainly cognitive chain (such as a chain of beliefs or associations), to one or more arguments that are religious in one of the above senses, or to one or more propositions that are either religious in content or evidentially dependent on a proposition that is religious in content.

There are, as our example about the permissibility of suicide suggests, at least two interesting subcases of historically religious arguments. Some are *persuasively autonomous,* in the sense that their persuasive power does not depend on their historically religious character. Others are *persuasively dependent,* in that some of their persuasive power derives, whether evidentially or otherwise, from one or more religious sources to which they are traceable. Since persuasive power may depend on the audience, an argument can be persuasive in one case and not another, or persuasively autonomous with one audience and persuasively dependent with another.

Consider the argument that monogamous marriage should be the only legally permissible kind, since the only normal marital relation is between females and males. This normality assumption might, in turn, be partly based, evidentially or historically or in both ways, on the idea that only parents, or potential parents, or at least people who can identify in a certain way with parents, of the same child or children, should marry. Either idea might be historically religious, tracing to religious injunctions about marriage as divinely ordained for men and women from the Garden of Eden onward. The latter idea, however, might be partly based on some religious view and partly founded on a supposed moral obligation of parents to rear their children and a supposed right of children to be reared by both of their parents – a supposition that could also lead to resistance to cloning of human beings, since there would then be only one "parent." An argument can thus have a mixed lineage: deriving, evidentially or historically or in both ways, from both a religious and a moral basis.[18] A mixed lineage is not intrinsically a strength; it *is* intrinsically a complexity and can be a strength.

The interest of the notion of a historically religious argument resides partly in this. Sometimes we cannot account for the plausibility of an argument without so conceiving it: it convinces, as it were, by its pedigree or its associations rather than by its evidential merits. Take the marriage argument just stated. Whether it has any persuasive force apart from its religious historical connections is debatable. Note, however, that even if it has none apart from those connections, its *conclusion* could still be supported by any number of powerful considerations; and yet it is neither epistemically religious nor, necessarily, motivationally religious. To say, then, that an argument is historically religious is not, even from a secular point of view, to imply that its conclusion is not justified (or known). Of the four kinds of religious arguments, it is only those that are evidentially religious that depend on religious considerations for the justification of some essential element in them.

Five Major Uses of Religious Arguments

Given the variety of religious arguments as just described, it should be no surprise that they can play an indefinite number of roles, and some of them are perfectly compatible, such as expressing oneself and guiding someone else. There is no hope of providing an exhaustive list, but we should consider some of the roles most important for an account of the appropriate uses of religious arguments in a liberal democracy that observes a separation of church and state.

One role of religious arguments is *expressive,* not merely in the sense of putting something forth, but in the sense of 'self-revelatory': to set out one's perspective on an issue, to articulate one's feelings on a major event, to evince attitudes, to get something off one's chest, and the like. This point has a major implication. A society that protects free expression must protect the freedom to express one's religious views, even in contexts in which there are good reasons to offer a wholly secular case for those views, as in certain kinds of public forums. Thus, *any* constraints we establish as reasonable for religious arguments must operate *within* these freedoms: the constraints will apply to the appropriate discretion in exercising our freedoms, rather than restrict our right to do so.[19]

A second, closely related role is *communicative:* for instance, to get across to someone certain of one's deepest feelings or to show someone else where one is "coming from." This kind of communicative argumentation will also be in some way expressive; yet the aim of argument is not mainly to articulate one's own position, but to change the understanding or information base of someone else. There will be times when one cannot convey one's special sense of an issue or one's distinctive approach to a topic without using religious arguments, at least implicitly. Even if I do not expect a religious argument to persuade you, I may want to offer it as an indication of how deeply I feel and of the sources of my views. Far from necessarily seeming dogmatic or insular, this practice might suggest some common ground between us, whether religious or secular.

Still another role of religious argument is *persuasive:* above all, to get people to agree with our view, or follow our prescriptions, or identify with us. Persuasion may often be best when one is communicative and self-revelatory, but it need not have either characteristic. There are at least two major cases: first, persuading people who accept one's general religious view, and second, persuading those who are either non-religious or religiously different from oneself. Often, in the second case, some arguments with religious *conclusions* are needed first, by way of partial conversion. But it may be sufficient simply to get the other person(s) to acknowledge the importance of one's conclusion if only because it is religious. In the first case, redirection is usually the main strategy, for instance showing others how a shared religious premise leads to one's so far resisted conclusion. In the second, one must create enough common ground to support the conclusion.

A fourth role of religious argument is *evidential:* to offer supporting reasons for a view or course of action. It may be that only religious people will accept religious reasons as good; but that is not at issue here, and we may leave open the question of actual evidential value. It would be quite wrong to omit this purpose of using religious argument: it is an important underpinning for many instances of religious argumentation by conscientious people. That *they* regard their arguments as good is important for how those arguments should be received, even by those who reject them.

Fifth, religious arguments may play an important *heuristic* role: they may stimulate the discovery of new truths, say by raising the question what God would command, or what is implied in the Gospels or the Talmud or the Koran. The value of this approach should not be underestimated. The appeal to God's intellect or will as standards of knowledge or value can open up hypotheses, and clarify assumptions, that might otherwise be lost; and the great religious texts are inexhaustible sources of ideas, standards, and practical wisdom. To exclude their study from public education is neither good academic policy nor required by a reasonable separation of church and state.

All five roles can be played by religious arguments in social-political contexts. The theory of church-state separation defended here does not in the least imply that such arguments should not be used in public as well as in private. Even in public policy discussions, religious arguments can be used without in any way tending to produce coercion of those who disagree or even violating any sound principle of separation of church and state. My separation principles in this book constrain *how* such arguments should be used, but neither prevent their use nor require only very occasional uses.

A great deal of discretion is required, however, to use religious arguments in public policy discussions without undermining the very framework of church-state separation that is needed to preserve the freedom to use such arguments in shaping one's society. Some of the elements needed to exercise such discretion have been suggested in Chapter 2. The state should support religious freedom without favoritism toward the religious; the church should seek political neutrality at least in public activities. In both cases, moral neutrality is neither required nor, in general, desirable or even achievable. Moreover, when governmental coercion is necessary, it should be justified by considerations of a kind that do not alienate those affected, and I have argued that here it is important that the justification accord with standards that any fully rational and adequately informed citizen can understand and identify with.

If these ideas concerning church-state separation and the restrictions on governmental coercion are sound, they should be extendable in certain ways to individual conduct. In different ways, the ideals central for the structure of a liberal democracy may be expected to bear on standards for the conduct of individual citizens. Individuals, like institutions, should observe certain principles directing a kind of separation of religious and political considerations. The business of the next chapter is to develop the overall theory of this book in application to individual as opposed to governmental conduct.

PART TWO

THE ETHICS OF CITIZENSHIP AND THE BALANCE OF RELIGIOUS AND POLITICAL ARGUMENTS

CHAPTER FOUR

RELIGIOUS CONVICTIONS AND SECULAR REASONS

The separation of church and state is not the only aspect of the relation between religion and democracy that is a central topic in political philosophy. There is a related battery of issues concerning the role of religious considerations in the conduct of ordinary citizens, people who may be politically active but are not government officials. These issues, almost as much as institutional separation of church and state, have been brought into great prominence by the growth, in recent decades, of religious fundamentalism. It is a powerful force in many parts of the world, and, in some of its forms, it is inimical to democracy.

There is division of judgment regarding the question whether fundamentalism is undermining democracy in the United States, but there is little disagreement on the powerful influence of the "religious right," as it is often called, in American political life. The reference is usually to conservative Christian groups, whether fundamentalist or not, but similar concerns have been expressed about fundamentalist elements in other religions and in other cultures. I propose no assessment of the sociological issue of the actual effects of religious fundamentalism; even the risk of an imbalance between religious and secular considerations in democratic societies is reason enough to indicate a need for principles that help to preserve a good balance between them. Defending such principles is the main concern of this chapter. If all of the citizens in a democracy adhere to sufficiently good ones, these principles should be able to guide their conduct in a way that can accommodate both a variety of fundamentalist movements and the aggressively secular forces we also find in contemporary Western culture. In Western Europe, Scandinavia, much of Britain, and other countries where there is no "complete" separation of church and state, these principles may seem less important. But they remain important. The recent history of Ireland and Lebanon makes this evident.

It must not be thought that liberal religious groups are not also politically active, nor should it be assumed that religiously conservative people as such are less than strongly committed to preserving democratic government. I shall indeed assume that in the United States, at least, reflective religious people, particularly those in what we might loosely call the Hebraic-Christian tradition, are on the whole committed to preserving not only democratic government but also religious liberty, including the liberty to remain outside any religious tradition.

Both democratic government and religious liberty are values that, from the point of view of any sound political philosophy, are eminently worth preserving. Their joint preservation, however, is far from easy, particularly when politically active religious groups are passionately convinced that certain freedoms are religiously forbidden or are immoral or, as in the cases of abortion and physician-assisted suicide, both. It is in part to achieve that joint preservation that liberal democracies characteristically observe a separation of religious institutions and the state. It is also partly in the interest of this joint preservation that many conscientious citizens seek a related separation between religious and political considerations, for instance between grounds for laws affecting all citizens and standards of purely personal conduct.

The need for this separation brings us to the task of this chapter as building on the previous three. Chapter 1 set out a basis for church-state separation – though one could endorse such a separation, as well as liberal democracy itself, even apart from the groundings of democracy set forth there. Chapters 2 and 3 outlined an account of the main principles that should guide church-state separation. Now suppose that, between religious institutions and the state, there ought to be the kind of separation I have defended, under the libertarian, equalitarian, and neutrality principles at the level of government and the principle of ecclesiastical political neutrality among religious institutions. Should there also be, in our conduct as citizens, a related separation between religious and secular considerations?

RELIGION, POLITICS, AND THE ETHICS OF CITIZENSHIP

By way of background for understanding the rationale for certain principles governing citizens in political matters on which their religion has significant bearing, recall that there are broadly moral arguments supporting liberal democracy as a form of government. If any of these succeeds, then insofar as separation of church and state and, more broadly, of religious and political considerations is crucial for liberal democracy, there is at least indirect support, from broadly moral premises, for preserving that separation both in the design of institutions and in the political conduct of individuals.

Chapter 1 laid out a number of frameworks for grounding liberal democracy, all either moral or aimed at providing a basis for a democratic state that is at least morally acceptable in terms of ideals of liberty and equality, and each warranting a separation of church and state and, by implication, of religious and (secular) political considerations. Let me develop this position further to prepare the way for the principles central in this chapter.

Moral Grounds for Liberal Democracy

On the basis of any of the approaches detailed in Chapter 1, one might mount some version of the following broadly moral arguments, which I state only in outline, that bear on the kinds of principles of sociopolitical conduct one might endorse as part of the ethics of citizenship. A liberal-democratic state might be held to be the only kind that preserves freedom and provides adequate scope for individual autonomy. Second, it may also be thought to be the only kind that can sustain legitimate government, which may be broadly construed as the sort of government that rational citizens are willing to consent to. And third, it may be held to contribute best – or to be essential – to human flourishing.

There are (as we have seen) other rationales for preferring liberal democracy over alternative forms of government. Some are moral, appealing for instance to the virtues of statecraft in those who govern and to correlative virtues of citizenship on the part of the governed. Some are economic, for example the case for liberal democracy as the only suitable framework for free-market capitalism. Some are pragmatic, such as the argument that entrenched power corrupts and democratic succession is the only way to minimize its deleterious effects. And there are eclectic approaches combining these and other sorts of considerations. I assume that some broadly moral rationale for liberal democracy will succeed. But it also seems that religious institutions might, for internal reasons, want to subsist in a liberal state. They might, for one thing, religiously endorse a moral case for a liberal state. But they might also see such a state as best for their own flourishing – indeed, even for their own safety – especially in a world of inescapable religious pluralism.

Individual citizens, religious and non-religious alike, often have a similar considered desire to live in a free and democratic society in which religious liberty is assiduously preserved. I consider this desire to be reasonable, but I will not argue directly for the preferability of liberal democracy over other forms of government. My task here is to explore some appropriate liberal-democratic principles in the conduct of individual citizens.

As individuals living in a liberal democracy, we are less constrained by principles that restrict sociopolitical conduct than are governments and institutions. It is indeed arguable that a citizen in such a society may properly vote or engage in other political conduct on any conscientiously chosen basis.[1] But some of the same grounds – including protection of religious liberty – that underlie separation of church and state at the institutional level may, at the individual level, warrant a measure of separation of religious and secular considerations. I want to explore the extent to which this is so.

Liberal Democracy from a Religious Perspective

Despite the connections between the institutional and individual levels and the bearing of liberal democratic theory on both, I think it is instructive to begin not (as is common) with the implications of some liberal theory of the state for the conduct of citizens or institutions, but instead with the point of view of a morally upright religious citizen who wants to live in a free and democratic society. This strategy will confirm the point (made in Chapter 1) that despite appearances, a theological approach to providing a framework of good government might well lead to the choice of liberal democracy.

Let us initially ask, then, whether a version of liberal-democratic theory of a kind favoring a separation of religious and political considerations can be reasonably reached from a certain range of religious perspectives. My main question here is this: What should conscientious and morally upright religious citizens in a pluralistic society want in the way of protection of their own freedom and promotion of standards that express respect for citizens regardless of their religious position?

Suppose that I am devoutly religious and that my faith (a Christian denomination, let us suppose) implies much about how a good life is to be lived. I might subscribe to the Ten Commandments, to the do-unto-others rule, and to Jesus's injunction to love our neighbors as ourselves. I thus have far-reaching, religiously grounded prima facie obligations relevant to my conduct as a citizen, and I might try to lead my daily life with such religious standards in mind.[2] May I, as a conscientious citizen, pursue these obligations as vigorously as possible within the limits of the law? This is a plausible view; but – as is appropriate from a religious point of view – let us go beyond taking legal limits as our baseline for acceptable conduct. The law may be either unjustifiably restrictive or unwarrantedly permissive.

The better question for our purposes is this. May I, as a conscientious citizen, pursue my religious obligations and aspirations so far as possible within the limits of my moral rights? An affirmative answer to the second question also seems plausible, at least if the issue is *moral* propriety; for if I were violating anyone else's moral rights, I would presumably be going beyond mine. If I am not, why should I limit my zeal?

One answer that may occur to me if I am aware of religious diversity in my society is that I should limit my zeal because I would like people in other faiths, with different sociopolitical ideals, to limit theirs. There are surely moral considerations bearing on this issue that go beyond the question of what we have a moral or legal right to do. There are ideals of moral virtue that require of us more than simply acting within our moral rights. In particular, there are, in the sociopolitical domain, *ideals of citizenship* that are supported by the most plausible kinds of groundings of liberal democracy (such as those set forth in Chapter 1), and demand of us more than simply staying within our rights. These ideals can be attractive to religiously committed citizens as well as to those whose standards are determined within a secular perspective such as one of those outlined in Chapter 1.

The standards I have in mind are what might be called *involuntary ideals:* their non-fulfillment (under the conditions to which they are relevant) subjects citizens in a liberal democracy to criticism, even if one may in various cases avoid it because of, say, a stronger conflicting demand. This does not hold of voluntary ideals, such as literary excellence or athletic prowess, which do not obligate us unless we undertake to realize them. There is a sense in which citizens in a liberal democracy *ought* to meet standards of, for instance, mutual concern and mutual respect, even if they have a right not to.[3] Insofar as what we ought to do in this sense is a constitutive element in liberal democracy, a rights-based theory of such democracy is deficient.

Despite appearances, the "ought" in question is not an unusual one; it is commonly recognized that those with enough resources to do more than comfortably sustain themselves ought to make charitable donations, but scarcely anyone thinks they have no right to choose otherwise. As is evident from this example, the kind of ideal in question is not utopian; it simply represents a high standard. In the main I shall speak here of prima facie obligations; but given that I recognize a moral right to act in ways that fall short of the relevant standards, the terminology of ideals may at times be preferable provided we distinguish between voluntary and involuntary ideals. (We could also speak of standards, but that term seems less apt for the purpose.) Let us consider some of the principles that partially express the ideals of citizenship that concern me.

TWO PRINCIPLES OF DEMOCRATIC CITIZENSHIP

If citizens in a democracy do no more in shaping their society by their political participation and in contributing to public service than they must do by law, their society will at best languish. A liberal state, however, not only protects free expression but also leaves the basis on which one votes – as well as voting itself – up to individual citizens. In this vast area of protected conduct there are high and low standards, and there is virtue and vice. What principles might citizens with high standards – including high standards grounded in their religious commitments – wish to abide by in relation to harmonizing religious and political considerations? I will defend two in particular. In doing this, I will have religious citizens foremost in mind but speak largely in more general terms applicable to citizens irrespective of religious commitments.

Secular Rationale

The first principle I want to discuss – the *principle of secular rationale* – says that one has a prima facie obligation not to advocate or support any law or public policy that restricts human conduct, unless one has, and is willing to offer, adequate secular reason for this advocacy or support (say for one's vote). Adequate secular reasons may be considerations of, for instance, public health, public safety (as with gun control), educational need, or national defense. It should be stressed immediately that this principle implies no exclusion of the religious, such as that one not also have a religious reason, nor does it imply that no such reason may be offered. It is equally important to see that the adequacy condition by itself is not intrinsically tied to secularity: it may rule out many secular reasons as well as many religious ones, but does not automatically rule out any specific kind of reason. There are difficult questions concerning secularity, adequacy, and the appropriateness of offering reasons of various kinds, not just those that are rooted in a particular religion. I address a number of these below. First, it will help to illustrate the principle of secular rationale in a case where religious considerations are central.

Suppose I want to advocate mandatory periods of prayer or meditation in public schools. According to the secular rationale principle, I should have adequate secular reason for this, such as its being educationally and psychologically essential for the nation's youth.[4] If my only reason is to promote my own or other distinctively religious ideals, then I would not satisfy this principle. Without an adequate rationale independent of my own religious commitments, I would (according to the principle) be moving improperly toward reducing the freedom of students who prefer to avoid such sessions. This might not disturb me insofar as I think of what I am doing as essential for the spiritual well-being of students. But if, for example, I imagine being forced to observe certain dietary laws or to dress in a certain style because another religion gains a majority and makes this legally binding, I may begin to see the advantages of adhering to the principle of secular rationale in matters of coercive law or public policy. I would feel alienated if coerced through the majority vote of another religious group acting as such. My sense of fairness will tend to restrain me from doing likewise.

Advocacy is so common in political action that one may lose sight of the other forms of political support in question. Voting is crucial; so is contributing to political campaigns, encouraging political candidates, preparing letters, pamphlets, and other written material supporting one's view, and attacking a political opponent. The list can be expanded. The principle of secular rationale applies to all of these kinds of conduct, though in different ways and to differing degrees. Nine additional points of clarification are in order immediately.

Two Kinds of Coercion. First, most laws and public policies do restrict human conduct to some extent, and the more restrictive the laws or policies in question, the stronger the relevant obligation. It is useful to distinguish *primary coercion* and *secondary coercion.* The first requires a particular action, such as paying tax at a certain level or submitting to inoculation. The second occurs in at least two ways. It may operate on the basis of the former, as where one's tax payments – already legally required – are spent partly in ways one disapproves of, so one is in a sense funding something against one's will. Secondary coercion may also be only conditional, as where it applies in circumstances that citizens may avoid, say by deciding not to drive and so avoid being forced to go through the process of licensing. Other things equal, primary coercion is more in need of justification than is secondary coercion: showing that a kind of coercive action, such as taxation, is warranted in the first place, tends to be more difficult than showing that, *given* a presupposition of its justification, the appropriate authorities may (within limits set by the justifying grounds for the coercion) use the funds in ways that contravene the will of some citizens. One might think that the secondary coercion is permissible wherever the corresponding primary coercion is; but the other things equal qualification is crucial. If, for instance, a tax revenue is to be used for a purpose inconsistent with the rationale for imposing the tax, then the secondary coercion in question is (apart from some special excuse) impermissible.

Positive versus Negative Restrictions. Second, my main concern is what I propose to call *positive restrictions* – roughly, coercion or restriction of the conduct of ordinary citizens – as opposed to *negative restrictions,* which are roughly the coercion or restriction of the enforcement of positive restrictions, chiefly by governmental or institutional officials. Negative restrictions are second-order, being restrictions of restrictions, and they amount to *liberalizations.* Restricting the government's power to investigate individuals, for instance, enhances civil liberties. For enhancing liberty, a free and democratic society does not ordinarily require special reasons; nurturing liberty is one of its constitutive purposes. This is why a civil rights movement does not need a special rationale beyond a justified claim of unwarranted restriction of liberty. But consider restricting government from investigating individuals even in legitimate law enforcement; here liberalization might engender exploitation of some individuals by others and thus produce restrictions of freedom that would be justified only if an adequate secular reason can be given for them. Negative and positive restrictions are, then, interconnected, and this must be kept in mind even though the former will not be discussed further here.

Non-restrictive Laws and Policies. Third, the secular rationale principle seems to have some force even when widened to apply to non-restrictive laws and public policies (those that, like laws enabling a certain kind of agreement to be a legal contract, impose no significant positive restrictions); but these less troublesome cases do not concern me here. It would be quite enough to speak adequately to those issues involving religion and politics that raise questions of substantially burdensome coercion, such as the issue of state-sponsored school prayer, as opposed to a city government's decision to give a face-lift to one old building rather than another. Still, a law is a kind of social statement, and a public policy may be that and more, even apart from coercion. It is thus desirable for citizens in a liberal democracy to have adequate secular reason to support such measures, even if it may not be obligatory.

The Notion of a Secular Reason. Fourth, I am taking a secular reason as roughly one whose normative force, that is, its status as a prima facie justificatory element, does not evidentially depend on the existence of God (or on denying it) or on theological considerations, or on the pronouncements of a person or institution *qua* religious authority.[5] Roughly, this is to say that a secular reason is a ground that enables one to know or have some degree of justification (roughly, evidence of some kind) for a proposition, such as a moral principle, independently of having knowledge of, or justification for believing, a religious proposition. Evidential independence of God on the part of reasons does not imply independence of God in general.[6] Nor does it imply that the "faculty" of reason is secular, in the sense that it is not capable of reaching religious knowledge or is not in some way intrinsically religious. My concern here is with *reasons,* not with the faculty of reason overall, except insofar as my points about reasons presuppose certain rational capacities. Moral skeptics may think there *are* no adequate reasons for moral judgments, but I assume that this is not so, that, for instance, an adequate secular reason for making murder and rape punishable is that they violate central moral principles, they constitute serious threats to the security of society, and they require legal punishability at least on grounds of adequate deterrence. Not every category of moral principle is so close to being uncontroversial among civilized people, and there remain disagreements on significant matters of detail, such as the appropriate severity of punishments. But similar moral principles basic to a liberal legal structure can be seen (by non-skeptics) to be adequately justified by secular reasons concerning enslavement, theft, fraud, and many other behaviors that every free and democratic society prohibits by law.[7]

Secularity versus Publicity. My fifth point concerns the contrast between what is appropriately independent of religion and what is simply "public." There may be a use of 'public' in which my position implies that public reasons should have the role I attribute to secular ones. But I do not think it wise to substitute 'public' for 'secular'. In addition to the risk this poses of assimilating my position to others (such as Rawls's), the term 'public' suggests intelligibility or even likely acceptance, on the part of the general public, perhaps even ready intelligibility or even an appropriate familiarity. But a public could be ill educated or blinded by prejudice. Second, in the work of Rawls and others the term often rules out reliance on "comprehensive views," something that my principles do not do (for reasons indicated in Chapter 3 and developed further below).[8] There is, however, a kind of public accessibility, in the sense in which scientific evidence is supposed to be publicly accessible, that is implicit in the notion of a reason which is *adequate* as well as secular. Let me clarify the notion in question.

Adequacy of Reasons. To say that a reason is adequate for a position or action is roughly to say that the reason (if true) justifies it, as the proposition that without inoculations we will have a deadly epidemic might justify requiring (minimally risky) inoculations. My sixth point, then, is that adequacy is chiefly a matter of justification. The kind of justification will differ with the kind of issue, for instance political or moral, and I take it that an adequate reason provides enough justification to make it at least minimally reasonable to do (or believe) the thing in question. As the example of an epidemic indicates, technical knowledge may be required to obtain such a reason; but the reason itself need not be difficult to understand. I cannot here propose a complete theory of the adequacy of sociopolitical reasons, but the following seems a plausible element in such a theory. If such a reason is secular, no special religious qualifications are needed to understand it; if it is adequate, any appropriately educated person can understand it; and if it is an adequate reason for a law or public policy, then either it or something it clearly implies will at least normally be intelligible to a normal adult with a good high school education. As this suggests, I do not take it that one has adequate reason only if one can adduce the deepest available ground to support it. We can be well supported by a foundation too deep for us to find and exhibit for skeptical inquiries. This is why one need know little about the technical side of public health to appreciate an adequate reason for inoculations.[9] Even in biochemistry, knowing the danger does not require knowing the cause. One should, however, be willing to say more than simply that a kind of action, say cloning of human beings, is wrong or that another, say imposing high taxes to relieve poverty, is obligatory. It is widely realized that actions are not morally wrong or obligatory for no reason, and forthrightness often requires that we indicate why we consider a type of action wrong when we are using the point to justify important conduct. It is required at least by the spirit of the principle of secular rationale that one be ready to do so. In a sense, to say simply that something is wrong is not to give a reason but to express a commitment to there being one.

Having an Adequate Reason. In allowing that one can have a reason without being able to give the deepest available ground to support it, I am acknowledging not only that we may sometimes properly rely on experts to assure us that there is a justification for a position we take to warrant political action, but that we may also rely more generally on testimony. The conditions for justifiedly doing this are complicated and controversial.[10] The point needed here (my seventh in clarifying the principle of secular rationale) is that we do not qualify as *having* adequate reason for a position or action merely by virtue of accepting a set of propositions that *constitute* one; we must also rationally accept the proposition(s) in question and see the relevance of the proposition(s) to the action or position. If I should see that someone giving me information supporting a public policy is not credible (say because of inconsistencies and gaps in the presentation), and, from the person's testimony, I unjustifiedly accept a reason for adopting the policy, then I do not have adequate reason to support that policy and I should presumably seek to verify the testimony before acting on it. And of course, if I do not believe *any* proposition that constitutes a reason for the policy and I could not by reflection arrive at one from what I do believe or from information accessible to me through reflection or memory, I do not have a reason at all, not even a weak and inadequate one. There are of course excusable errors, as where one is ill or simply cannot hear the testimony well and must act on it before there is time to reconsider; nor am I suggesting that we must scrupulously check the credibility of everyone who gives us important information. But it is appropriate to a principle expressing an ideal of citizenship to place conditions both on the evidential force of a reason and on the citizen's warrant for accepting it.

Prima Facie Obligation. Eighth, I am taking a prima facie obligation to be one that provides a reason for action which is strong enough to justify the action in the absence of conflicting considerations, but is also liable to being overridden by one or more such considerations. Among the overriders of the obligation to be willing to offer secular reason are special circumstances in which secrecy is necessary, as where one would be in serious danger if certain people knew what legislation or candidate one was supporting. Under repressive conditions (which, especially in a small community, can exist within a larger liberal democracy) the prima facie obligation to be willing to offer adequate secular reason may also be overridden. As to the obligation to *have* an adequate secular reason, one possible case of overriding would be a kind in which one suddenly finds one must vote, sees that the opposition is voting on a conflicting religious basis, and has confidence that adequate secular reason for one's vote can be found when one explores the issue further. (Other overriders will be considered later.)[11]

The Varying Strength of the Obligation. My last point here is that the obligation posited by the principle of secular rationale may be stronger in some kinds of cases than in others, even for the same person, and it tends to be stronger for government officials acting as such than for private citizens. My main interest in this chapter is ethical standards appropriate to ordinary citizens in a liberal democracy as opposed to government officials therein, but the latter are citizens as well and sometimes act as ordinary citizens. In some such cases, the greater information and social responsibility that go with government positions, or the wide visibility or significant influence of such people as role models, make the prima facie obligation in question stronger for these citizens even when they are not acting in their official capacities. Moreover, even for ordinary citizens, the strength of the obligation varies with circumstances. One must in general be more careful in making a public speech on national television than in a preliminary precinct meeting concerning a primary election. Moreover, the principle of secular rationale applies to officials (in their official conduct) more than to ordinary citizens. Even local officials with little authority are more constrained here; the judiciary, and especially the highest court, are perhaps most constrained.[12]

Returning to the point of view of a religious citizen who wants to live harmoniously in a liberal democracy, consider how one might regard the principle of secular rationale from the perspective of theological assumptions that are standard in Western theism. Might one not think that the principle is one that is religiously acceptable, given God's having created a world in which religious differences are pervasive and secular protections of liberty can be seen to appeal to all normal persons? One might also note that the principle does not preclude appeal to religious considerations, and one might find that often they are harmonious with secular ones (a pattern that, in Chapter 5, I argue is expectable given major elements in at least Western theism).

One might reply, "If people are told that, at least in the absence of adequate secular reasons, they should not rely on religious beliefs to vote for candidates who will protect animals, this is a serious constraint on the free exercise of their religion. As a modern statement of the Presbyterian Church (U.S.A.) puts it, it is a 'denial of faith not to seek its expression in both a personal and a public manner . . .'"[13] This ignores the point that the obligation expressed in the principle of secular rationale is compatible with a right to do otherwise: a right of "free exercise." But countenancing this right does not imply that every exercise of it is beyond moral criticism. Rights are (in large part) protections against interference. Rights are not a moral license to do everything they forbid others to prevent.

That brings us to a second reply: the objection ignores the point that there are ways to enhance protection of animals without appreciable restrictions of human conduct – nor is the example one in which there is any shortage of good secular reasons for advancing the relevant aim. Thus, the exercise of the right of freedom of action here might be unnecessary as well as criticizable if exercised without appropriate grounds.

Let us, however, pursue the idea that an exercise of a right of freedom of action can be morally criticizable. Suppose that much money must be spent in enforcement of the animal protections in question and that many jobs are lost through the changes in the food sector of the economy, so that human conduct is significantly restricted, even if meat consumption remains legal. Then one might ask the religious voters supporting the protections whether they would accept comparable restrictions of conduct, as well as similar job losses or mandatory changes in their daily work, on the basis of coercive legislation protecting the dandelion as a sacred species or prohibiting miniskirts and brief bathing suits as irreverent. Such examples are perhaps not realistic for Western societies, but they bring out the advantages that the principle of secular rationale offers for a plurality of peoples and faiths. It allows a great deal of expression of faith "in both a personal and a public manner." Its limited constraints on religious expression by some are protections of liberty for others – including the religious. A liberal democracy's restraints of some are liberations for others, and they are intended for the benefit of all.

Another objection is that at least for religious people who do not think in secular terms, the principle would restrict democratic participation. They would, for instance, be unable to engage in public discourse in secular terms.[14] A number of points should be made in reply. One is that there is much democratic participation that does not require advocacy or support of restrictive laws or policies. One can, for instance, query opponents and criticize their objectionable positions; formulate guiding ideals, religious as well as secular; discuss the quality of the records of the people or political parties in question; arouse concern about the issues in question.

A second point is that the principle of secular rationale does not restrict freedom of speech or the content of one's vocabulary. It does not even treat as prima facie objectionable the kinds of speech needed for the religiously influenced political activities just described; and the requirement of adequate secular reason does not constrain the expression of religious reasons, much less the use of religious language. There are reasons of prudence that often indicate the wisdom of conducting political discussion in secular terms; but these reasons would have force independently of the principle of secular rationale, and nothing in its content accords them exaggerated weight.

Something should also be said about the idea that some people cannot think in secular terms (at least not about weighty matters in human life) or may find it impossible or unduly burdensome to "separate" the secular from the religious in their thinking. The relevant kind of thinking in secular terms does not require suspending one's theism, at least for any kind of theism of major importance in the world today. Even if one thinks of everything as created by God or under God's sovereignty, one will have ways of referring to people and (non-religious) things without mentioning God, and one can appeal to moral principles – including the ethical imperatives among the Ten Commandments – without depending on religious descriptions. This is entirely compatible with taking those principles to depend on God as much as anything in the Creation.

The point here is not that thinking or speaking in secular vocabulary is required by the principle of secular rationale (a restriction I do not endorse for liberal democracy); it is that such vocabulary is available to normal religious people for the sake of conceiving and formulating reasons in a minimally secular fashion. Those reasons can *be* both secular and adequate even if the person having or offering them would not accept them on a secular basis. The only sense in which the principle calls on religious people to separate the religious from the secular is conceptual and, in some cases, verbal. As the Commandments themselves illustrate, one can take a standard having secular content to be theologically grounded without its cogency as providing a secular reason being undermined in the least.

It may still seem that the principle of secular rationale would sometimes have unacceptable consequences. Imagine a person who cannot think of an adequate secular reason for her religiously grounded pacifism and, too quickly to provide time to find a secular reason she can endorse, must vote on whether to go to war. It might seem that my view requires her "to vote against her conscience," since she should vote yes or abstain.[15] This misses the significance of the point that she not only has a *right* to vote no, but also has only a prima facie obligation to abstain from voting. But *given* the importance of her religious convictions to her, and given her intellectual and psychological capacities, voting no may be, from her perspective at least, the rational thing to do. In that case she is not "required" by any moral principle I endorse to vote yes or abstain.

Suppose it *is* rational for the pacifist, on the basis of her overall commitments as a generally rational religiously committed person, to vote against going to war, but she still lacks an adequate secular reason. We may excuse her voting without it; but we need not for that reason consider it praiseworthy or even best, any more than we need so view someone's breaking a promise on the basis of considerations that, although understandably compelling from the agent's point of view, are objectively mistaken. The case is one in which either her prima facie obligation under the principle of secular rationale is overridden or its non-performance is at least excusable. What my view requires of conscientious citizens like her who knowingly act against the principle of secular rationale is that they be aware of what they are doing and have conscientious grounds for taking their religious commitments to be overriding or at least excusatory. This is the kind of requirement that is generally implicit in prima facie moral principles (such as the rule requiring the keeping of promises). Here, as in that more general case, morality does not dictate that one never depart from the principle, even if it is in fact true.[16] It does require that one scrutinize departures; but that does not seem too much to ask.

The principle of secular rationale is, then, not unduly burdensome for religious people. Indeed, it may also be expected to have good effects for people *within* a religious tradition, for instance in different denominations, and possibly even in the same denomination, as well as to facilitate good relations *between* different religious traditions, and between religious and non-religious people. Intramural strife can be deadly. History has shown that, and we can surely see it in the contemporary world. It seems less likely to occur where this principle is adopted.

Secular Motivation

Reasons we have for actions or beliefs, reasons we give for them, and reasons we are actually moved by are all important, and in different ways. The second principle I suggest asks citizens to consider not just what they want to do and what reasons they have to do it, but *why* they want to do it. I propose, then, a *principle of secular motivation,* which adds a motivational condition to the rationale principle. It says that one has a (prima facie) obligation to abstain from advocacy or support of a law or public policy that restricts human conduct, unless in advocating or supporting it one is sufficiently *motivated* by (normatively) adequate secular reason. Sufficiency of motivation here implies that some set of secular reasons is motivationally sufficient, roughly in the sense that (a) this set of reasons explains one's action and (b) one would act on it even if, other things remaining equal, one's other reasons were eliminated. Roughly, the idea is that one should be advocating or supporting the law or policy in question in part *for* some adequate secular reason, where the role of this reason is sufficiently important to explain why one is so acting (even if some other consideration is also sufficient for this). This second principle is less important than the secular rationale principle to the partial ethics of citizenship I am proposing for liberal democracies, but it is still quite significant. It is also more difficult to interpret and apply. Let us explore it in a concrete case.

To begin with, since an argument can be tacitly religious, say evidentially or motivationally, without being religious in content, we might fail to adhere to at least the secular motivation principle even when we are offering arguments that on their face are neither religious nor fail to provide an adequate secular reason for their conclusion. Think of the genetic argument for the personhood of the zygote: roughly, the argument that since all the genetic information needed for its development into a person is present at conception, the zygote *is* a person at that point. It might be held that some people who offer this argument are not sufficiently motivated by the secular considerations cited in it, those just mentioned, and (quite apart from whether it is objectively sound) would not find the argument convincing apart from their underlying religious beliefs. They might, for example, think of the zygote as ensouled by God at the moment of its formation or might simply have been brought up to think of all human life as sacred.[17]

There are two cases here. In one, the person realizes that the secular reason does not motivate. I might realize that, for instance, the idea of ensoulment is what really convinces me on the abortion question. Here the secular reason is presented as a rationalization for the position held on a religious basis. In the other case, I do not realize that the secular reason is not motivating. There the presentation of the reason is an unconscious rationalization. A rationalization *can* be good, in that the ground it invokes may actually justify what it is intended to support. But it is quite characteristic of rationalizations to be unsuccessful attempts to provide justification where – as is common in difficult matters or where we are influenced by prejudice – we doubt we have one independently. That the reasons we offer in giving rationalizations do not motivate us may be a sign of their failure to justify. It is at least a sign of their failure to convince us; that is one reason we do not like giving them if we can avoid it, and do not like being given such reasons by others in their attempts to convince *us*.

There is another kind of case in which the principle of secular motivation applies. Suppose I believe that assisted suicide is morally wrong, but my only ground is my religious belief that God giveth life, and only God should take it. That this kind of act is morally wrong is not a religious view, and let us assume for the sake of argument that it can justify a legal prohibition of assisted suicide. But if I am motivated by it essentially on account of my theistic ground, then under the principle of secular motivation I have a prima facie obligation not to support legal coercion on the basis of it. Adherence to that very principle, however – even if the adherence itself is partly religious, as it may be owing to, say, acceptance of the do-unto-others rule – may lead me to seek an adequate secular reason that motivates me in the same direction. If I find it, the fact that my search for it was in part religiously motivated does nothing to prevent my now satisfying the principle.

It may be thought that the principle of secular motivation burdens only the religious, but it in fact applies to those who oppose religion in certain ways. The principle is meant to rule out a certain kind of *anti*-religious motivation as proper in coercive sociopolitical action. A free democracy should be wary not only of religious domination, but also of anti-religious domination. Imagine a scientific argument aimed at excluding creationism from discussion in public school science courses: the secular considerations it cites might not be motivating, and if the exclusionary policy is proposed on the basis of anti-religious motivation of a kind that does not count as secular, then even if it accords with the rationale principle, offering it does not accord with the motivation principle. Its proponent lacks a set of secular reasons that is both evidentially adequate and motivationally sufficient.[18]

Consider, by contrast, a case in which someone argues for a voucher system on the ground that parents, and especially religious ones, should be free to educate their children in academically adequate schools of their choice, including those that teach a particular religious point of view, and so should receive a voucher for each child, which can be used toward the costs of their children's attending *any* accredited school.[19] Here the *content* of the proposed legislation, unlike that of proposed restrictions of abortion, includes a concern with religion and even envisages some likelihood of promoting its practice; but the *ground* given for the legislation is not intrinsically religious: one could support a voucher system on this ground without specially favoring the religious over, say, non-religious people who are simply dissatisfied with the general quality of public education, just as legislators can take account of the religiously based preferences of their constituents *as* their deep-seated preferences without thereby favoring the religious as such over other constituents. One might support such a system even if there are no church-affiliated schools at the time. This system is less far-reaching than government's directly supporting religious as well as secular schools, as in the Netherlands. That policy probably cannot satisfy the neutrality principle (defended in Chapter 2), as a voucher system might be argued to do,[20] since the former both directly supports religious institutions as such and, by comparison with a voucher system, would be more likely to create a presumption that there should be religiously affiliated schools. If, however, pressing for a voucher system is to conform to the principle of secular motivation, then some such secular consideration should be both (normatively) adequate and sufficiently motivating. If one's *only* reason for supporting vouchers is to promote the religious devotion of one's children (or of other children), then even if one is expressing a kind of religious virtue, one is not exhibiting civic virtue.[21]

Granted, if there is an *adequate* secular reason for a policy, then no overall harm need be expected from instituting the policy; this is in part why the principle of secular rationale is the more important of the two. In this light, it may be thought that one may offer the reason as justifying one's conduct even if it does not motivate one. One may. But harm can come from the way a policy is instituted even if not directly from the policy itself, and harm certainly may come from habits that allow one to support coercion of others for religious reasons so long as one can find an adequate secular rationale.

Let us also apply the do-unto-others rule to this case: one would not like having a different religious group, with which one deeply disagrees, press for its religiously preferred policies solely for religious reasons of its own, even if a good secular reason could be offered for those policies. It matters greatly to us *why* people do what they do. If we have too little sense of it, we do not know what to expect from them. To be sure, someone who has both motivating and non-motivating reasons can present both, and this might seem to solve the problem. It does not. Indeed, if, in supporting a law or public policy, we present a set of reasons in the usual way, hence without taking special care to imply that none of them need be motivating, the normal presumption is that they are all motivating. We can say, as a paid advocate might, something like, "Here are the arguments," but if we do this in a way that distances us enough from the reasons to rebut the presumption that they are motivating for us, there is a sense in which we conceal from others in the discussion or debate *who* we are. There is a place for such concealment, for instance in criminal trials, but it should be generally avoided in policy discussions in a liberal democracy.

Where one takes it that someone with both secular and religious reasons is not sufficiently motivated by a secular reason offered, one's tendency to disapprove may be modified, if only slightly, where, the secular reason motivates to *some* degree, but is inessential to determining support for the policies, which would have been promoted in its absence. We are especially likely to be wary of the dominance of religious motivation if, as with illegal euthanasia, the policy or law in question is backed by severe punishments. If we think the law or policy unjustified, we may feel coerced by someone else's religious views; but even if we agree, we may well think that *others* may feel coerced – or we may wonder how we will fare in later legislation. As elsewhere in ethical matters, there can be a wrong way to do the right thing. The right way in cases of coercion must (for additional reasons to be given shortly) incorporate appropriate motivation.

Some Important Aspects of Religious Reasons in Politics

The stress on secular reasons as evidential and motivational elements important in the ethics of citizenship must not be taken to imply that no other constraints on appropriate reasons are required, such as prohibitions of racist grounds for public policy. This is not the place for an account of what makes certain reasons appropriate overall. Religious reasons, conceived (for instance) as reasons for human conduct that are ultimately grounded in God's nature or commands (or, at least from the point of view of religious persons, are rationally believed to be so grounded), are a major subject in their own right. There are some respects in which they are special in relation to liberal democracy even by contrast with other reasons – such as certain "intuitive" deliverances about other people – that are not accessible to any normal adult and are often inadequate though clearly secular.[22] Here are some salient points that help to distinguish religious reasons from certain secular ones, such as a number of moral reasons.

Infallible Supreme Authority. First, the kinds of religious reasons of greatest concern in this book are directly or indirectly viewed as representing an infallible authority, in a sense taken to imply that the propositions expressing them *must* be true.[23] A further implication which many feel in such cases is that not to act on such considerations is a violation of divine command and is seriously wrong or even punishable by damnation. Some who think this do not require that the religiously deficient person need have any *moral* guilt at all in order to merit negative treatment, such as disapproval, rejection, or damnation. If moral guilt is not required, then even coercion of the virtuous might seem warranted – and perhaps reinforced insofar as they may be seen as eminently worth saving. Furthermore, it is not just that one must act in some way to achieve the desired result, say by proselytizing; one must do *any* deed commanded by such a supreme authority.

Condemnatory Tendencies. A second, closely related point is that very commonly those who identify with what they regard as the ultimate divine source of religious reasons believe that anyone who does not identify with it is forsaken, damned, or in some other way fundamentally deficient. This disapproval is often enhanced or even inflamed by others' openly rejecting the relevant command or standard, as is common in, for example, sexual matters. Nor are religious people always consoled by knowledge that the disagreement with their religiously inspired views is respectful; this can be so even if they think those rejecting the views do so on the basis of *their* religious convictions. Following a false God – or misunderstanding the true one – can be even worse than secular error.

The Threat of Religious Domination. Third, religious reasons often dictate practices that are distinctively religious in content (such as prayer) or intent (such as preserving a fetus on the ground that it is a gift from God), and therefore are plausibly seen in some cases as forcing others who are either not religious or differ in religious outlook to observe a religious standard. This applies particularly where a religious consideration is used in favor of a practice for which there are no secular reasons persuasive to most reflective people not antecedently sympathetic on religious grounds, as in the case of most of the currently popular restrictions of abortion. Religious reasons for laws or public policies, then, can threaten, or be widely seen as threatening, not only coercion in general but *religious coercion:* coercion of religious conduct.

Cults and the Specter of Fanaticism. Fourth, for at least many religions – and commonly for cults – rational, relevantly informed outsiders are unable to discern effective checks on certain possible tendencies for clergy (or, in some cases, votaries) to project, whether consciously or otherwise, their own views or preferences into their interpretations of one or another authoritative religious source, including even God.[24] In this case there is, in addition to the possibility of some people's cloaking their prejudices with absolute authority, the possibility that the views and motives of those who follow them lack the minimal autonomy that citizens in a liberal democracy may hope for in one another. Even if at the polling place the rule is one person, one vote, it might be argued that people under the influence of cult leaders or certain other kinds of dominating religious figures may be casting votes that not only fail to be independent but are also even less open to reconsideration than most of the votes unduly influenced by secular figures.

Dangers of an Inflated Sense of Self-Importance. Insofar as the liabilities that go with cults and fanaticism are a serious problem – as they surely have been both historically and in the contemporary world – we can see a fifth point. There is a danger not only of one religion's dominating others or non-religious people, but also of one person's doing so, or one religiously powerful coterie's doing so or even of a single individual's doing it, or at least of one or more zealots taking themselves to be important in a way that makes them uncooperative as citizens. This may be in or outside politics. The belief in a supreme God with sovereignty over the world should induce humility, but it need not. Indeed, the better one thinks one represents God – especially when God is being ignored or disobeyed – the more important one may naturally think one is oneself. Who has not heard preachers apparently enthralled by their voices? There is a kind of zeal that, in influential clergy or religiously influential laypeople, can erode citizenship and, sometimes, substitute a personal vision for genuine religious inspiration.

Passionate Concern with Outsiders. Sixth, owing to some of these points (among others), religious people often tend to be, in a way that is rare in secular matters, highly and stubbornly passionate about the importance of everyone's acting in accordance with religious reasons (whether because they are accepted or not), even in private conduct, and non-religious people often tend to be highly and stubbornly passionate about not being coerced to do so. If many who are religious are vehemently opposed to the sins of a multitude outside their fold, many who are not religious are incensed at the thought of manipulation in the name of someone else's nonexistent deity.

The Centrality and Delicacy of Religious Liberty. Partly because religious liberty is a constitutive foundation (or at least a cogent rationale) for liberal democracy, citizens in such a state are naturally and permissibly resentful about coercion by religious factors (which may lead to restrictions of their specifically religious behavior), in a way in which they are not permissibly resentful concerning coercion by, for instance, considerations of public health. Even the moral errors of others are, for many, easier to abide as supports of coercion than religious convictions having the same result. Perhaps the thought is that one can argue with others concerning their moral or economic or philosophical views in a way one cannot argue with them about their religious convictions. And if religious considerations are not appropriately balanced with secular ones in matters of coercion, there is a special problem: a clash of Gods vying for social control. Such uncompromising absolutes easily lead to destruction and death.

Intergenerationality. It is more characteristic of religious commitment than of other kinds of institutional commitment that one tends to want to bring up one's children (if one has any) in the faith. With this desire often comes a sense of alienation or even betrayal if they reject the faith once brought up in it. In the present age, many have learned to live with such alienation, but it remains a source of deep concern, normally more so than counterpart reactions to apostasy in aesthetic, political, and sometimes even ethical matters. In many cases religious people can tolerate what they take to be profound ethical differences with their children, but this may be in part because those differences do not seem profound to them unless they contravene the morality of the religion in question. Many Christian parents, for instance, can live with their children's ethical liberality in sexual matters and departure from church membership largely because they see the children as retaining a commitment to the "social Gospel" of love and service.

There may be other kinds of reasons to which each of these eight points (or close counterparts) applies; but if there are any non-religious reasons to which all of them apply, it is in a different way and is in any event a good prima facie reason to impose similar restrictions on the use of those reasons. Given that I have treated religious reasons as special in important respects, I should add that nothing I have said about them entails that religion is necessarily either "esoteric" or in any way irrational, or even that there cannot be cogent arguments for God's existence from non-religious premises. One can hold that there are such arguments, and even that they should be compelling to any rational person who properly considers their premises in the light of the data, yet still consider the principles of secular rationale and motivation to be sound commitments in political philosophy.[25]

Virtuous Action versus Merely Permissible Conduct

It might still seem that motivation should not matter if the quality of one's reasons is good enough. This is a very difficult issue. But I would stress that insofar as we are thinking of the advocacy or other public behavior as supposed to be action *from virtue,* we should look not just at what kind of act it is and what can be said for it abstractly, but also at how it is grounded in the agent's *character.*[26] As Kant distinguished acting merely in conformity with duty and acting *from* duty, and Aristotle distinguished – as any virtue theorist should – actions that *express* virtue from those not virtuously performed but merely "in the right state," that is, of the right type, we should distinguish actions that proceed from civic virtue and actions that are merely in conformity with it. I am granting that morally, one may, within one's rights, advocate a coercive course of action without being motivated by an adequate secular reason for that action; my contention is that to do so is not always consonant with virtue.

The principle of secular motivation, then, may be viewed as a *virtue principle,* whereas the principle of secular rationale is better viewed as a (minimum) *justification principle.* Action in accord with the latter, being supportable by adequate reason, may be considered to be at least minimally justified, in the sense that it is permissible even if not obligatory (some alternative may, e.g., be equally warranted). But this does not imply that the action is virtuously performed, or indeed performed for any remotely admirable reason; nor does it imply that the agent is virtuous. Actions in accord with the principle of secular motivation, being sufficiently motivated by adequate reason, may be considered to be (at least to that extent) not only justified but also (civically) virtuous. Even if the agent is not habitually virtuous, the occasion in question is one on which an evidentially adequate set of reasons is also motivationally sufficient, and so produces action that is to this extent virtuously performed.

It is a main contention of this book that justification for sociopolitical action can be readily combined with motivation sufficient to produce such action, and that where this combination does not occur, conscientious citizens – whether religious or not – are prima facie obligated to resist supporting coercive laws or policies even where they feel confident that they have an adequate rationale. Even if one could act virtuously where one's justifying reasons are not motivating, when a rationale that one takes to be adequate does not motivate one there is a significant chance that this is because it does not deserve to carry one's conviction, either objectively or in the light of one's own best standards.

One may wonder, of course, whether principles weaker than those I have defended may accomplish much the same results. This may turn out to be so, but so far I have not found preferable principles. One might think that in place of adequate secular reason we might mention just plausible secular reason; or one might suggest that it is enough for an adequate secular reason to be necessary (as opposed to sufficient) for motivating the conduct in question. Here it should be remembered that we are formulating a kind of ideal; that, partly for this reason, there is a right to act otherwise; and that non-conformity to the principles may be warranted by overriding considerations or excused. Given these qualifications, the notions of a plausible reason and the weaker motivational condition are too weak to provide good ideals. If this is not already evident, it should gain further support, particularly in the motivational case, when we consider civic virtue in more detail in Chapter 6.

SOME PROBLEMS OF APPLICATION

Application of the principles of secular rationale and secular motivation can be complicated because there may be considerable difficulty in determining whether a reason one has for doing or believing something is secular, or constitutes an evidentially adequate ground, as well as in deciding whether it is in fact motivating. These difficulties merit extensive study. Here I simply offer three suggestions.

First, we should be guided by what we can learn from considering paradigms of both kinds of reason, evidential and motivational. There is much to be learned from asking, of what seem our most cogent reasons, why they justify, and, of our most moving reasons, why they influence us. Second, wherever the two kinds of reason (evidential and motivating) diverge on a major issue, we should inquire why. If I think that capital punishment is sometimes morally justified but believe it is wrong on religious grounds, I should ask why, and I may learn much from reflection on the matter. Third – and this suggestion may require one to seek outside help – in borderline cases where the secular status of a reason is in question, we should consider whether it would be taken to be secular by a reflective person who sincerely and comprehendingly claims to be non-religious and considers it carefully.[27] A religious consideration, viewed from inside a religious tradition to which it belongs, need have no theological identifying marks and easily seems to be second nature, or perhaps a dictate of purely natural law, as heterosexual preference appears to many people to be; but from the outside such an element can sometimes be seen to be rooted in a tradition that the outsider recognizes as religious and may find alienating. Dialogue with other citizens of diverse backgrounds may help greatly in reducing the incidence of such alienation.

The difficulty of determining whether a reason one has is a motivating element in one's sociopolitical conduct is especially likely to occur long before the relevant action or long afterward. But what the motivation principle (beyond the rationale principle) requires of conscientious citizens contemplating support of restrictive laws or policies is making the following three (and perhaps at most these three) manageable efforts.

First, conscientious citizens should try to formulate all the significant reasons they have for each major option – itself often a very useful exercise even apart from determining motivation and especially in assessing the weight of one's overall evidence. We revise, often improve, and commonly unify our views in the process of seeking to ground them in reasons. Until we have a good sense of what reasons we have, we are in a poor position to determine which, if any, is motivating.

Second, where one or more reasons is religious, conscientious citizens facing decisions of the kind in question should consider the motivational weight of each reason taken by itself as well as in the context of the others (if none is religious, the principle does not imply any need to go any further into motivation, though some other principle may). In examining motivational weight, there are a number of questions we can consider. How persuasive does a consideration seem to us? Are we influenced by it through commitment to some authority backing it or by its content, and how important to us is this basis of its persuasiveness? How concerned or upset would we feel if it were challenged or could not be realized in action? How did we acquire it, and does this show anything about the strength of its grip on us?

Third, citizens in the relevant position should attempt to ascertain, by considering hypothetical situations and felt motivational or cognitive impulses or tendencies, whether each reason is motivationally sufficient. We should ask ourselves, for example, what really impresses us as supporting the proposition or action; what occurs to us first (or most spontaneously) on the matter; whether we would believe something if we did not accept a certain premise for it; and whether a given reason taken by itself seems persuasive to us, in the sense of providing a feeling of surety.

In short, my two principles imply that we should ask of our reasons certain evidential, introspective, historical, and hypothetical questions. One must, with any such principles, use practical wisdom in deciding how much effort to expend in a given case of contemplated action. But once inquiry is focused by a commitment to these principles, much can be accomplished in even a few moments of reflection.

Practical wisdom is also crucial in determining how much of one's public discourse should be couched in religious terms (a matter considered in some detail in Chapter 6). Even if one is scrupulously abiding by the secular motivation principle, one may still have and present religious reasons for one's sociopolitical views. The principles of secular rationale and secular motivation concern advocacy and support of a certain range of laws and public policies; they do not restrict freedom of speech or preclude using religious reasons in major ways. Nor do they imply that religion should be "privatized," as if it had to be kept to oneself, or that it should be marginal in influencing public life.[28] It is not a necessary consequence of adherence to these principles that the religious ideals and efforts of the citizens in question are any less effective in changing society.

The rationale and motivation principles do not even imply that one need hesitate to appeal publicly to religious reasons in support of a widely contested view if it is purely moral, as where abortion is said to be morally wrong because it destroys a gift of God. Neither the crucial premise for this moral conclusion nor the conclusion itself entails that abortion should be *illegal* in a free and democratic society, and stating the premise, even publicly, does not automatically count as supporting a coercive law or public policy. There are, moreover, ways to offer the argument even in public policy contexts (e.g., by taking care to bring these limitations out) that do not imply one's supporting restrictive laws or public policies.[29]

One may, however, easily be wrong in thinking that bringing religious reasons to bear on a moral question or, especially, a public policy issue, will make one more convincing; one may instead polarize the discussion. It can well turn out that advancing religious reasons for a controversial social policy leads the opposition to advance conflicting religious reasons. This, in turn, can lead to suspicions about the motivation or the cogency of even the secular reasons on each side. It is true that people who seek equilibrium between their religious and their secular views may often be prepared to revise the latter as well as the former; but this disposition is not always present, and deadlock may occur where compromise would have been possible.

Fortunately, if the motivation principle is widely accepted by the parties to a dispute – indeed, perhaps even if it is not – and if one is in good communication with people who disagree on the issue at hand, one will likely get substantial help from them in determining what one's motivating reasons in the dispute are. Whenever religious reasons seem to them motivationally too strong, people who disagree on the issue in question should be expected to help one probe one's grounds. Others hear our voice better than we do. They may also think of revealing questions about us that we ourselves overlook, or observe words or deeds that teach us something we did not realize about our own thinking or motivation.[30]

It could be that most people are not usually good at forming reasonable judgments regarding even what reasons they have, much less which of these reasons, if any, are motivating.[31] If this is so, the effort to find out may be all the more needed: if, through self-examination, I cannot tell what my reasons for a belief or desire of mine are, I should probably wonder whether I have any normatively adequate reasons for it; and I am likely to make better decisions if I try to find some good reasons for the relevant belief or desires. If, moreover, I cannot tell pretty accurately which reasons motivate me and about how much they do so at least relative to other reasons, I cannot adequately understand myself or reasonably predict my own behavior.

Given the self-examination that, for some people, may be required for conscientious adherence to the rationale and motivation principles, it may appear that they would exclude some religious people from "full participation in political debate and action on some important issues."[32] To assess this, we must distinguish the two quite different cases of debate and (other) action, such as voting for more restrictive abortion laws. We should also distinguish *full* participation in debate from *unrestricted* participation. I can participate fully in political debate – even dominantly – whether or not I use all my arguments or express all my sentiments. To be sure, if I have only religious considerations to bring to such a debate – something that, as Chapter 5 will argue, seems unlikely to hold for informed, reflective religious people – then the rationale principle may lead me not to use them in certain ways. I may, for instance, point out their bearing, but I may not advocate coercive legislation on the basis of them. That, however, is a restraint I would wish to be observed by people who, for *their* religious reasons, want to restrict my liberty.

To see the issue in perspective, we have to keep in mind that *any* moral principle applying to sociopolitical conduct will restrict it in some cases. But I can adhere to the rationale and motivation principles and still fully participate in a significant range of political actions even concerning abortion and even aimed at producing its rejection: I can prominently and forcefully support policies, candidates, and parties that seek to *dissuade* people from doing it. What I may not do without adequate secular reason (unless my obligation regarding secular rationale is overridden) is advocate or support *coercive* laws or public policies on this or other matters that concern me. That, too, is a kind of restraint I would wish to be observed by members of other religious groups who would want to coerce my behavior in the direction of their religiously preferred standards.

THE ETHICS OF CITIZENSHIP AND THE ACCOMMODATION OF RELIGION

This is a good place to emphasize a number of further interpretive points about the rationale and motivation principles. Together these points help to show what the principles do not exclude and how large a role they accommodate for religious considerations in the political arena.

Leveraging by Reasons versus Arguing from Reasons

Contrary to appearances, in special cases the principles allow presenting reasons that one is not motivated by – or even does not believe evidentially adequate. I have in mind cases in which one is not arguing *from* those reasons but presenting them as considerations acceptable to one's audience and supporting a position that (typically but not necessarily) one *does* take to be sound. Call this *leveraging*. In the common case in which one accepts the conclusion oneself, it is a way of trying to achieve agreement on something by working from premises to which one's interlocutor is already committed. Here one's point is not that the premises are true (something one may or may not believe), but that the interlocutor already believes them, or should believe them, say because they are either plainly true or clearly follow from what the interlocutor believes.

There is no question that leveraging occurs and is widely accepted in debate and advocacy. But how can one present reasons that are not one's own in this way without insincerity or "dissembling"?[33] One possibility (which may or may not be combined with leveraging) is simply saying such things as "Here are two good reasons for this position," where one takes both to be convincing to one's audience but is not oneself moved by them. This case is troubling: we have to imagine the speaker thinking a reason for a position to be good, yet not having that as a reason for holding the position or even pulling the speaker in the direction of holding it. This is extremely rare in rational persons, especially if they *hold* the position, which normally one will if one is sincerely trying to persuade others of it. If I think the reason I give is good, and if I hold the position that I adduce this reason to support, it will normally be at least in part *for* this reason that I hold the position.

A second possibility is pointing out reasons the audience already has that support the policy, whether one thinks they are good reasons or not. This second case, by contrast, is really not one of offering reasons *for the position;* it is giving reasons *for the audience to hold the position.* This is leveraging: one tries to move an audience to a view by noting one or more reasons there are for it from the audience's point of view.[34] Leveraging is compatible with not holding the position and even with thinking that the reasons do not in fact support it.

A third possibility is to offer reasons one thinks will convince one's audience but does not believe good (this need not be leveraging, since one may be persuading the audience of a new point of view as opposed to appealing to one the audience antecedently holds). At best, this practice manipulates people; it also tends to undermine good reasoning in those who are taken in; and thirdly, it tends to be deceitful, since it is very difficult to present reasons for a view in a convincing way without implying that one takes them to support it.

The first and last objections seem also to apply to presenting *good* reasons that are not one's own: doing this tends to manipulate others – whom one is in effect asking to accept something on a ground that does not move oneself – and certainly a convincing presentation of the reasons will make it appear (contrary to what is the case) that they are one's own.[35] As to leveraging by appealing to reasons the audience already has, consider a case of a common kind, in which it is done so as to avoid giving the audience warrant to conclude that one is offering reasons one accepts as genuinely supporting the position in question – as we normally do accept reasons we offer in promoting a position we hold. Here it is likely to be evident that it *is* leveraging; for plainly one is pointing out why, from the audience's point of view, the position is worthy. That may or may not undermine one's effectiveness in persuading.

Political Argument, the Public Persona, and the Participant in a Community

Leveraging has an important place in political discourse. But if it is all I do, the audience cannot see *who* I am. I am like a lawyer representing a client in court: my job is to represent the client's point of view within certain limits, and my personal view does not matter. This is not generally a good way to relate to fellow citizens. As communitarians have perceived, I should be an individual who participates in the life of the community, not a political persona identified chiefly with my abstract position. It tends to conceal much of my perspective and so may well fail to promote understanding of me or my view; and it tends to arouse suspicion and so is likely either to undermine my efforts at persuasion or to make me seem an unknown quantity whose future conduct may be unpredictable.

There are, then, good grounds for thinking that in the main the reasons one offers for a position in public should be among one's own reasons for holding it. They may not be *all* of these; but if it tends toward insincerity to offer reasons for a position one holds that are not among one's reasons for holding it – say because they are believed by one's audience but not oneself – it also tends toward insincerity to offer (without qualification) reasons for it that, though one accepts them in the abstract, are not (motivationally) sufficient for one's holding it. If one successfully adheres to the principles of secular rationale and secular motivation, two good consequences follow: first, one is presenting reasons that are evidentially sufficient, and so should tend to be persuasive to a rational audience irrespective of its point of view; and second, one is being sincere, and so should not arouse the suspicion that easily arises from offering reasons that are not one's own.

These considerations about the importance of sincerity may illuminate an insightful critical comment that Nicholas Wolterstorff has made about liberalism, notably Rawls's version, but not restricted to that: the liberal "is trying to discover, and to form, the relevant community. He thinks we need a shared political basis . . . I think the attempt is hopeless and misguided. We must learn to live with a politics of multiple communities."[36]

I agree that it is hopeless for a pluralistic society to operate as a single community in the sense in which that implies a shared overall view of the world, including religious and sociopolitical outlook. But suppose we distinguish first- and second-order communities. Why is it not possible to seek a *second-order community* whose members are the different and overlapping religious, ethnic, professional, and other communities of which Wolterstorff speaks? Members of the second-order community will tend to have less in common than those of a first-order one; but a commitment to principles of mutual self-government and civic activity, such as those I have proposed, can do much to nurture understanding and tolerance.

Motivational and Evidential Cooperation of Religious and Secular Reasons

Like the principle of secular rationale, the principle of secular motivation is in one way quite inclusive. It allows that one may have and be motivated by religious reasons *as well as* secular ones. One may indeed believe the former more basic than the secular reasons that motivate one in sociopolitical matters, as in the case of someone who thinks that the most basic reasons for a principle, though not the only adequate reasons for it, are religious (here one might again think of the Ten Commandments). The ideal for religious citizens is a special kind of cooperation between the religious and the secular, not the automatic supremacy of the former over the latter. That cooperation requires that some secular reason play an essential role, but not that the person *regard* that role as primary or *take* the secular to be more important than the religious or even independent of it.

It should also be stressed that my use of such separationist principles by no means presupposes that religious reasons cannot be evidentially adequate. One need have no view on their adequacy to see the grounds for requiring that they be accompanied by adequate secular reason wherever they are used to advocate or support coercive laws or public policies. The principles also allow that religious reasons may be motivationally *sufficient* for a political stance (though not motivationally necessary, since secular reasons could not then be motivationally sufficient – they would be unable to produce belief or action without the cooperation of religious elements).

There is still another role my principles allow religious reasons to play, one that is easily overlooked. These reasons can be *causally sufficient* for producing a secular justification of a law or public policy, in the sense that one's having such reasons can, say through one's thinking about them or about related considerations, lead one to discover an evidentially adequate secular reason. That reason in turn can be motivationally sufficient (even independently of its continuing to receive support from the religious factors leading to its discovery). A bridge initially raised on one set of pillars may or may not continue to rest on them, in whole or in part. In the orders of discovery and motivation, either religious or secular reasons can be primary, and each kind can cooperate evidentially or motivationally with the other.

The rationale and motivation principles not only allow a conscientious citizen's judging the religious reasons in question to be more important than the secular ones, they also allow being more *strongly* motivated by them; this is perfectly consistent with one's being sufficiently motivated by adequate secular reason. Holding such judgments is also compatible with adhering to the principle of ecclesiastical political neutrality. The principles simply aim at preventing a certain kind of domination by religious reasons in contexts in which citizens should constrain them. Moreover, for both individuals and institutions, adhering to the principles makes it much easier to speak in public in a way that is both intelligible and persuasive to a diverse citizenry.

To be sure, in public advocacy of laws and policies that restrict human conduct, it seems *generally* best to conduct discussion in secular terms; but there may be special contexts in which candor or other considerations require laying out all of one's main reasons.[37] If one does articulate religious reasons in a public debate, it should help to be able to express both commitment to the principle of secular rationale and reasons that accord with it. This would show a respect for a religiously neutral point of view that any rational citizen may share.[38] The principles of secular rationale and secular motivation may, however, be adhered to without being stated or even consciously endorsed. It is the reasons one has and is motivated by that matter most, not what one would say about one's reasons or about the principles those reasons should satisfy.

Although the rationale and motivation principles (and indeed everything I have contended here) are entirely consistent with religious reasons' being evidentially adequate, the evidential adequacy of those reasons is not a presupposition of liberal democracy – nor, of course, is their evidential inadequacy.[39] Indeed, it may be that the absence of both presuppositions is a negative commitment of liberal democracy, a special kind of neutrality regarding religious matters, one that seems to go somewhat beyond neutrality toward religious institutions. This view is supportable, to differing degrees, from the perspective of any of the paths to liberal democracy described in Chapter 1. Even apart from that, I think it would be inappropriate for a theory of liberal democracy to contain either epistemological claim, just as it would violate the neutrality of a liberal state toward religion to support anti-religious practices or institutions as such.[40] This epistemological neutrality perhaps need not be a positive plank in even a fully articulated democratic constitution, but it is an important strand in much liberal-democratic theory.

Ideals, Rights, and Democratic Respect

In closing this chapter, I want to reiterate that my position as applied to individual conduct is above all one that lays out what we ought to do in something like an ideal case. It describes an aspect of civic virtue (a notion to be treated in detail in Chapter 6), not a limitation of civil (or other) rights. I have not claimed, for example, there is no *right* to base one's votes on a religious ground. But surely we can do better than guide our civic conduct merely within the constraints imposed by our rights. An ethics that directs us merely to live within our rights gives us too minimal a guide for daily life.

One important way in which my position is highly consonant with theistic religion, and in particular with the Hebraic-Christian tradition, is its insistence that morality speaks to the heart and mind, not just to the hand and mouth: our thoughts, attitudes, and feelings can be morally criticizable or praiseworthy, as well as our words and deeds. And our deeds, however well they can be rationalized by the reasons we can offer for them, *bespeak* the reasons that motivate them. We as agents, as opposed to our deeds, are judged more by the reasons *for* which we act than by the reasons we had for which we *could* have acted. Loving one's neighbors as oneself implies appropriate motives as well as good deeds, and it is far more than just respecting their rights of civic courtesy.

It is also worth reiterating that the domain of application of my principles is primarily contexts of political advocacy and of public policy decision. The principles are addressed especially to citizens as voters and supporters of laws and public policy, to legislators in their official capacities, to judges in making and justifying decisions, and to administrators, especially government officials, laying down and interpreting policies. But the principles apply differently in different contexts; less, for instance, in the classroom than in the statehouse, less in private discussion than in corporate board rooms.

There are, to be sure, proceduralist models of democracy that are less demanding than the conception I endorse. I have been thinking mainly of a constitutional liberal democracy. My claim is that a substantially weaker separation of church and state than I have defended is not fully consonant with the ideals of liberal democracy; and I think that sound ethics itself dictates that, out of respect for others as free individuals with human dignity, we should always have and be sufficiently motivated by adequate secular reason for our positions on those matters of law or public policy in which our decisions will (or might be reasonably expected to) significantly restrict human freedom.

If my fellow citizens are fully rational and are adequately informed concerning the matter at hand – an ideal combination many do not often realize – and I cannot convince them of my view by arguments framed in the concepts we share (or can readily share) as rational beings, then even if mine is the majority view I have a strong prima facie obligation not to coerce them. Perhaps the political system embodies a legal right for the majority to do so; presumably there is even a moral right to do so, at least given a certain mutual understanding of and commitment to majority rule. But the principles I am suggesting still make a plausible and weighty claim on our allegiance. They require, in certain contexts and for certain purposes, partial secularization of our advocacy, argumentation, and decisions. But they do not restrict our ultimate freedom of expression, and they leave us at liberty to fulfill our cherished religious ideals in all the ways compatible with a system in which those with differing ideals are equally free to pursue theirs.

CHAPTER FIVE

RELIGION AND ETHICS: TOWARD INTEGRATION

The principles of conscience defended in the last chapter may, in spite of all I have said in interpreting them, still appear to require more of religious citizens than an optimally liberal society should. Although the principles are consistent with both moral and legal rights to act otherwise, they nonetheless express prima facie obligations whose non-fulfillment is a basis for criticism from the point of view of the ethics of citizenship. A sound ethics may at once prohibit coercing people to meet a certain standard and provide for criticism of them if they do not adhere to it. This is how I have represented the principles of secular rationale, secular motivation, and ecclesiastical political neutrality. This chapter will show that these principles can be viewed in a plausible framework of combined theological and ethical standards which, taken together, indicate that the principles do not ask more of religious citizens than a free and democractic society should. Since my concern is largely to show the compatibility between the principles and the religious obligations of conscientious believers and to establish that the principles should be acceptable to a great many believers, it is appropriate to begin by considering sources of religious obligation.

THE DIVERSE SOURCES OF RELIGIOUS OBLIGATION

Religious obligation has at least five kinds of sources and of corresponding evidential grounds. In describing these sources, and indeed in discussing religious obligation in relation to the ethics of citizenship, I am thinking above all of the Hebraic-Christian tradition; but the points that emerge will apply, to varying degrees, to other traditions, including certain non-theistic religious traditions. The five sources I have in mind are

(1) scripture; (2) non-scriptural religious authority, especially that of the clergy, but including the authority of the relevant community, such as the religion's theological community if there is one; (3) tradition, which may be quite authoritative, including as it does presumptions regarding one's religious obligations and also habits that, whether or not they have scriptural or theological endorsement, can have strong momentum in a community; (4) religious experience; and (5) natural theology, for instance the philosophical kind illustrated by Thomas Aquinas's famous five arguments for the existence of God, each proceeding from non-religious premises. Divine command is of course distinct from any of these sources of religious obligation and may be conceived as a sixth source of religious obligation, but I am supposing for the sake of argument that *evidences* of divine command will come from one of the five sources. Several further comments are called for.

Direct and Indirect Religious Obligations. First, a source of religious obligation may require a kind of conduct directly – as by commanding it in the way God is biblically described as commanding the actions that Moses singled out in the Ten Commandments – or indirectly, as where Jesus exemplifies a kind of conduct and the text presents it as incumbent on us. Second, there are both direct and indirect obligations that go with a general commitment to an institutional religion. These include both *religious obligations* in the narrow sense, for example to engage in certain rituals, and *obligations of a religion* (some of which are non-religious in content), such as Christians' obligations of charity. Third, there are special obligations, such as those arising from what is revealed in a religious experience, which may fall not only on the person in question, chiefly the one having the experience, but perhaps also on those addressed in it. A whole family might, for example, be singled out in a religious experience of one member and might acquire a religious or other obligation through what is credibly reported as revealed to that one person. Fourth, there are what might be called *supererogations* – types of conduct that are highly desirable (and so are often presented in a favorable light) but not obligatory: they represent going beyond the call of duty.[1] All four cases are relevant here, but it will not be necessary to address them separately.

Grounding versus Content of Religious Obligation. It is also important, in discussing religious obligation, to distinguish its grounds from its content – its basis as contrasted with the conduct it requires. An obligation can have religious grounds without having religious content, such as theological or liturgical content. This is illustrated by the non-theological commandments among the Ten, for instance the prohibition of bearing false witness. Here a principle with secular content is presented as based on religious grounds. If, however, we take this distinction to imply that we should not in any circumstances call the obligations imposed by those commandments religious, we lose contact with an important constraint: an obligation whose non-fulfillment is religiously criticizable is to that extent a religious obligation. It is an obligation *of* a religion, even if not an obligation having religious content.

Secularly Aligned Religious Obligations. We should also distinguish those religious obligations that are *aligned* with non-religious ones, such as the obligation not to murder, from those that are religious in content (and from those that are neither), and I will generally use the term 'religious obligation' to refer to obligations that are clearly grounded wholly or primarily in a religious source.[2] I leave open whether these must be objective, externally grounded obligations, as opposed to obligations that are, say, reasonably *believed*, from the point of view of a person's religious commitments and relevant non-religious beliefs, to be objective obligations. This leaves open the possibility that there can be religious obligations even if the associated religious presuppositions (such as theism itself) should be mistaken, but it does not force us to attribute to a people just any religious obligation they believe they have, nor to adopt any specific account of the nature and force of any subjective religious obligations there may be. There are, for at least the religious traditions most important to this book, internal standards for responsibly determining when one has a religious obligation.

The Mutual Independence of Religious Sources of Obligation

It seems clear that the five sources of religious obligation I have listed are, though historically interdependent, logically independent, in the sense that "endorsement," by any one of them, of a proposition favoring some conduct does not entail its endorsement by any other source among the five.[3] A scriptural interpretation may yield an obligation that may not be reaffirmed in religious experience; a clerical directive given in a sermon may depart from tradition; and there may be myriad tensions, as well as common threads, connecting two or more sources of religious obligation.

The close historical association of the five sources may tend to hide their logical independence, but the latter is of great importance. It suggests the possibility both of conflicts between the sources and of mutual support among them. If the sources are independent, then on the one hand, their deliverances or indications regarding human conduct need not agree; but on the other hand, their agreement, especially when it is clear and unqualified, may greatly enhance the justification conferred on the conduct or point in question by any one of the concurring sources.

The possibility of converging support among the sources is particularly important because the support that any one of them gives to an action may be merely partial. One or more sources may provide some degree of support for a kind of conduct, yet not imply the strong conclusion that conduct of this kind is obligatory. Biblical examples often illustrate conduct that is arguably of this sort. It can be unclear just what such an example (such as Jesus's injunction to turn the other cheek) should be taken to show; and even where this seems clear, the support it implies for certain kinds of actions may – for some Christians, at least – be only partial. One case is the kind in which the support falls short of justifying an action. A second kind is justification without requirement: even if the injunction implies, for instance, that turning the other cheek is always justifiable, it might not entail that doing so is always obligatory.

It is also possible for two or more sources to be jointly but not individually sufficient: no one of them implies that action of the kind in question is obligatory, but, taken together, they do imply this. Still another case is obligational overdetermination, so called because more than one determinant operates. It may occur in the religious as well as in the moral domain. Two or more independent religious sources may each be sufficient to imply (and in that sense may determine) an obligation. It should not be surprising, then, if some religious obligations are stronger than, or even override, others, whether because two or more sources coincide in requiring the act in question as against one source prohibiting it, or because one source is clearer or more weighty than some other single source. This differential strength of religious obligations is indeed reflected in the way they are sometimes presented in scriptures.[4]

Suppose, then, that multiple religious sources can converge in favoring the same obligatory behavior, such as giving to the poor. Suppose further that a religious obligation can be aligned with a secular one – one that is secularly grounded (which in principle could also have religious content, since one might, for example, promise to pray with someone and thereby have a moral reason, based on a duty of fidelity, to do a religious deed). We should now expect that there is sometimes not only a plurality of different obligating grounds for a kind of conduct, but also religiously and secularly mixed obligational overdetermination, the kind that occurs when there are both sufficient religious reasons *and* sufficient secular reasons for a kind of conduct, for instance truth-telling.

Logically, neither the religious nor the secular ground for a kind of conduct they both require is necessarily stronger than the other, either evidentially or motivationally. Genetically, neither kind of obligation need be prior in the order of learning. Some people learn at least some of their moral principles first through religious education and later see a secular rationale for them; other people first learn at least some of their moral principles through secular education and later see a religious rationale for them.

Connections among Religious and Secular Sources

If we think of the Hebraic-Christian tradition, it is clear that there is much overlap between religiously and secularly grounded obligations. In the main this tradition is not opposed to taking secular grounds seriously, nor even to looking to them for purposes of, say, better understanding the conduct required by both sets of grounds, or of enhancing one's motivation to produce that conduct. Granted that a person's faith can and should inform aspects of secular life, including especially the treatment of others, reflective secular living can also lead to enhanced understanding of one's faith. Taken together with the multiplicity and independence of religious grounds, their internal diversity, and the unclarity (in some cases) of their bearing on conduct, this complicated, mutually enriching relation between religious and secular grounds has important implications. Two implications in particular concern me: one regarding religious individuals themselves, the other concerning their relations to their non-religious fellow citizens.

Consider rational individuals who are aware (as many educated people are) of the independence of religious sources, of the overlap between religious and secular obligations, and of the extent of religious diversity within and, especially, among traditions, both religious and non-religious. Should we not expect such individuals to seek confirmation of, or at least mutual support among, some of these justificatory sources, as they bear on judgments of far-reaching obligation? Some of those judgments, after all, are controversial or unclear or difficult to live up to; hence, combined evidence for a judgment by mutually supportive sources to which one is committed should normally be felt to be at once confirmatory, clarifying, and motivating. That joint confirmation can increase the likelihood that the judgment is true, clarify what it means, since different groundings can elucidate meaning, and enhance one's motivation to act on it.

Furthermore, if the grounds one finds for a religiously inspired judgment or a religiously required kind of conduct include secular considerations, there is the special satisfaction of being able to maintain that one's religious perspective leads to a truth (such as a principle of conduct) that can be supported independently of it. Such a truth, or at least one's secular grounds for it, can sometimes be a route by which others may join one, from outside one's tradition, in some project that this truth supports.

My suggestion, then, is that mature, rational, religious people living in circumstances like those of a contemporary liberal democracy will seek at least a measure of reflective equilibrium among their beliefs and attitudes grounded in religious sources of obligation and, in some cases, among those elements *and* beliefs and attitudes which they hold or find plausible, that they take to be grounded in secular sources. Roughly, this effort is a search for a reflective cognitive balance in which the elements in question – chiefly one's beliefs, attitudes, and desires – are mutually consistent and, so far as possible, mutually supportive. One can seek such an equilibrium in quest of a better religious understanding of one's religious obligations or mission or in search of a better moral understanding of one's ethical obligations or secular world view, or both. Given the richness of integration that is possible through such an equilibrium, multiply diverse concerns can join hands to lead one to it.

The more rational we are and the more complicated the moral issues we face, the wider the equilibrium we are likely to seek. The equilibrium may reasonably extend, though it need not, to theology, ethical theory, and even scientific considerations.[5] Thus, preferring to use one's resources reserved for charity to support an orphanage over a symphony orchestra might fit best with one's religious commitments, moral priorities, and scientific sense of how to strengthen the social fabric, whereas the thought of contributing to a candidate who favors most of one's sociopolitical policies but is also stingy regarding foreign aid may produce an ambivalence that precludes reaching reflective equilibrium in making a contribution.

In the social arena, a mature, rational, religious person is likely to be sensitive not only to overlapping moral views but to moral and other disagreements that have at least potential religious significance. It is likely to seem quite appropriate in such cases to seek common ground with fellow citizens with whom one disagrees in major moral or sociopolitical matters. One might hope that one's view is supported by secular grounds that people of any religious persuasion can accept, even if appealing to those grounds means questioning some aspect of one's own outlook. Indeed, I may find that I should revise something in my religious view: after all, once I take seriously the possibility of my religious sources yielding mutually conflicting results, I will surely be a fallibilist about my views of my religious obligations. I will also recognize the possibility of making errors in identifying or interpreting those obligations, particularly if I must rely on authorities in doing so – sometimes on authorities who themselves need labored interpretation. Their writings and sermons, for instance, may be complex, elusively metaphorical, or ambiguous.

I may, to be sure, feel very confident of some particular religious obligation, such as the obligation to try to love others and to spread the word of God among those who have not received it. The sense of my fallibility need not in all cases reduce my confidence. But this sense may still moderate – and it certainly bears on – what I should be willing to *do* on the basis of that confidence, particularly as it affects those outside my religious tradition.

Fallibilism about one's conception of one's religious obligations is particularly significant where two conditions jointly hold: first, the issue is what we are morally permitted or obligated to do in *non*-religious matters, and second, one can find no good secular ground for one's religiously based view. For although no secular reason need be expected for engaging in the special rites and rituals appropriate within a religious community, there is something of a presumption that such reasons may be found for our *general* moral obligations, including obligations to prevent or promote certain kinds of social conduct.[6] I shall return to this issue. For now, it is enough to have argued that both an effort to achieve reflective equilibrium on certain important matters and an attitude of fallibilism are appropriate to mature, rational practitioners of a religion for which, as is typical, there are multiple, independent, and sometimes unclear or ambiguous sources of authority regarding human conduct.[7]

RELIGIOUS COMMITMENT AND POLITICAL PARTICIPATION

If fallibilism about one's religious obligations – particularly in sociopolitical matters as opposed to the conduct of spiritual life – is appropriate to mature theists aware of the diversity and independence of the sources of religious obligation, then we can begin to see why such believers should tend to endorse the standards for justifying coercion that I have suggested are central to (or indeed partly constitutive of) liberal democracy. To reiterate a central idea, a liberal democracy by its very nature resists using coercion, and prefers persuasion, as a means to achieve cooperation. What we are persuaded to do, by being offered reasons for it, we tend to do autonomously and to identify with; what we are compelled to do constitutes both a reduction in our freedom and something we tend to resent doing. Thus, when there must be coercion, liberal democracies try to justify it in terms of considerations, such as public safety, that any rational adult citizen will find persuasive and can identify with.[8]

This last point expresses one reason why religious grounds alone are not properly considered a sufficient basis of coercion in a liberal democracy even if they happen to be shared by virtually all citizens. If fully rational citizens in possession of the relevant facts cannot be persuaded of the necessity of the coercion – as is common where that coercion is based on an injunction grounded in someone else's religious scripture or revelation – then from the point of view of liberal democracy, the coercion lacks an adequate basis. This is a point that religious citizens can well appreciate, particularly if they belong to a minority faith. A liberal state exists in good part to accommodate a variety of people irrespective of their special preference for one kind of life over another; it thus allows coercion in such major matters only where necessary to preserve civic order and not simply on the basis of majority preference, even when that preference is religiously authorized.[9]

As advocates for laws and public policies, then, and especially for those that are coercive, morally conscientious citizens will seek grounds that include reasons of a kind that any rational adult citizen can endorse as sufficient for the purpose. Virtuous citizens tend to be motivated in this direction in proportion to the burdensomeness of the coercion they support, for instance to be more concerned with the rationale for military conscription than with the basis for requiring hunters to be licensed.

From Theology to Ethics and Back Again

I have already suggested that there is in fact a great deal of overlap between the content of certain religiously based obligations and that of widely recognized secularly based moral obligations. I think that there is substantial overlap with respect to major moral principles, such as those prohibiting murder, assault, injustice (including political oppression), theft, and dishonesty, and those requiring some degree of beneficence toward other people, say in cases where one can help others with no significant sacrifice to oneself (this conception of moral overlap is similar to Rawls's idea of an overlapping consensus, though that notion includes sociopolitical principles as well as basic moral ones). I now want to go further than the overlap thesis regarding religiously based obligations and widely recognized secularly based moral obligations. I begin with a conception of God that seems at least implicit in what we might loosely call standard Western theism. I have in mind chiefly Christianity, Judaism, and Islam, the Abrahamic religions, as they are sometimes called; and I am speaking from the point of view of natural theology, the kind available to any rational informed inquirer, not the theology of any particular religion.[10]

If we assume a broadly Western theism, we can take God to be omniscient, omnipotent, and omnibenevolent. Might we not, then (at least given this set of divine attributes), expect God to structure us free rational beings and the world of our experience so that there is a (humanly accessible) secular path to the discovery of moral truths, at least to those far-reaching ones needed for the kind of civilized life we can assume God would wish us to live? Let me develop this idea.

It must first be granted that if God has created an ambiguous world in which evil looms so large that even many theists are tempted to doubt that God created it, then it would seem possible that there is no secular path to moral truths (at least not one created by God). But it is one thing for God to test us and provide conditions for our freely choosing to become children of God; it is quite another thing to make it virtually impossible for those who do not so choose, even to be moral in non-theological matters.[11] Why would God compound the incalculable loss suffered by rejecting one's beneficent creator with the impossibility of even discovering how one should behave in the absence of such a supreme authority who can guide one's daily life?

If the freedom preserved by the religious ambiguity of the world is valuable enough to explain God's permitting that ambiguity, should we not expect God to provide for access to rational standards, discoverable by secular inquiry, for the proper exercise of that freedom, as opposed to its abuse or waste in immoral, wrong-headed, or ignorant behavior? If God cares enough about us not to compel us toward theism, but instead to allow our free choice or rejection of it, would it not seem that we would be equipped with standards for the use of our freedom in the ways appropriate to God's creatures? Even if one thinks that much of our misfortune is a result of our own sin, one might reasonably expect that God would not allow us to be deprived of the minimum standards required to understand our own wrongdoing and use our freedom to rectify it.

Some theologies might imply that punishment requires this terrible fate. But not every theology need regard all who reject belief in God as deserving such severe punishment, and a plausible natural theology centered on omniscience, omnipotence, and, especially, omnibenevolence, surely need not. Some theologies, moreover, might consider the loss of a proper relation with God punishment enough, perhaps indeed the ultimate punishment; and even a theology that sees non-believers (or some of them) as needing further punishment might reasonably view the deprivation of secular paths to moral truths as at best incongruous with God's nature. This deprivation would be much like imprisoning people for a wrong (or otherwise imposing a painful sentence) and making it impossible for them, while they serve their sentences, to conduct themselves with moral dignity and with proper respect for their guards and fellow prisoners. Such prisoners would have neither religious nor even moral grounds for treating others in many of the ways God is widely believed to have commanded.[12]

Moreover, if one thinks, as a great many theists do, that natural theology yields a rational, non-religious route to religious truths, it is reasonable to expect that there might be a counterpart secular route to at least some basic moral truths. It seems altogether appropriate that in ethics as in religion, God should provide more than one path to truths essential for living a good life. The existence of multiple paths to a truth increases the likelihood of our finding it; the availability of many independent grounds for a truth makes it more likely that we will believe it with conviction and act on it when the going gets hard. A passage from Saint Paul is relevant here:

> When Gentiles who have not the law do by nature what the law requires, they are a law to themselves . . . They show that what the law requires is written on their hearts, while their conscience also bears witness . . . (Romans 2: 14–15)

One implication of this is apparently that, for Saint Paul, God has provided a sense of right and wrong that does not depend on religious teaching.

There is a scientific analogy pertinent here. If there is already a plurality of grounds for some major theological propositions and, in a different way, for some important theoretical conclusions in science, and if plurality in those domains is suggestive of God's provision for our discovering, in our individual ways, genuine religious and scientific truths, why should there not also be plurality with respect to grounds for major ethical truths? A plurality of grounds for important truths contributes to the likelihood that we will discover them, to our understanding of them when we see them in the multicolored light the diverse grounds provide, and to our commitment to act on them. It is altogether harmonious with the divine nature that there be such a plurality.

The possibility of secular paths to moral truths raises the question, at least for those who take natural theology seriously, whether there might not be a secular path not only to theism, but *through* it, to moral truths. In that case, at least for someone who could mount the appropriate natural theological arguments, there would be, as it were, a secularly certified theological route to sound moral principles. It should be granted that a non-religious route to religious truths could conceivably lead through them – for instance through divine commands ascertainable from secular premises – to moral truths. One problem with this idea is that there is a great distance from (a) discovering natural theological arguments, as accessible to secular reason, that ground knowledge of God's *existence* to (b) discovering such arguments that ground knowledge of God's *moral commands*. The crucial natural data for ascertaining those commands would seem to be the same data that, in the most plausible secular ethical theories, can justify moral principles: moral intuitions, facts about human flourishing, and other morally relevant sources of knowledge. In that case, the theists in question should be quite able to achieve an equilibrium between theological and ethical standards of human conduct – or should at least think it important to be able to achieve it – and their secular fellow citizens should have no great difficulty seeing the force of the relevant non-theological data. Communication and even moral agreement between these two groups of people should be approachable.

Suppose, however, that there is a pathway through natural theology, conceived as having entirely secular starting points, to divine command (as some natural law theorists may think there is). This pathway to moral truths, however impeccable logically, still runs through religious territory, and some rational non-religious citizens in a liberal democracy might be permissibly unwilling to follow it as an essential path to those moral truths, say as their only way of grasping why they have an obligation to give up a liberty. Some of them might accept an invitation to traverse it, but nearly all of them would resent being forced to take it or to occupy the position it leads to if they see no other route to that position. For other such citizens it might be objectionable to be asked to proceed through religious premises even voluntarily. For some religious citizens, on the other hand, it might be *religiously* inappropriate to be so led by someone *else*.

The Accessibility of Moral Truth to a Secular Use of Reason

Even if one does not agree that, given standard Western theism, we should expect there to be accessible, adequate secular reasons for (sound) major moral principles, one may well grant (on other grounds) that there are such reasons. I believe that there are. One ground for thinking this is the existence of moral principles that seem on careful reflection to be compelling.[13] This is not the place to state and defend moral principles on this kind of ground, but nearly everyone concerned with the issues under discussion will regard some ethical theory or other, say Kantian or utilitarian or intuitionist or Aristotelian theory, as highly plausible on non-religious grounds.

There is also one very general consideration that provides significant reason to think that there are secular paths to moral truths.[14] Suppose, as is widely held, that moral properties are based on natural ones (supervene on them, in a terminology common in ethical theory), roughly in the sense that the moral properties of a person or an act are possessed by it in virtue of its natural properties, those we might somewhat loosely call its factual (descriptive) ones. These are the kind ascertainable by scientific procedures, including ordinary observations of behavior. A person is honest, say, in virtue of a tendency to tell the truth (for an appropriate range of motivating reasons), and an act is obligatory, for instance, in virtue of being an avoidance of running over a child; and if a person is morally good, then so is any other person (e.g., a perfect duplicate) who is exactly similar in natural properties, such as psychological makeup taken to include intentions to treat people in certain ways, dispositions to share, aversions to fighting with others, and so forth.[15] Now, if there are natural properties determining moral properties, it is reasonable to think that in principle we can discover the presence of moral properties through discovering the presence of the natural properties on which they are based. Natural properties are (as normally – and non-skeptically – conceived) accessible to secular reason.

To be sure, apparently we are sometimes unable to tell *what* moral properties a person or act has even when (a) we know that the person or deed has certain natural properties and (b) these are in fact the ones that underlie the moral properties. For we may not know this latter fact. The psychological basis of some types of deceitfulness, a skeptic might note, need not wear its moral significance on its sleeve. A person might have a special tendency to be ambiguous or misleading that only careful inquiry can show to be a producer of the moral defect we call *deceitfulness.* We could, then, lack an appropriate principle for connecting the former with the latter. But this does not in general happen: if, as a mature moral agent with a normal range of human experience, you have a thorough knowledge of my personality, views, and motives conceived non-morally, you are in an excellent position to discern my moral character.

Mature moral agents also have a good sense of what *sorts* of natural properties are relevant to moral decisions, for instance their properties affecting people's pleasure and pain, freedom of movement, and mental capacities.[16] We know, for instance, that equality of effort and output are relevant to the justice of remuneration, that being truthful with people is essential to treating them with respect, and that brutality to children is unjust treatment. Doubtless many young children know such things too, though they lack the vocabulary to put them this way. These are, moreover, the kinds of moral truths that most reflective rational people can agree on even if they do not accept any particular ethical theory. There are, then, many natural properties that are at least of the sort through which we can know moral truths about the people or situations having those properties.

On the assumption that for major moral principles, there are secular reasons sufficient to warrant accepting them (a possibility that, incidentally, does not depend on the supervenience just hypothesized as supporting it), we can appreciate a further connection between the conception of God as omniscient and omnibenevolent and the possibility of a rational secular path to moral truths – *any* cogent argument, including an utterly non-religious one, for a moral principle *is* in effect a good argument for (1) God's knowing that conclusion – since God knows all truths – and hence, presumably, for (2) God's wishing or requiring conformity to it. How could God, conceived as omniscient and omnibenevolent, not require, or at least wish, our conformity to a true moral principle? And given that God should be believed to wish us to conform to true moral principles, it is at best difficult to see how God could *both* allow some people to reject all forms of theism and leave them unable to find a secular path to moral truths.[17]

To be sure, it cannot be assumed without argument that religious (or moral) obligations outweigh all others. Hence, on the assumption that God wishes us to fulfill our strongest obligations, it cannot simply be assumed that God must wish us, on balance, to prefer realizing a religious obligation over a moral one where the two conflict. What then of the case of Abraham and Isaac? Does it not present a religious obligation (to sacrifice a son) as taking precedence over a moral one? This is one reading, but even if we knew that God placed (one or more) religious obligations over moral ones, we could still have better reason for believing that God commands, say, protection of one's children than for believing that God commands any particular action inconsistent with this. Should Abraham, however – insofar as he (reasonably?) believed that it was God requiring the sacrifice – have believed that sacrificing his son was inconsistent with protecting him? That is not clear: God's ways of protecting us are infinite. Note, too, how the story ends: the morally prohibited action is not required after all, perhaps suggesting that despite appearances, there cannot be an inconsistency between religious and moral obligations.

If mutual reinforcement between a plausible theology and a sound ethics is as likely to be achievable as I suggest, it may turn out that the theological significance of some moral arguments may be at least as great as the moral significance of some theological arguments. If, for instance, there are sound arguments for pacifism or at least the position that only purely defensive wars are permissible, then a theology that represents God as commanding conquest for the faith is mistaken.

I should think, moreover, that in some cases, good secular arguments for moral principles may be *better* reasons to believe those principles to be divinely enjoined than theological arguments for the principles, based on scripture or tradition. For the latter arguments seem (even) more subject than the former to cultural influences that may distort scripture or tradition or both; more vulnerable to misinterpretation of religious or other texts or to their sheer corruption across time and translation; and more liable to bias stemming from political or other non-religious aims. Granting, then, that theology and religious inspiration can be sources of ethical insight, we can also reverse this traditional idea: one may sometimes be better off trying to understand God through ethics than ethics through theology.[18]

The Integration of the Theological with the Ethical

If these considerations from philosophical theology and ethical theory are sound, then the ethics of citizenship on the part of the religious should embody a commitment to *theo-ethical equilibrium* – a rational integration between religious deliverances and insights and, on the other hand, secular ethical considerations, including sociopolitical principles of the kind that determine the level of permissible freedom in a democracy. Thus, a seemingly sound moral conclusion that goes against one's scriptures or one's well-established religious tradition should be scrutinized for error; a religious demand that appears to abridge moral rights should be studied for such mistakes as misinterpretation of what it requires, errors in a translation of some supporting text, and distortion of a religious experience apparently revealing the demand; a major moral principle derived from only one of the five sources of religious obligation should, in many cases, be tested against one or more of the other four and perhaps also against some secular source. Given the conception of God as omniscient, omnipotent, and omnibenevolent, the possibility of theo-ethical equilibrium is to be expected; and a mature, conscientious theist who cannot reach it should be reluctant or unwilling to support coercive laws or public policies on a religious basis that cannot be brought into that equilibrium.[19]

If we take a commitment to seeking theo-ethical equilibrium to be (or at least to merit being) a major element in the ethics of citizenship of the religious, are we deifying reason? I think not. Notice that although secular reason can lead to modifying one's religious views, religious considerations can also lead to revision of one's secular moral views. This applies especially to moral theories, but it extends even to "intuitive" moral judgments. Moreover, a commitment to seeking theo-ethical equilibrium leaves open whether one gives either kind of reason evidential priority or any other kind of priority. Any precedence that either one may have, however, is not license to ignore the other: a conscientious religious person aware of the relationships outlined here should not in general approve of any deed that is either morally or theologically impermissible.

A commitment to seeking theo-ethical equilibrium may be thought to split the self into religious and secular personae,[20] but it need not, and it can have the opposite effect. The intelligibility of separate grounds for action does not require different agents or subagents to grasp those grounds. Such intelligibility does not even imply different obligations to act on the separate grounds, as opposed to a single obligation with a plurality of supporting reasons. One's strongest obligation may be an integration of moral, theological, pragmatic, and indeed other elements. It need not be a triumph of a single one or a mere coincidence of two or more.

An action's being supported by two different kinds of grounds is not merely possible, it is sometimes welcome. It can be a good occasion to connect those grounds as allied considerations. In some such cases disparate grounds may even be merged into a unified point of view, especially when theo-ethical equilibrium is achieved or, where it is not, when the grounds support the same or complementary actions. Moreover, each of several disparate grounds may be embraced from the standpoint of the others, as where secular benevolence is a fulfillment both of divine command and of a secular ethical commitment. This benevolence may issue in both individual acts of charity and a national policy of foreign aid.

For some religious outlooks, a commitment to seeking theo-ethical equilibrium, or even to the aspect of it that requires only seeking secular as well as religious grounds for major moral principles, may seem to go against the view that the whole of one's life must be devoted to doing God's will.[21] On two plausible assumptions, even this view can be accommodated by the position I am suggesting as a way of harmoniously combining the religious and the secular in a wide range of moral matters. The first assumption is that a property – such as that of being commanded by God – can appear to human intelligence in more than one guise, say in a Kantian guise as the property of befitting the dignity of persons or in an agapistic guise as the property of being appropriate to loving treatment of others. The second assumption is that if God either has ordained the coincidence of the property of being commanded by God with a property appearing in a secular guise, or has at least allowed us to discern the equivalence of the two or, minimally, to grasp the reasonableness of taking the property appearing in a secular guise as an adequate basis of action, then our being guided in our actions by the property in its secular guise is not irreverent. If, for instance, God has created me so that I grasp the dignity of other people as dictating just treatment of them, and I am motivated by that to treat them justly, then my doing so on that basis is not irreverent.

We may go further. Suppose that the property that I am morally responding to *is* that of being commanded by God, as would be expected on a version of divine command ethics for which the property of being obligatory for human beings is identical with that of being commanded by God.[22] Then, even if I were a non-theist, my conduct would be appropriately and non-accidentally in conformity with reverence. (It would even be – unconsciously – reverent, insofar as reverence is possible without awareness of the theological ground to which one is responding.) To be sure, I myself would not thereby be a reverent person; but if my actions are reverent, I may come to appreciate their consonance with divine will.

If I can, as is certainly possible for a theist in the Hebraic-Christian tradition, *conceive* my acting justly as also doing God's will, then from a religious point of view, so much the better. Moreover, nothing stops me from so conceiving it even if I am independently motivated by the moral sense of dignity as demanding justice. If the world that God has created exhibits divine will in a multiplicity of guises, why should I not appreciate that will in the variety of God's creation and allow those aspects of creation that attract my rational approval or allegiance to contribute to my motivation to be moral?

It should also be stressed that reason itself can be considered a gift from God and thereby divinely sanctioned for our use. Furthermore, even divine commands about its use – such as to love God with all one's mind – must be carried out under the guidance of the very faculty they are to regulate. A significant degree of autonomy of reason in governing human life is presupposed in any religious perspective. Extending a good measure of that autonomy to the ethical and religious domains seems in any case to be quite consonant with piety.

The Possibility That Human Reason Is a Corrupted Faculty

To some people, the view just expressed is much too optimistic. Some may object that reason is or certainly might be corrupted by sin or, as it is sometimes put, "fallen."[23] But what can this mean? Not that we cannot adapt means to ends and even reason at a high level philosophically and scientifically. This is plainly false. Not, surely, that we cannot at least make a rational effort to apply scriptural imperatives, such as the Ten Commandments and the injunction to love one's neighbor as oneself, to everyday life – no easy task, particularly since the requirements of some of them can apparently conflict with those of others. This is also plainly false.

If the basis of the view that reason is defective is scriptural, maintaining the view presupposes rational powers sufficient to interpret the relevant texts. If its basis is special revelation, maintaining it presupposes someone's having at least reason enough to understand the message. Given how obvious it is that we operate rationally at high levels in these as well as myriad other tasks, this is certainly a far-reaching presupposition. These points may not satisfy those who take the view, derived from Saint Augustine, that without grace our reason is too corrupt to discover basic moral truths. One response is that an omnibenevolent God would give the (presumably limited) measure of grace required (or appears to have given it); another is that the degree of reason required to arrive at this sophisticated a theological view is itself sufficient for such discovery (and may also be evidence of a measure of grace); and still another is that the realization of sinfulness needed to seek grace in a properly penitent way implies sufficient rational powers to grasp basic moral standards – which, one might argue, are no less difficult to comprehend than the theological standards required for recognition and rejection of sin. These points will not meet every objection of the kind I am considering, but for most people, whether religious or not, they should go a good distance toward reducing its force.

To be sure, there is no doubt that we are not only fallible but capable of using reason to rationalize both error and injustice. Insofar as this is the point of calling reason unreliable or corrupt, I accept it. But is it not by the use of reason that we most easily detect its own abuses? And is reason not equipped to correct them – or at least an indispensable element in that effort? I cannot see that there is a plausible interpretation of the idea that reason is corrupt or unreliable that does not presuppose its soundness in a great variety of cases central for the conduct of human life.

Supposing this reply to the corruptedness objection is basically sound, it raises for some the question whether the liberalism it represents is theologically neutral.[24] Although I cannot argue the point here, I am not aware of any seriously developed theology that does not presuppose the use of reason to a degree that undermines any claims it may make to the effect that reason *in general* can never be trusted. But suppose someone claims to have a revealed theology on which our *only* imperative is to follow its own directives. Much would depend on what these directives are; but such an approach lends itself to irrationalism, and at least in the wrong hands it would tend to permit wanton human sacrifice and unpredictable abuses of any living thing that runs afoul of the Sacred Word.

A theology of that kind, and indeed any theology that does not endorse certain protections of innocent people, lends itself to abuses by demagogues and fanatics, tyrants and megalomaniacs. A Hitler could think himself specially privileged in receiving the revelations. The appropriate theological neutrality of liberal-democratic theory, or of any plausible political philosophy, operates within broad moral boundaries. I do not think there is any seriously developed major theology whose conscientious adherents, if they are living in a well-ordered liberal democracy, would be seriously disadvantaged by this constraint. I am certain that a political philosophy that does not observe similar broadly moral constraints will not command the assent of either the major theologies of the world today or reflective rational persons.

The very notion of the ethics of citizenship, as contrasted with religious virtue, suggests that secular reasons will play a major role in the former. One reaction would be to say that if so, then the deeply religious are within their rights in rejecting the obligation to strive for the ethics of citizenship as understood here. They *may* be within their religious rights, but that depends on the very issue we are discussing: on what implications their overall religious view has for the treatment of others, especially people outside their religious community. Thomas Aquinas's emphasis on natural law, and indeed Jesus's emphasis on loving one's neighbors, on nonviolence, and on forgiveness, would suggest that the ethics of citizenship, especially when taken as embodying a commitment to theo-ethical equilibrium, should not (from within at least the major Christian traditions) be rejected.[25]

If, on the other hand, the question is whether we are within our moral rights in rejecting the proposed ideal of the ethics of citizenship, I would say that the answer is not clear. A major second-order moral obligation that we all seem to have is to take (first-order) moral obligations and principles seriously and to seek accommodation with those with whom we are obligated to live in peace despite our disagreements, whether they are outside our own religious tradition or within it.

Suppose, however, that we would be within both our moral and our religious rights in rejecting this ideal of the ethics of citizenship. Is doing so morally desirable, and would it be morally virtuous? My answer to both questions is negative. Whether, from a religious point of view, this answer is reasonable depends on the conditions for achieving theo-ethical equilibrium within that point of view and on what sorts of principles support granting such equilibrium a serious place in sociopolitical conduct. I have suggested that given omniscience, omnipotence, and omnibenevolence as elements in the conceptions of God prevalent in standard Western theism, a major factor in the equilibrium should be good secular arguments for moral principles. To connect samples of these arguments with any specific religion is too large a task to undertake here. But the next section will suggest some principles of conscience that commend themselves both as aids to achieving theo-ethical equilibrium and as elements in the ethics of citizenship.

THE PRINCIPLE OF THEO-ETHICAL EQUILIBRIUM

Given the importance of the cooperation of religious and secular motives, it is appropriate to formulate a principle that facilitates application of, and adherence to, the principles of secular rationale and secular motivation. This principle is based on the idea that there is much to be gained, intellectually and motivationally, from seeking theo-ethical equilibrium in deciding a wide range of questions. For those who are religious, then (and possibly even as a heuristic principle for some who, though not religious, can think fruitfully in religious terms), I propose a *principle of theo-ethical equilibrium:* where religious considerations appropriately bear on matters of public morality or of political choice, religious people have a prima facie obligation – at least insofar as they have civic virtue – to seek an equilibrium between those considerations and relevant secular standards of ethics and political responsibility. I take the obligation to seek this equilibrium to be strongest where support of a law or public policy that would restrict human conduct is in question, but I believe that some obligation may remain even apart from such cases.[26] It is certainly supported by the do-unto-others rule.

Much is still left unspecified here. How readily should the bearing of religious considerations on the matter at hand be discernible in order for the obligation to seek theo-ethical equilibrium to become operative? How much effort should one expend in connection with decisions regarding law or public policy in order to discern whether there is any such bearing? And what ethical and political standards must one consider in relation to such decisions? A great deal could be said, but I leave the issue for another occasion. I would reiterate, however, that one may seek a still wider equilibrium, for instance where the application of a moral standard to a concrete case requires a knowledge of many facts, say medical facts about an elderly population needing help and sociological facts concerning their patterns of life. Here one may properly seek an equilibrium that yields a sociopolitical judgment which is at once morally and religiously sound and scientifically informed. It should be no surprise that a principle of virtue is not quantifiable and requires finding an Aristotelian mean between excess and deficiency.

The Normative Force of Theo-ethical Equilibrium

If I have been right so far, then the wide range of the cases in which theo-ethical equilibrium is achievable by mature rational theists supports my contention that the principle of secular rationale is not unreasonably demanding toward religious citizens. Indeed, the theory of theo-ethical equilibrium can also support a principle that may give religious citizens (and perhaps some non-religious ones) both better justification and more incentive for activism. Suppose that for rational adherents to at least some religions, this equilibrium is possible. Then there is reason to think that in many such cases the ethical and sociopolitical principles that the equilibrium yields are normatively reasonable. They at least gain some support from surviving the scrutiny and integration the equilibrium requires. If they gain enough, one might plausibly hold a counterpart of the principle of secular rationale – call it the *principle of theo-ethical rationale,* to the effect that citizens in a liberal democracy who have reached a reasonable theo-ethical equilibrium with clear implications for sociopolitical conduct have a prima facie justification, and may have a prima facie obligation, to act accordingly.

To be sure, if a prima facie obligation I have under this principle comes into conflict with one I have under the principle of secular rationale, as where I want to legalize assisted suicide on my secular evidence and to illegalize it on my overall evidence in theo-ethical equilibrium, then as a citizen in a liberal democracy I should question whether my theo-ethical equilibrium is reasonable or is, for instance, based on a hasty inference or false premise. But I should also question whether, for example, my secular reason for the position in question is adequate. Is it, for instance, the protection of a liberty that I would want to preserve if I were the one to be coerced, or is it instead one whose exercise is destructive or degrading toward human life, a kind that, on the basis of my religious views as they stand in equilibrium with my secular moral principles, I reflectively want to restrict?

In such a case of conflict, I have a moral right to act on my religious conviction, as indeed on my secular conviction. Morality surely protects our freedom in such a matter, and in a liberal democracy law follows suit. But it does not follow that, all things considered, I should act on my religious conviction. The question of which prima facie obligation takes priority may be complex, and it need not be automatically answered in favor of either religious conviction or secular judgment. Civic virtue (to be discussed in the next chapter) may normally favor preference for the latter; but a rational agent need not automatically take that virtue to be the dominant normative standard in sociopolitical conduct. A citizen who does not, however, is liable to criticism from the point of view of that virtue, even if the conduct in question is considered reasonable, or at least excusable, from the agent's perspective.

Institutional Applications of Theo-ethical Equilibrium

The notion of theo-ethical equilibrium has institutional applications; its application is not restricted to the deliberations of individual citizens.

Like an individual citizen, a church might, in supporting a law or public policy, often both have and be sufficiently motivated by a moral consideration bearing on a political issue. This ecclesiastical moral engagement is surely desirable in a liberal democracy, and it is quite likely to occur if, in moral matters, churches abide by an *institutional principle of theo-ethical equilibrium,* which says that religious institutions, at least insofar as they are committed to citizenship in a free and democratic society, have a prima facie obligation to seek such equilibrium in deciding to advocate or support laws or public policies that restrict human conduct. This equilibrium principle is a plausible candidate for a principle of institutional citizenship and is quite far-reaching.[27]

A counterpart principle has some application to those secular private institutions, such as colleges and universities with many religious faculty and students, for which it is appropriate to bring religious considerations into certain public policy decisions. Serving the religious needs of faculty and students, for example, even if done for secular reasons, can often be best achieved if the activities by which it is accomplished are selected in part in the light of reasoning that seeks a theo-ethical equilibrium. A principle we might take as a guide here would be that secular institutions in a liberal democracy (particularly private ones) that must determine policies affecting their religious members are well advised (even if they do not always have a prima facie obligation) to consider their alternatives in the light of an effort to find a theo-ethical equilibrium that reflects both their institutional ideals and the considered religious convictions of the members affected. Consider a decision concerning whether prayer should come into the commencement ceremony and, if so, how and with what sort of content. Here considerations drawn from the various religions represented among faculty and students are quite relevant, and they should be placed in equilibrium with such concerns as whether prayer, or a certain kind of prayer, would alienate or offend the non-religious people attending.

The case for seeking theo-ethical equilibrium, whether individual or institutional, should not be taken to imply that there is nothing to be learned from disequilibrium.[28] Many insights and theoretical advances come from reflection on or experience with conflicting elements and from the effort to reconcile them. But disequilibrium is not mere confusion or perplexity; and at least in a form in which one is likely to learn from it, it is unlikely when there is no concern to reach equilibrium, as with many for whom sociopolitical decisions are mainly cut and dried.

Disequilibrium may occur spontaneously, but it is more often an effect of an unsuccessful attempt to reconcile elements in tension.

Theo-ethical equilibria differ in unity, scope, depth, stability, and other dimensions. Some are, moreover, better than others. Some are more reasonable in terms of comprehensiveness, grounding of basic premises that figure in them, soundness of relevant inferences, and explanatory power. A reasonable equilibrium in a complex sociopolitical matter may be hard-earned; but a spontaneous one arising from internalization of a good moral theory and an adequate grasp of relevant facts is also possible and, once achieved, can be often maintained by reflection. Wisdom here consists in part in knowing how much, and in what ways, to reflect on one's commitments.

THEOLOGY AND THE AUTONOMY OF ETHICS

If I have suggested significant restrictions on the use of religious arguments in liberal-democratic politics, I have nonetheless said nothing incompatible with the idea that there *can* be religiously grounded knowledge in ethical and sociopolitical matters. Liberal democracy, however, is committed, at least in its best-developed forms, to the *conceptual and epistemic autonomy of ethics,* in the broad sense in which ethics encompasses normative political philosophy. This commitment does not imply affirming the ontological independence of ethics; it is above all a commitment to the possibility of our achieving moral knowledge or at least justified moral beliefs or attitudes (this is the epistemic side); and it implies that we can understand moral concepts independently of theological ones (this is the conceptual side). It is compatible with the possibility that such beliefs cannot be *true* apart from God's existence (an ontological matter). Knowledge of moral standards may be achieved independently of theology, even if those standards are in an important sense rooted in divine command. The foundation may be below ground.

Consider an aesthetic analogy. Just as, regardless of whether a poem must have an author, one might understand it, and know its aesthetic merits, without knowing who its author is (or even that it has one), one might understand, and know the truth or at least justification of, a moral principle without knowing who its author is, or even whether it has one. If, with many divine command theorists, I believe that God necessarily exists and is indeed the ultimate ground of moral truths and the ground of the existence of anything, I can still embrace liberal democracy and defend the full sociopolitical rights of atheists. But this would be at best difficult for me if I thought there is no non-theistic route to justifying moral and sociopolitical standards.

For reasons already given, I have argued that liberal democracy is also committed to the possibility of justifying, on secular grounds, any coercion necessary for maintaining civil life, even where the conduct subject to coercion is defended by a religious justification, as with some religiously rationalized persecutions of religious minorities. Here secular coercion may have a justification that, in a liberal democracy, overrides a sincere and articulate religious rationale for allowing the proscribed conduct. Granting this sociopolitical ascendancy of secular argument in justifying coercion in a liberal democracy does not imply a commitment to its being evidentially better than all religious argument. Agreeing on the principles – and referees – of a game does not entail believing that, from a higher point of view, there can be no better game, or no superior referees.[29] But at least as long as we consentingly play the game, we have a prima facie obligation to abide by its rules.[30] We may of course protest against the rules; but there are standards of conduct governing protest, and the mere fact of sincere protest does not automatically override the obligation to adhere to the rules.

Teachers of ethics, and indeed teachers in general, should, I think, presuppose the epistemic autonomy of ethics.[31] It is a further question whether specific moral principles, such as the principle that people must be allowed free expression except where harm to others would result, must be presupposed by liberal democracy and by teachers therein. I believe that some of them must be, if only because they reflect underlying premises of such a system, and (as noted in Chapter 1) the very name 'liberal democracy' indicates the same conclusion; but perhaps only a pragmatic assumption to this effect is presupposed.

The largest single issue here is whether liberal democracy must be in a sense *morally constituted,* as opposed to being grounded, for instance, in instrumental considerations concerning the preference satisfaction of, say, the founding parties or the current citizens. I am not certain that it must be morally constituted. I believe it is best that a liberal democracy should be so constituted, say by its commitments in its founding documents or at least its unwritten normative standards; but as argued in Chapter 1, a commitment to equality in liberty and basic political power, and to the kind of standard for justified coercion I have proposed, seems defensible on non-moral grounds, for instance on instrumentalist principles or even on various religious lines.

The epistemic autonomy of ethics does not imply its disconnection from other conceptual domains, including theology. Everything I have said is intended to be compatible with the existence of a religious grounding of ethics, and even of moral knowledge – there can be evidential overdetermination here: two routes that, from the point of view of knowledge and justification, are independent ways to reach moral principles. Moreover, on the assumption of a broadly Western theism, I have argued that we can say at least this: God would surely provide a route to moral truth along rational secular paths – as I think Aquinas, for one, believed God has done. Given how the world is – for instance, containing so much evil – it would seem cruel for God to do otherwise. If there were no secular path to moral truth, the plight of the world would be even worse than it is, and in ways there is good reason to think God would not allow.[32]

If I have been right about the possibility, and indeed, the desirability, of a theo-ethical equilibrium for religious citizens in a liberal democracy, then separation of church and state, together with a corresponding separation of religious and secular considerations in the thinking of individual citizens, may seem far less a detriment to the sociocultural influence of religion, especially of traditional monotheistic religion, in proportion as the moral requirements of religion are properly understood in the light of the divine attributes. Not only should traditional theists expect there to be secular routes to moral truth (roughly, routes neither religious in content nor epistemically dependent on religion or theology); these same paths should also be secular routes that lead to divine truth, whether or not those who traverse them so regard the truths they find at the end of the journey.[33] It is not too much to ask of conscientious religious citizens, then, that they sometimes seek these paths; and in part because of the strong case for their existence, it is not too much to ask of them that they abide by the principles of secular rationale and secular motivation.

PART THREE

CIVIC VIRTUE AND POLITICAL ACTIVISM IN A RELIGIOUSLY PLURALISTIC DEMOCRACY

CHAPTER SIX

CIVIC VIRTUE

A democratic society cannot flourish if its citizens merely pursue their own narrow interests. If it is to do more than survive, at least a substantial proportion of citizens must fulfill responsibilities that go beyond simply avoiding the violation of others' rights and occasionally casting a vote. The vitality of a democracy requires that many citizens – ideally all of them – contribute something to their communities and participate responsibly in the political process.[1] The disposition to do these things is a large part of what constitutes civic virtue. But that virtue encompasses more. My task here is to explore civic virtue. I first outline a broad conception of virtue and, with that set out, pursue the question of what makes a virtue civic. My special concern is to articulate what constitutes civic virtue in relation to the central problem of this book: how to determine a proper relation between religion and politics and, in the lives of religious citizens, an appropriate balance between religious and secular demands. I have already argued for a partial ethics of citizenship that can help in resolving this problem. Here I want to show how such an ethics can be plausibly reached from a conception of civic virtue.

This virtue-theoretic route to the principles I have proposed is entirely compatible with the arguments so far given; but even if one had certain doubts about those arguments, one could reach much the same standards by working from a conception of civic virtue that apparently has independent moral force. Whether it does have independent moral force may be controversial, but insofar as it does it provides considerable support for the principle of secular motivation. I have argued for that principle on other grounds, including considerations of respect for persons, mutual trust, democratic stability, and justification of concrete deeds as opposed to types of conduct considered in the abstract. Virtue theory, more than any other major ethical orientation, emphasizes the character and motivation of agents rather than the types of actions they perform. This is one reason for its considerable bearing on the principle of secular motivation.

The revival of virtue ethics since the late 1950s stems in good part from dissatisfaction with the prevailing rule theories, above all utilitarianism, Kantian ethics, and intuitionism, all of which can provide a basis for the theory of church-state separation defended in this book. But one need not reject rule theories in order to see the value of the concept of virtue as an important element in any ethical theory and as a focus for both moral education and the support of ethical standards.[2] A good rule theorist should indeed recognize the power of virtue theories. Even if their normative force turns out to depend on some rule standard or some general theory of value, an appeal to aretaic notions ("virtue notions") can both clarify and support sociopolitical standards in a distinctive way.

There is a further reason to consider the principles and standards proposed in this book from the point of view of virtue theory. Quite apart from holding any ethical theory, people of good will – and especially those who care about their responsibilities as citizens – can deeply want to have and be guided by the kind of character that exhibits virtue (whether or not they would so describe it). This chapter will show how a plausible concept of civic virtue supports the framework of standards I have been defending.

VIRTUES AS NORMATIVELY STRUCTURED ELEMENTS OF CHARACTER

We can best understand civic virtue if we first achieve an adequate general conception of virtue. This will require both an outline of what it is to have a virtue and an indication of how virtues manifest themselves in action. We can then see what constitutes a specifically civic virtue.[3]

A virtue is a certain kind of character trait, one appropriate to pursuit of the good with respect to which the virtue counts as such. The well-being of others, for instance, is essential for determining what counts as beneficence. A virtue may be more or less deeply rooted; more or less dominating in the agent's behavior; and variable in many other ways. Moreover, both cognitive and motivational elements are central in any virtue. A virtuous person, say one with veracity, must have certain beliefs; some would say, indeed, that these must constitute knowledge, such as knowledge of when it is appropriate to avoid an unjustified question rather than either answer it truthfully or lie. Virtuous people must also have desires appropriate to the virtue, for instance, in the case of fidelity, a desire to stand by friends.[4]

There are at least six conceptually important dimensions of a virtue of character.[5] These correspond to situational, conceptual, cognitive, motivational, behavioral, and teleological dimensions of the trait itself and the actions proper to it – actions from virtue, as we might call them.

The first dimension is the *field* of a virtue. This is roughly the kind of human situation, such as voting in an election, in which it characteristically operates. The field for civic virtue is open-ended, but encompasses the wide range of actions affecting one's immediate or wider community, particularly as they bear on people's freedom or well-being.

The second dimension is the characteristic *targets* the virtue aims at. For civic virtue (conceived in a democracy), a major target is election of the best candidate, though there are other targets that are non-political, and there are some, for elected officials, that do not pertain to citizens as such. In the case of honesty, there is avoidance of deceit; for humility, there is appropriate restraint about one's accomplishments; and so forth. If there is a single overarching target, say the good of the community, or perhaps even a unified set of targets, we may speak of the *telos* of the virtue, as writers on Aristotelian virtue ethics often do.[6]

The third dimension is the agent's *understanding* of the field of the virtue – for instance, in politics, an understanding of criteria for being the best candidate. Virtue is consistent with limited understanding of this field, but one can hardly find a target with no sense of where it is or what means will lead to it. Civic virtue requires some understanding of one's community and its political structure.

Fourth, there is the agent's *motivation* to act in that field in a certain way, to engage in a kind of conduct appropriate to the virtue. Given civic virtue, we will be motivated by, say, a desire to contribute to the well-being of the nation as opposed to wanting just our own enrichment. The former but not the latter desire is appropriate to civic virtue.

Fifth, there is the agent's acting on the *basis* of that understanding and motivation, for instance on the basis of a concern with national prosperity rather than with one's own personal projects. This notion is important for distinguishing actions merely in conformity with virtue from those performed *from* it and hence truly virtuous, in the sense implying that they bespeak an element of good character.

The sixth dimension is the *beneficiaries* of the virtue, above all the person(s) who properly benefit from our realizing it (virtue may certainly benefit its possessor, but I have in mind civic virtues, for which external beneficiaries are primary). For civic virtue, the beneficiaries are compatriots in general.[7]

These six notions are specially appropriate to explicating action from virtue, including political action that stems from it and hence is grounded in the right kind of motive. These notions apply, moreover, to religious as well as secular virtues. Let us first consider the field of a virtue.

The field of, say, the virtue of justice, which must be possessed in some measure by anyone with civic virtue, might be roughly retribution and – more important – the distribution of goods and evils; that of fidelity might be conduct required by explicit or implicit promises; and so forth. Such fields may overlap other aretaic fields. Justice without honesty would be at best accidental; justice without compassion is possible, but would be unnecessarily harsh. Still, each virtue has some distinctive features.

How does a civically virtuous person understand the field of, say, citizenship? It would be natural for the appropriate understanding to manifest itself in believing that elections create a duty to vote, that listening to the candidates provides information citizens ought to use in judging the issues, and so on. But suppose someone did not use the concepts of duty or obligation (at least here) and thought simply that it is *good* to vote and to criticize people who do not. A virtuous person could even be skeptical about moral concepts or might think them indistinguishable from aretaic concepts in general. We need not claim that virtuous citizens approach citizenship with any specific aretaic or other normative concepts, only that, as citizens, they operate with any of a range of acceptable concepts and commitments.

Civic virtue, like most other virtues, is a practical success, not a theoretical achievement. Its intellectual requirements are quite latitudinarian and can be met by a self-conscious rule theorist or by a moral skeptic suspicious of ethical concepts. A conscientious citizen must have a sense of when to endorse a social policy that will relieve poverty, or to oppose one that will lead to war, but need not derive this sense from a theory. Having such a sense of appropriateness is part of what it is to understand the field of a virtue, and – more broadly – to have practical wisdom. Without that understanding, one would not act from virtue.

It is useful to conceive the relevant traits – at least traits of broadly *moral* character, which is where I would place civic virtue – as constituted by fairly stable and normally long-standing wants and beliefs, or at least beliefs, proided they carry sufficient motivation.[8] Surely civic virtue, for instance, requires appropriate wants, such as desires to treat others decently, and certain beliefs, say the belief that participating in elections is morally required.

The more self-consciously virtuous an agent is, the greater the moral content of the appropriate wants and beliefs, or at least the greater the tendency for the agent to entertain the relevant content; but even being spontaneously virtuous is more than a matter of simply doing the relevant kinds of deeds. The deeds must be appropriately aimed, in terms of what the agent wants and believes, or they are not moral – in the sense of morally performed – but merely consistent with morality. If I vote merely to avoid the criticism of peers, then even if the vote is informed I am not exhibiting civic virtue in my voting; if my resulting vote is civically justified, that is quite coincidental so far as my motivation is concerned.

One of the challenges in understanding virtue is to determine how objective the notion of virtue is. If one were always wildly mistaken about what the issues of the day are and about the character of the candidates, it would be at best unlikely that the motivation appropriate to civic virtue and the right *kinds* of beliefs – say that Janet Victor is the most competent candidate running for mayor – would qualify one as having civic virtue. Some errors, however, are compatible with possessing that virtue, and some virtues, such as generosity, are less restricted by objective standards, while still others, such as humility, apparently demand even less in the way of factual accuracy.

THE GROUNDS OF CIVIC VIRTUE

To bring out what constitutes civic virtue in a liberal democracy, I want to consider it in relation to the grounds of the trait, where these, in turn, are viewed in relation to the plausible kinds of grounding that can be offered for liberal democracy in the first place. Doing this presupposes that we have *some* conception of civic virtue; but it will probably be uncontroversial to say that whatever else civic virtue is, it is a trait appropriate to citizens as such. It is roughly that virtue whose possession makes one a good citizen.

Let me briefly recall the seven kinds of grounding of liberal democracy that were presented in Chapter 1 and then schematically connect each with civic virtue as the main virtue citizens in such a society should have. It would be a major undertaking to show how each kind of grounding is related to civic virtue in each of the six conceptual dimensions of virtue just described. For our purposes, the main dimension to be noted is the target of civic virtue: roughly, the good that its exercise is properly aimed at achieving.

There is good reason to consider civic virtue to be at least in large part moral. First, it requires respect for fellow citizens. Second, its possession is clearly incompatible with gross immorality in the social arena – pillaging, fraudulent voting, cheating on taxes, and the like. If it can be grounded in non-moral elements, they must be of a kind that can account for these basic points. That constraint, however, does not rule out any of the perspectives considered in Chapter 1 as candidates for grounding liberal democracy. Let me indicate in outline why this is so.

An instrumentalist will argue that a population that does not exhibit a minimal level of civic virtue cannot constitute a well-ordered society, certainly not a liberal democracy. The emphasis will be on the elements of character whose expression tends to produce the ends for which civil society exists. The target of civic virtue, then, will be to achieve the constitutive end(s) for which society exists, such as the peaceable pursuit of individual plans of life. For this rather pragmatic approach, on the basis of our fundamental desires, such as desires for a comfortable life under peaceful conditions of social interaction, we presuppose certain goals and we seek the best means to achieving them. This line of thought may recall Hobbes and indeed Hume; both seem to me instrumentalists about the *original* ground of social justice, whatever other views (perhaps not clearly consistent with instrumentalism) they held.

From a broadly instrumentalist point of view, one might consider our present sociopolitical situation and seek a conception of citizenship which yields a notion of civic virtue that would command wide assent. If one is pragmatic, one need not even assume a great deal of overlap in people's fundamental desires. People with very different ends can sometimes agree on the same means. This instrumentalist approach might also be eclectic, and might constrain conditions for assent in various ways, for instance to agreement under relevant information. Thus, one might consider a specific society, note how it operates and what constitute some of its major problems relative to the fundamental goals of citizens, and construct a conception of citizenship that addresses those problems in the context. If this approach seems to many to need grounding in something more fundamental, or at least the backing of a contractarian argument to corroborate its results, a strength of the approach is that it does not require, and arguably does not even invite, agreement on fundamentals. That kind of search for consensus may easily divide us.

Utilitarians will argue that civic virtue, as in large part an internalization of sound utilitarian ethics, conduces to the well-being of society. The emphasis is on enhancement of pleasure and reduction of pain, which are the target of the virtue. Social programs will reflect this. Civic virtue is guided by a network of "secondary rules" (as Mill called them) subordinate to the utilitarian master principle, and civic virtue is achieved when certain of these, such as those calling for beneficence – are internalized in such a way that they direct one's conduct as a citizen. The relevant rules are determined by applying the secondary rules – or if necessary the master principle – to the field of the virtue, such as selection of candidates for office.

For a Kantian view, civic virtue will be to the categorical imperative roughly what for utilitarians it is to the principle of utility. In both cases, there is a similar appeal to secondary rules, categorical imperatives (with a small *c*) in Kantian terminology. The central principles will be those that bear on social relations and political activities. But, in contrast to utilitarianism, the emphasis will be on just treatment of fellow citizens – always as ends and never merely as means – rather than on promotion of overall non-moral good. Liberties, then, will never be traded off for "utility," say for enhancements in material flourishing.

With virtue theories in moral philosophy, by contrast, there will be no master principle; and even if there is a master virtue, as perhaps practical wisdom (*phronesis*) is for Aristotle, the relation of civic virtue to it will not be governed by any formula. There is, then, no general illuminating description of civic virtue as conceived from a virtue-theoretic base; each virtue theory will have its own conception. But clearly any full-scale virtue theory will make a place for it, most plausibly (if Aristotle is our guide) as shaped by an overarching account of human flourishing (or the common good), in whose civic dimensions it plays the central governing role.[9]

In the communitarian tradition, civic virtue will be conceived, as to its target, in terms of the kind of community that represents the relevant ideal. For our purposes, the important cases are those in which liberal democracy is the framework of this community. The communitarian tradition (which can accommodate a rule ethics as well as a virtue ethics) tends to treat civic virtue as important for sustaining democratic participation and as deriving its targets from an appropriate conception of the common good.

When we come to theological approaches to grounding liberal democracy, we find perhaps even more room for diversity in the resources available to account for civic virtue. An otherworldly theology may require a minimum from its votaries as citizens; a politically activist theology may demand proselytizing; and a pragmatic one or one stressing service may require extensive charity and volunteering in support of the poor and the sick. But there are limits to the demands inherent in any civic virtue appropriate for liberal democracy. A religion or a moral position may appropriately ask much, but some demands go beyond what civic virtue can require in a liberal democracy; such a society limits the extent to which virtue requires giving up one's personal liberty. One could lack civic virtue because one pursues religious goals in the wrong way, but a different kind of pursuit of those goals could lead one to develop excellence as a citizen that goes well beyond the minimum standards for civic virtue. I believe, however, that it is quite possible for religious citizens in many faiths to find an appropriate balance here and to aspire to civic virtue of the kind this book portrays as appropriate for liberal democracies.

The last path to grounding democracy I want to consider, the intuitionist approach, will share with the other rule theories a commitment to explicating virtues in good part as internalizations of rules; but there is not likely to be an appeal to any master rule,[10] and there will certainly be an emphasis on internalization of the social side of virtue, for example beneficence and (social) justice. These two ideals are likely to be the main targets of civic virtue so conceived.

Since the intuitionist stresses the lack of hierarchy among the central moral principles and the need for practical wisdom to deal with their application or with conflicts among them, the same need is likely to appear in the conception of civic virtue. The two main targets cannot always be reached – or directly hit – by the same conduct. As Ross viewed morality, its central demands come in principles expressing prima facie duties: of fidelity, reparation, justice, non-injury, gratitude, beneficence, and self-improvement.[11] Now clearly duties of non-injury, reparation, fidelity, justice, and beneficence go a long way (though not the whole way) toward indicating how one should (prima facie) behave as a citizen.[12] (Self-improvement and gratitude play a significant but lesser role in citizenship, though Ross argued that duties of gratitude at least partly account for political obligation.)

I have so far not mentioned the possibility of contractarian underpinnings of civic virtue. One could take civic virtue as the kind of trait appropriate to citizenship of the sort that would be agreed to under proper contracting conditions. One might follow here a Hobbesian, Lockean, Rawlsian, or other line; and one might be guided by a moral theory or might simply make instrumentalist assumptions that do not substantively constrain the crucial contracting. This is why a social contract argument by itself is not a basic mode of grounding a political system: it does not yield definite results until some independent theory supplies the constraints – say instrumentalist, Kantian, or intuitionist – on the contracting. Once these are supplied, it can be a mode of justification of a political system and can motivate allegiance to it. If, for example, one followed Rawls and made his two principles of justice (both discussed in Chapter 1) fundamental to the constitution of civic virtue, that virtue would imply at least a disposition both to permit the greatest liberty all citizens can mutually enjoy and to nurture a system of distribution in which inequalities satisfy his difference principle and are thus in the interest of the worst off and attach to positions filled by fair competition. In addition, one would construe Rawlsian "public reason" as the primary mode of thinking appropriate to civic behavior, and the only kind appropriate to certain official conduct, especially that of the judiciary.[13] There would be other elements implicit in civic virtue conceived on a Rawlsian approach, but my purpose here requires only specifying in outline how any of these approaches would work.

A quite different approach to civic virtue may appeal to people for whom tradition and continuity with the past are central to good citizenship. This approach is substantially historical: one seeks to find part of the basis of civic virtue, and even of political obligation in general, in the historical conditions of the society in question, say in long-standing agreements to which the people have at least tacitly consented. On the assumption that either initially – say, on contractarian grounds – or at some point in the past, the overall conditions of a society merited allegiance to its government and civility among citizens, one can identify injustices thereafter for rectification, and (given continuity in the social conditions meriting allegiance to the state) one might establish the permissibility of other patterns (say of ownership and control) as arising by just processes such as legitimate transfer between generations. To be sure, this approach is severely limited if one does not have adequate standards for determining what *merits* allegiance and what constitutes an injustice. But given an adequate set of such standards, a historical conception can lead to insight about what is appropriate to civically virtuous conduct at a given time. Such a historical exploration might reveal injustices so severe as to require changing the prevailing governmental structure; it might also reveal less serious deficiencies, for instance that some patterns of distribution, say high rates of taxation, are unwarranted; and it might provide some justification for elements in the status quo that would otherwise seem objectionable.[14]

Any of the non-theological approaches to civic virtue so far described can be combined with a theistic approach. A pure instrumentalist, to be sure, could not consider theistic goals rationally binding on all, but could recognize them as in fact basic in determining the appropriate political system in a given society. Pragmatically, then, the instrumentally rational thing to do would be to maximize the fulfillment of these goals and of whatever others, such as material well-being, are presupposed. Further, if we think of the Hebraic-Christian tradition, we can see that certain ethical theories, such as Kantianism and some versions of intuitionism or virtue ethics, are readily combinable with a biblically based theology. The injunction to love one's neighbor as oneself, for instance, can be taken to require both wide-ranging beneficence *and* a kind of equal treatment. There are various combinations with that theology, for instance Aristotelian, neo-Thomistic, and Lockean, that can provide both a rationale for liberal democracy and a conception of civic virtue appropriate to it.

If there are high standards of conduct, such as some based on religious commitments, that go even beyond the requirements for achieving civic virtue, the latter requirements nonetheless go beyond the standards set by merely conducting oneself as a citizen in a way that violates no one's rights. Civic virtue requires doing more than merely living within one's rights, hence more than one can be properly coerced to do. The limits of governmental coercion do not set the upper boundaries of virtue. Even though civic virtue does not require doing all that a religious ideal may demand, it does call for a measure of supererogation, in the sense of good conduct not morally or (properly) legally required.

My own approach is to articulate a conception of civic virtue, and of related principles expressing an ethics of citizenship, that takes account of theistic as well as secular conceptions of the proper foundations of the state, but does not presuppose any one conception. I find something of value in all of the approaches to civic virtue considered in this section, and despite their conceptual differences there can be much normative convergence among them when they are conscientiously applied in the light of the same relevant data, such as socioeconomic information about the working of the kind of society in question.

One way to see the possibility of convergence among diverse approaches to civic virtue in a liberal democracy is to consider the appeal to universal moral standards as a ground for such a society. Invoking universal moral standards may to some smack of a dogmatic dependence on intuition. If, however, we recall the distinction between agreement *in* reasons, which is simply a matter of accepting the same first-order prima facie normative judgments on the same grounds, and agreement *on* reasons, which requires agreement on some theoretical or other general proposition about those grounds, this worry diminishes greatly. An extensive agreement in moral practice is compatible with absence of agreement or even sharp disagreement in moral theory. Consider a policy of nuclear waste disposal that exposes a community to a cancer risk. We are much less likely to disagree about whether this danger provides us with a reason to oppose the policy than on a theory of reasons showing why it does so. Rather than argue for the significance of this distinction,[15] I shall proceed to frame and defend a conception of civic virtue and to show how it provides further support for the principles defended in Chapters 4 and 5.

CIVIC VIRTUE AND THE GROUNDS FOR SOCIOPOLITICAL ACTION

If what I have so far suggested about civic virtue is correct, at least this much may be said of it. It is constituted largely (though not entirely) by two kinds of traits. In the first category are habits of conscientious political participation, a wide-ranging respect for the political rights and quality of life of others in one's society, and an enduring disposition to contribute to such community projects as public education, public health, and environmental preservation. These traits we might call *civic virtues proper.* The second category includes fairness, veracity, loyalty, and a measure of benevolence toward fellow citizens. Those traits we might call *civically essential virtues;* their scope ranges far wider than the civic domain, but the narrower, specifically civic virtues are of limited effectiveness without them. Civic virtues can be more or less cultivated, and their cultivation is no trivial matter. Civic virtue has a distinctive field and can demand much in the way of self-discipline, particularly in relation to balancing religious commitments with secular obligations. Why that is so can be best determined in the light of a more detailed conception of what constitutes civic virtue.

If virtue is conceived as I have suggested, it is essentially connected with reasons for action, in both the normative and the motivational senses of that phrase. A loyal person must, for instance, have or at least recognize normative reasons why people *should* be treated in a certain way and, sufficiently often, must do an appropriate kind of thing *for* some such reason,[16] in a sense implying being motivated by the reason. Given this double-barreled requirement, we have at least two kinds of question to consider: what normative reasons should guide citizens insofar as they have civic virtue, and what motivational role should the relevant reasons play in their civic conduct? I take these in turn.

Civic Virtue and Publicly Comprehensible Reasons

Some of the relevant territory has already been covered, at least if we may take Ross's commonsense list of prima facie moral duties, such as those of justice and non-injury, as a reasonable starting point in the ethics of citizenship – the broad area of ethics of which the theory of civic virtue is part. If, however, we think of the civic context, in which one may need to speak (in a public meeting, say) to others who may be total strangers, at least one further requirement also arises. It concerns what might be called *public comprehensibility.*[17]

Particularly where one's civic behavior, such as a vote to pass a new law, would substantially restrict the behavior of citizens, as with enactment of a military draft or prohibition of abortion, it is important to be able to explain it, and if possible justify it, in terms comprehensible to normal adult citizens (taking them as they are in the English-speaking world today to get a baseline – since a standard relativized to normality in just any historical situation could be too low); in short, to meet a certain standard of public comprehensibility. This rules out relying wholly on technical language as well as appealing only to esoteric terms drawn from a subculture or intelligible only within a certain religious community.

Granting that there may be special conditions under which secrecy is needed, the health of a democracy requires that by and large citizens speak to each other both comprehensibly and honestly about their preferences and, often, about their judgments favoring one or another specific policy or candidate.[18] Presented with reasons by the opposition, we are often content to be outvoted; persistent loss with no explanation can easily produce alienation among the outvoted minority. And if one does not understand the reasons given – if, for example, they are expressed in obscure terms or presented simply as deliverances of a sixth sense – both alienation and civil strife may result.

The comprehensibility standard is different from a secularity standard but supports it in the form it takes in the principle of secular rationale. Religious reasons are by no means intrinsically incomprehensible to the non-religious. But they include such things as religious intuitions or feelings, as well as being or feeling spiritually inspired. To some people, there may be a religious intuition in virtue of which various kinds of consensual sex seem wrong. One could also have a religious experience that one takes as a reason for opposing a public policy or even a candidate for office. Although the words reporting these are understandable, the experiences they report are not publicly comprehensible, particularly considered as reasons. Furthermore, one cannot tell in such cases whether one's opponents get what they wanted when the candidate in question takes office or the law or policy in question is in force. Not perceiving a comprehensible reason for preference, one can only conjecture on this matter, whereas one can reason with people much better regarding their resistance to a change when one knows why they prefer the status quo and whether it gives them what they want.

There is, then, a public comprehensibility requirement that belongs to the conception of civic virtue. I would now add a further consideration so far left implicit in discussing the conception: that a comprehensible reason should be (evidentially) *adequate* to the use made of it. Such adequacy does not require guaranteeing the soundness of the law or policy it is taken to support, but it must imply at least providing a basis on which their soundness is rationally expectable with confidence. The corresponding principle – call it the *principle of civically adequate reasons* – might be put thus: civically virtuous citizens in a liberal democracy have a prima facie obligation to have, and under appropriate conditions to be willing to offer, publicly comprehensible, evidentially adequate reasons for their support of laws and public policies. This applies especially where the laws or policies in question would restrict the behavior of citizens, but it applies to some degree in any case of such support, since the principle specifies virtuous citizens.

Naturally, a fully conscientious effort to find a comprehensible and adequate reason may fail. If this is so, the failure is excusable, though it is a further question whether the agent is excusable for acting on a reason that is not comprehensible or not adequate.[19] To say just that one simply prefers a candidate one is voting for is not in general to give an adequate reason for the deed (though it may suffice to break a tie where one has equally cogent reasons favoring each of two competing candidates); to say merely that the candidate was born on the first Friday of a year that begins a decade is not to offer a comprehensible *or* adequate reason. The words are intelligible, of course, but *as* expressing a reason they are neither comprehensible nor adequate. The comprehensibility of a reason is not merely a matter of the intelligibility of the language in which it is expressed but also of its force as a reason. If it cannot be seen to have any force given the powers of an adequately informed rational citizen, if, for instance, it cannot be so understood apart from initiation into a subculture, it is not publicly comprehensible in the relevant sense.

Public Reasons, Accessibility, and Comprehensive Views

What I mean by 'public comprehensibility' is similar to what others have meant by 'accessibility', but the latter term has often been taken to imply that the reason in question is not dependent on a person's comprehensive view of the world but draws only on something like (in Rawls's phrase) public reason.[20] This independence requirement is not entailed by public comprehensibility as I understand it; for there might be comprehensive views that at least in the relevant parts are comprehensible to normal adults in the required way even if they hold quite different comprehensive views.

Comprehensiveness is a matter of scope, and a comprehensive view need not even be highly theoretical, much less esoteric or incomprehensible to normal adult citizens who take the time to consider it carefully. For liberal democracy, however, the importance of public comprehensibility, like that of accessibility insofar as it is different, is largely a matter of communicability in a sense appropriate to avoiding alienation and civil strife. Even a comprehensive view that includes religious doctrines may have non-religious segments that are both secularly groundable and intelligible to normal adults with no religious commitments.

To be sure, if one thinks of a "comprehensive doctrine" as Rawls does, there is plausibility in saying that it is only "in certain situations" that citizens may "present what they regard as the basis of political values rooted in their comprehensive doctrine," and that they may do so only "provided they do this in ways that strengthen public reason itself."[21] For he has in mind outlooks on the world, particularly religious ones, that are not compelling to rational persons in general and among which a liberal democracy should be neutral. But if comprehensiveness is understood non-technically and is a matter of scope, then we surely cannot say a priori that there is no comprehensive view – at least in a limited domain, such as the moral or sociopolitical – from which one may, even apart from Rawls's restriction, draw reasons or principles appropriate for public justification of laws and public policy.[22]

It may be best from the point of view of civic virtue if, in adducing reasons or principles to justify laws or public policies, one not introduce them *as* belonging to an overall view that is not universally accepted, but that is a different matter. My concern that citizens recognize a prima facie obligation to have and offer adequate secular reasons is intended to accomplish much of what Rawls wants to accomplish by restrictions that are in principle more stringent and would often be so in practice as well; and as argued in Chapters 3 to 5, adequate secular reasons for coercive laws or public policies will in general be understandable to normal adults of an educational level by no means too high to expect in citizens in a contemporary liberal democracy.

More recently, Rawls has revised his view to allow that "reasonable such [comprehensive] doctrines may be introduced in public reason at any time, provided that in due course public reasons, given by a reasonable political conception, are presented sufficient to support whatever the comprehensive doctrines are introduced to support."[23] Three points will serve to bring out how this view differs from mine.

First (as Rawls is aware), much depends on how the view is specified as to "due course" and how "reasonable" the eligible comprehensive views must be. It is also important whether someone introducing a comprehensive view or part of one must have good reason to believe there *is* adequate public reason for the position in question. Without this requirement Rawls's view would surely be too permissive. It is one thing to have warrant for believing that there is good public reason available now, say through a combination of obtaining further (accessible) facts and reasoning carefully enough about them; it is quite another to have warrant for believing that there *will* be adequate public reason at some appropriate point in the future. The latter requirement probably is, and is likely to be perceived as, far weaker. Many people would think it applies to any view whose truth they feel in their bones.

Second, given any plausible understanding of these matters, the day-to-day control of a liberal democracy would be at best precariously protected by the due course standard from domination by religious or other majorities. It is commonly much harder to remove a law or policy than to prevent its passage, particularly if it strengthens the domination of its supporters – which is usually what happens in the case of unduly repressive laws. Even revising Rawls's proviso to require having a reasonable expectation of finding sufficient public reason would allow laxity: if reasonable expectation is possible for someone who does not have the actual justificatory reason, we would have to allow a considerable amount of time and could probably not discount a general optimism based on past experience that might or might not be predictive.

My third point is more comparative. Here as elsewhere Rawls puts his main emphasis on what kind of reason may be presented, but we should also look to the kinds of reasons people *have* and are *moved* by. This is particularly so if we are concerned to articulate and promote civic virtue. My principles of secular rationale and motivation address this dimension of reasons for sociopolitical conduct. They are more prescriptive than Rawls's in this domain, but less restrictive as to discourse (at least in comparison to his position prior to the proviso just considered). I believe that if we adopt a requirement of adequate secular reason in the way I propose, we can, on the one hand, countenance at least most of the sociopolitical reasons Rawls's latest work seeks to accommodate in providing a wider role for comprehensive views but, on the other hand, avoid a system of princples in which inadequately justified coercive laws and public policies can be instituted with a good conscience.

Two Kinds of Reasons for Laws and Public Policies

Suppose, as is reasonable in the light of any plausible version of the approaches to grounding liberal democracy we have considered, that we take avoidance of alienation and civil strife as important goals of citizens who have civic virtue. Suppose too, as is also reasonable, that such citizens positively seek to promote the flourishing of the civil society in which they live (where flourishing is understood largely though not entirely in terms of the physical and psychological well-being of citizens). We can now say something further about the adequacy of reasons for supporting or advocating laws and public policies. Roughly, I suggest that we call a reason *negatively, or preventively, adequate* provided that (in comparison with the alternatives) it indicates that without the law or policy the society will be worse off in relation to avoiding alienation or civil strife and *positively, or melioratively, adequate* provided it indicates that the law or policy will (in comparison with the alternatives) make the society better off in moving it closer to flourishing or further from an undesirable condition such as poverty or civil strife. A reason may of course be adequate in both respects; improved education may be both required to prevent backsliding and adequate to enhance prosperity.

Considerations of negative adequacy presumably tend to have priority over considerations of positive adequacy. In any case, virtuous citizens will give special attention and weight to negative and positive adequacy, probably preferring the former in cases of conflict (a preference that seems widely shared by people of differing theories, especially in similar cases of choice between relieving someone's suffering and improving the life of someone who is already well off). It is surely a civic duty to give substantial weight to such considerations in one's sociopolitical conduct. Taking this to be a civic duty is meant to indicate that it is essential for civic virtue.

The point is not, however, that there is never a moral *right* not to do one's civic duty, say to vote on a selfish basis – though a case can be made that there is at most a right not to be *coerced* to do the virtuous thing, as opposed to a positive right to vote selfishly. As I have stressed, virtue requires that we do things not strictly demanded by the narrow morality of rights, for instance by people's rights against us – the domain of morality in which we may be subject to morally coercive pressures such as wide disapprobation if we commit a violation, as where we encroach on someone's rights of free speech. These rights are often backed by legal coercion; but the appropriateness of that is not a defining property of a moral right, just as backing by the appropriateness of such action as strong moral criticism is not a defining property of a moral virtue.

Civic Virtue, Political Neutrality, and Personal Preference

Any of the approaches to the basis of civic virtue noted earlier could be invoked in grounding civic virtue, though each would do it differently. The details are not essential; my point is that my conception of civic virtue is largely neutral among the various kinds of accounts of the basis of political obligation and civic responsibility. The plausibility of this neutrality claim will emerge more clearly if we pursue in more detail what is involved in civic virtue.

Let us begin with a case in which mere personal preference is politically determinative. Suppose one simply likes one candidate more than another but thinks, from the impersonal point of view of adequate reasons, that the latter is appreciably better. Alan has a winning personality, but one sees that Ellen is better qualified. May one, consistently with civic virtue, support the former on the basis of mere preference? There is a moral and also a legal right to do so, but that is not at issue. The point is that although a liberal democracy protects the freedom in question – roughly, the moral right to exercise it – there is a sense of 'ought' that goes with ideals of citizenship, a sense in which the answer may be that one ought not to vote on the basis of sheer preference. In a way, it is selfish to allow a personal preference to outweigh a judgment of objective difference in how well the candidates will serve society. It is certainly not a manifestation of civic virtue.

To be sure, if the preference is not merely a matter of personal liking but of one's financial gain, then at least others can identify with it as a rational economic preference that is universally understood. Moreover, there may be those who believe democracy will work best, even by partly non-material ideals of flourishing, if each citizen honestly pursues self-interest within the constraints of mutual respect. I consider this a contingent matter and will not contest it, doubtful though I find it. But surely such motivation, as a pervasive feature of character and sociopolitical conduct, is not what constitutes civic virtue, and this is *not* a contingent matter. Perhaps civic virtue is consistent with indulging sheer preferences or selfish desires some of the time and where little is at stake sociopolitically; but the exceptions are limited.

The importance of public comprehensibility for sociopolitical reasons suggests something we have already seen: that religious considerations taken to provide such reasons constitute a special problem in a liberal democracy. For some of these considerations will not be comprehensible (as normative reasons) to some citizens, for instance either non-theists or certain radically disagreeing theists who, because of their own religious commitments, cannot see certain reasons offered from another religious point of view as (normative) reasons at all.[24] I want to pursue this problem in the context of what we have seen about civic virtue and to suggest how my account of that virtue bears on the kinds of principles defended in the last three chapters.

CIVIC VIRTUE AND THE BALANCING OF RELIGIOUS AND SECULAR REASONS

If we are to understand how civic virtue is realized in religious citizens, it is well to think about how sociopolitical issues are approached by a mature, rational religious person who is a conscientious citizen committed to a liberal democracy like that of at least some contemporary Western democracies. I have argued (in Chapter 5) that most such citizens will be aware of their fallibility in interpreting their religion as it applies to public life and will be sensitive to moral standards, as well as to specifically religious ones, differing from their own. Those in the Hebraic-Christian tradition, which encourages beneficence and charity, will also try to contribute to the welfare of others, including others beyond their immediate community. There are, to be sure, religious people who are not particularly sensitive to moral or religious standards differing from their own, but many of these can be persuaded to reflect on such differences. In any case, the principles of civic virtue I am proposing can be adopted by normal citizens.

Civic Virtue and Secular Reasons

The principle of secular rationale, in positing a prima facie obligation not to advocate or support any law or public policy that restricts human conduct, unless one has, and is willing to offer, adequate secular reason for this, might seem to require religious citizens to go well beyond the requirements of civic virtue. It would burden some citizens, to some degree, in some cases. But suppose we again assume a broadly Western theism. Then, as argued in Chapter 5, we can take God to have properties in the light of which there is reason to think that for a great many people in the Hebraic-Christian tradition, the principle of secular rationale, when conscientiously applied, would not be seriously burdensome.

If, given God's omniscience and omnibenevolence, there is as much reason to expect alignment between religiously well-grounded and secularly well-grounded moral standards as I suggest, then abiding by the principle of secular rationale should not generally put a religious person into disequilibrium over a conflict between religious and secular considerations except where there is an error of a kind that a virtuous citizen should want to eliminate. The error need not be on the religious side: it is not just that scriptures and clerical pronouncements can be misinterpreted; there are also unsound (secular) ethical views and invalid inferences even from sound ones.

If these points are rougly correct, we also gain perspective on the connection between civic virtue and the principle of secular motivation, which addresses the motivational side of virtue and reflects the point that in a virtuous person the normative reasons connected with the virtue also *motivate* the conduct they indicate. This point largely explains why virtuous citizens who take a reason to justify their sociopolitical conduct – particularly in advocacy or support of a coercive law or public policy – will strongly tend to be sufficiently motivated by that reason in doing the deeds in question. They will try to find adequate reasons in the first place, but in finding them they will not merely note the adequacy intellectually, but try to act accordingly. Civic virtue is not merely intellectual; it puts appropriate normative standards into civic practice.

Since an argument can be tacitly religious without being religious in content (as shown in Chapter 3), one might fail to adhere to at least the second of these principles even in offering arguments that many would not take to be either religious or lacking in cogency from the point of view of secular evidential adequacy. Some people might, for instance, offer a slippery slope argument against legalizing physician-assisted suicide (claiming that it will gradually lead to coerced suicide or even murder) when what motivates their conclusion is a conviction that only

God may take innocent human life. A person dying of painful inoperable cancer who notices that the same people are undeterred by the parallel slippery slope argument against permitting *passive* euthanasia – which, let us suppose, its proponents describe as "letting nature take its course" – may resent being restricted by what appears to them to be a religious conviction. Even in the absence of using similar reasoning for a welcome conclusion, proponents of this highly contestable form of argument may seem to be motivated by considerations that lie below the surface of the argument.

One might think the secular rationale principle is enough, on the ground that abiding by it will ensure justified sociopolitical actions. Why should motivation matter if one's justifying reasons are good enough? From the point of view of virtue ethics, at least, it does matter. Insofar as conduct is action *from virtue,* it matters greatly how it is grounded in the agent's character. The woman prevented from having an abortion, and the patient denied medical assistance in suicide, will tend to resent the preventive legislation as religiously motivated even if the secular arguments offered to support it seem plausible. Even if they are objectively cogent, moreover, passing the legislation on the basis of religious motivation will be only acting in conformity with civic virtue, not *from* it. Furthermore, those who acquiesce in the legislation for the cogent reasons given are still likely to wonder what might have happened if the religiously motivated supporters had not found a cogent secular case to offer to their opponents.

Civic Voice

The main point here may be more readily seen by reflecting on the difference between what we say to others and what we *communicate* to them. This difference is particularly relevant to public debate, where voicing, attitude, and even body language are important; but it also has significant application in private discussions. We speak with different voices on different occasions and for different purposes. Even when they carry the same content, say that a certain policy is required to protect innocent people, human voices can differ as radically as the timbres and resonances of different musical instruments sounding the same note; and, as it is the causal basis of those notes, and not their pitch, that produces the quality of the instruments that sound them, with human speech it is the causal basis of what we say, and not the content of what we say, that yields our voice. Our motivation in speaking is a crucial basis of what we say.

Our voice, then, is determined more by motivation and manner than by semantics, more by why and how we say what we do than by its content.[25] The hunger for power can be stentorian, like the blare of a trumpet; compassion can yield a voice mellow like the lower register of the cello; religious zeal can produce a rhythm and shrill intensity of its own. Both in public and in private we tend to listen for voicing as well as content. We try to hear more than just *what* people say, and quite commonly we accept – or reject – what others say because of how they voice it as well as because of what it is. Indeed, the less well we know someone – and we commonly do not know well many fellow citizens even in small towns – the more we may depend on voicing to help us get a sense not only of sincerity but also of credibility, cooperativeness, and other traits relevant to the kinds of things we have in common as citizens.

Part of civic virtue consists in having and using an appropriate *civic voice;* part of civic harmony in a framework of pluralism and disagreement consists in using that voice as the primary mode of communication in debating issues important for citizens, especially fundamental ones such as the extent of our liberties, but also lesser matters. It need not be any citizen's only voice, not even for argumentation, and certainly not for self-expression. But a civic voice is achievable by any rational citizen committed to liberal democracy, and to lack such a voice, or to use it too infrequently, is a significant failure in civic virtue. If, moreover, I am right about the prospects for achieving an equilibrium between religiously enjoined moral obligations and secularly grounded duties toward others, then a civic voice is available, in part through adherence to the principle of secular motivation, to most rational religious people without compromise of their basic religious commitments.

One has a voice as a writer and can also have a civic voice as such. In some ways the voice of a writer is less easily, in some more easily, discerned; but the same general points hold. If the writings in question are either expressions of legislative decision or, especially, judicial decision, then the need for a civic voice is even greater, and it becomes greater still in proportion to how high the relevant court is or how large a proportion of the population the legislative body represents. For in these cases there is a sense in which the legislative or judicial voice is supposed to be that of the people or at least representative of the citizenry as a whole.

Here it may be pointed out that on a different view of democracy, elected representatives regard themselves as primarily representing their immediate constituents (those who elected them) and may speak in virtually any way that the majority of them would approve of. This seems to me to go too far if it extends to using a voice that would avoidably alienate a minority of their constituents – or indeed would alienate people eligible to be their constituents who, for such contingent reasons as the place where they reside, are not among these constituents. The issue is whether civic virtue in a liberal democracy is tied more to a constitutional conception of proper conduct or to a more narrowly representative one. Given the broadly moral grounding of democracy that I prefer as a rationale for democratic government, and given the possibility that majority decisions may fail to preserve our moral rights, I favor a constitutional conception.[26]

Unfortunately, even a duly adopted constitution can be morally corrupt. I thus leave open that the prima facie moral duty to obey the law (which citizens of liberal democracies at least normally have) is not *basic* in a constitutional democracy and that a sense of that duty in relation to *every* law is not necessarily an element in civic virtue. Under a constitution permitting slavery there might be a law requiring the reporting of escaping slaves. One would surely have no prima facie moral obligation to obey it (though non-reporting could in any case also be justified by reference to an overriding incompatible obligation).[27] Even apart from this reservation and the preference for a constitutional conception of proper civic conduct, however, there are reasons to adopt the view of civic virtue I propose.

In bringing out further reasons to adopt this view it may help to stress that it does not imply that civic virtue is intrinsically better than religious virtue; they are good in different ways. One can also act from two (or more) virtues, just as one can act from two motives (a point stressed in explaining the principle of secular rationale). If one takes in a homeless family from a sense of religious mission *and* in order to keep the community safer and more peaceful, one might be manifesting both the religious virtue of agapistic love and the civic virtue of responsible citizenship.

As important as civic virtue is in motivating citizen participation of any constructive kind, it is needed above all where one is advocating or otherwise supporting coercive laws or public policies. Much of human life does not involve such conduct; much that does can be guided by cooperating religious and secular motives, motives that, like secular compassion and religious benevolence, urge one to roughly the same conduct. It is often noted how powerful religious considerations were in motivating the civil rights movement. Their prominence should not lead to underplaying the force of moral convictions entirely compatible with them, nor to thinking that those whose motivation might have been entirely religious would have been incapable of seeing and being adequately motivated by a moral case for the same social changes.[28]

Given the importance of such cooperating religious and secular motives, we can also see the appropriateness of the principle of theo-ethical equilibrium. Abiding by it facilitates application of, and adherence to, the principles of secular rationale and motivation. This principle is based on the idea that there is much to be gained, intellectually and motivationally, from seeking theo-ethical equilibrium in deciding a wide range of important questions. Even where no equilibrium can be found on a moral matter, for instance on the purely moral status of abortion, it may be possible concerning the associated sociopolitical issue of whether to prohibit abortion by law. This may be claimed to be highly unlikely, on the ground that many who oppose abortion morally must in conscience conceive it as murder, which is already a grievous crime. But if murder requires anything close to *intention* to kill a person, this conception seems questionable (a matter considered in detail in Chapter 7).

Three of the main principles defended in Chapters 2 to 5, then – those of secular motivation, secular rationale, and theo-ethical equilibrium – are good candidates for internalization in citizens, particularly religious citizens. This is not in the least to suggest that *genetically* the relevant virtuous conduct must arise from such an internalization. My point concerns only the nature of civic virtue. How that virtue is acquired – say from childhood imitation of good role models or from internalization of principles adopted in adulthood – is secondary.

THE PLACE OF RELIGIOUS CONSIDERATIONS IN CIVIC DISCOURSE

In most of this book my concern has been the reasons citizens should have, should be willing to offer, and should be motivated by in advocacy or support of laws and public policies. I have been at pains to do justice to the importance of religious reasons in the lives of citizens, but have said much less about the appropriate place of religious considerations in civic discourse, say in political settings or in conversations about the future of society. In case it might be thought that I favor a religiously naked public square,[29] and in order to extend my overall position on religion and politics, I want to consider the positive place of religious discourse in political contexts. How might such discourse contribute toward a civic harmony in which all elements, especially religious citizens, play a maximally constructive role?

Given the principles so far proposed in this book, one might think that I stand with those liberal theorists who would like to keep religion out of "the public square."[30] There is an ambiguity here. Keeping religion out of the public square might mean at least three things (or combinations thereof): (1) keeping religious language out, (2) keeping religious considerations from exercising sociopolitical influence, and (3) keeping concern *with* religion from exercising such influence. I do not think that any responsible liberal position endorses the third exclusion: one can take religion to be important, for instance as a basis for designing a social studies curriculum, without making any judgment on its intrinsic worth; and one must indeed take it to be important in according full respect to the abiding concerns of a vast number of citizens. As to eliminating the sociopolitical role of religious considerations, no plausible liberal position endorses that kind of exclusion. My principles call for a measure of constraint; but they neither deny a right to give those considerations a major role, nor restrict their role to a degree that prevents religious considerations from often determining conduct. It is the third exclusion, which goes with a kind of *rhetorical privatization,* that I particularly want to address. I begin with some distinctions that facilitate analysis.

Some Major Types of Religious Discourse

The notion of the religious is vague and problematic, and the concept of religious discourse is no more easily clarified. But it will serve our purposes to take as our paradigm the Western religions, Christianity, Judaism, and Islam, and to draw examples mainly from the Bible. It is useful to recognize at least seven cases.

Implicitly versus Explicitly Religious Discourse. Even apart from a focus limited to Western religion, it is clear that discourse may be religious without being explicitly so, as is typical of prayer. Whereas explicitly religious discourse openly uses religious language such as references to God's will or to the content of the Bible or the Koran, implicitly religious discourse is recognizable as religious only on the basis of an acquaintance with the religion or religious orientation or content in question, or by inference from some such acquaintance with a religion or religious concepts. There are also expressions that can be taken as religious or not depending on the context: phrases like 'It is not given to us to understand', 'the ultimate purpose of our existence', and 'the sanctity of life' may render discourse in which they occur implicitly religious. Sometimes, however, a mere allusion or a single metaphor can render a segment of discourse implicitly religious. Describing someone as believing that science is "the light of the world" readily evokes a New Testament metaphor for Christ. Arguing for expanded welfare provisions by saying that a society is judged by what it does for the poor and the sick may evoke Jesus's saying that what people have done to "the least" of society they have done to him. Here, as elsewhere, intonation and context are crucial.

Mixed versus Unmixed Religious Discourse. This second distinction cuts across the explicit-implicit one; implicitly religious discourse, for instance, might or might not be mixed with large secular segments. One can imagine a clergyman testifying on, say capital punishment, using either entirely secular language or, instead, both explicitly and implicitly religious discourse in an effort to harmonize them in a mixture with stretches of secular discourse about, say, scientific studies of deterrence.

Primarily and Secondarily Religious Discourse. This third distinction is not quantitative even to the extent that the previous one is; the primary-secondary contrast is mainly a matter of grounding and presuppositions rather than vocabulary. Mixed discourse that is secular in most of its vocabulary could be primarily religious because it constantly presupposes religious principles and concludes with a religiously based point that draws together its various elements. Such discourse is primarily religious because it is rooted in religious presupposition and its main thrust is one or more religious points. On the other hand, discourse pervaded by biblical allusions and metaphors could be primarily secular because of its underlying assumptions and main arguments. The use of these allusions and metaphors could be a literary device for explication or even parody. There are also intermediate cases: the language might, for instance, invoke a religious view about divine plan in arguing for something that, overall, the advocate defends far more prominently on a secular basis.

Persuasive and Descriptive Religious Discourse. Fourth, as in other contexts, we should distinguish the persuasive from the merely descriptive use of language and, within the persuasive category, between attempts to persuade *of* a religious view and uses of religious considerations to persuade of a secular view. Many biblical stories are, for instance, powerfully descriptive in sheer literary terms, but they need not be used persuasively and often are not so used. With an aim that is explanatory rather than persuasive, one could say of a man who, owing to divided loyalties, failed to realize his ideals, "He tried to serve God and mammon." Compare this with saying "You cannot serve God and mammon" to remind people that they are abandoning their ideals for money – something one can say even if the ideals are secular. Here one would be using religious language persuasively, but not religiously. By contrast, appeals to biblical or religious authority in support of a view one is pressing, or invocations of religious arguments to establish one's view, constitute a persuasive use of religious language. (Such persuasive discourse may not actually tend to persuade; the contrast is mainly a matter of apparently intended function rather than effect.)

Self-directed and Audience-directed Religious Discourse. A fifth distinction concerns the relation of discourse to the speaker more than its content: religious discourse may be simply about oneself, as where one indicates one's religious roots or commitments, as opposed to audience-directed. In the former case nothing need be explicitly indicated about where one stands on an issue under discussion. Religious believers may be as it were introducing themselves to a new friend, or (as is often appropriate) clarifying their own stance for themselves or others, or rededicating themselves by saying things that connect them with the crucial religious text or their religious tradition. In the case of audience-directed religious discourse, one seeks to move the audience, say to convince fellow citizens of something. Here, even if one is apparently endorsing religious premises, one need not be identifying oneself as a religious person, as opposed to a believer of those particular propositions as grounds for one's point. The guiding concern is to move the audience, and religious self-identification might not figure in the effort. One might, however, make such an effort by citing mutual religious commitments presented as such; there one would to some extent identify oneself religiously, though the discourse as a whole could be audience-directed.

Authoritarian and Moderate Religious Discourse. Cutting across all of the distinctions I have made is a sixth, closely connected with civic voice. I refer to the distinction between authoritarian and moderate religious discourse. Intonation alone can create an authoritarian character (as indeed with secular discourse), but that effect often comes from an implication or suggestion, through tone or content or both, that one in some sense must be right. By contrast, a fallibilist attitude tends to eliminate authoritarianism in tone or content. Authoritarianism can, of course, come from content as well as tone. The politest, most soft-spoken speech can simply cloak that attitude or stance. It should be added that the relevant kind of moderateness, the kind that contrasts with authoritarianism, is *cognitive;* passional immoderateness, for instance, might readily combine with a keen sense that one might be mistaken in the view (or vision) in question.

Directly and Indirectly Argumentative Religious Discourse. A seventh distinction (introduced earlier) is between arguing from religious reasons and leveraging by religious reasons. In the first case, one gives the audience to understand that one accepts the relevant reasons (say that ensoulment occurs at conception) and one represents the conclusion proposed as supported by them; in the second, one implies that the *audience* accepts or should accept the reasons and one represents the conclusion one is arguing for as supported by them. The latter is a paradigm of audience-directed religious discourse. It may, but need not, be manipulative. Religious discourse may also be indirectly argumentative in other ways. The conclusion argued for may be left implicit, or premises for it may be presented in separate places and not identified as such, whereas in paradigms of direct argumentation it is made evident both what the conclusion is and what the indicated grounds are.

Many other discourse-related distinctions might be reasonably made here, but these are sufficient to enable us to articulate some standards applicable to public discourse in free democracies. Let us consider some of them.

Standards for the Sociopolitical Use of Religious Discourse

The freedom of expression appropriate to liberal democracy permits citizens and – though to a lesser extent (depending on their office) – public officials to use religious language in the public sphere. But, as I have suggested, both should speak mainly with a civic voice in public discussion of law and public policy. Once we note how many ways there are to use religious language, we can see the complexity of determining to what extent publicly using such language is consonant with civic virtue. This is plainly a case for prudence. We need an Aristotelian mean between excess and deficiency. There are, however, several plausible guiding principles. It will be no surprise if I suggest that my principles of civic virtue, especially secular rationale, secular motivation, and theo-ethical equilibrium, apply here.

It has seemed to some readers that the principles of secular rationale and motivation severely constrain one's use of religious language in public.[31] This is not so. The most general point is that a constraint on the evidential and motivating reasons one should have is independent of the language one uses in making one's case – particularly if religious reasons are *also* given a major place in thought and action.

There is, moreover, one respect in which my perspective affords *more* freedom in one's choice of language than a number of other liberal positions, including that of Rawls at least prior to his qualification of his long-standing position, which now allows that comprehensive doctrines may be introduced at any time so long as "in due course" appropriate public reasons are offered.[32] Since adherents of a view can, if committed to my principles, honestly repudiate anyone's supporting governmental coercion without evidentially adequate and motivationally sufficient reason, they are (other things equal) *more free* to stress the religious elements in their thinking. If we are taken to be sincere in commitment to my principles – and particularly if there is as much alignment between secular morality and religiously grounded morality as I think there commonly is – we can explicitly bring forward religious considerations without offending enlightened people who either have no religious beliefs or belong to another religion.

To be sure, one is not likely to be thought sincere in endorsing the principles of secular rationale and motivation if one's public discourse is of an unmixed religious kind, or if reference to secular grounds for one's position seems perfunctory. This brings us to our first general rule: in public discourse, one should avoid making a sociopolitical issue appear to be a religious issue (the converse is also plausible, but not my concern here). Take assisted suicide. This is a moral issue as well as a religious one, and it is religiously as well as morally contested. One liability of treating it religiously in a public setting is *polarization along religious lines*. Polarization in the relevant sense is not merely sharp disagreement and is not even a necessary consequence of deep disagreement. I refer to (roughly) a difference of conviction that is, or is at least persistently felt to be, irreconcilable, is attended by hostile attitudes in each direction, and lacks common ground sufficient to make reconciliation promising.

Different religions may have more or less official stances on assisted suicide; a sociopolitical decision about legal limits need not prejudge the religious or even moral soundness of these stances. Free democracies may, for various reasons, legally permit conduct they consider immoral or religiously forbidden, such as (unexcusably) breaking a promise to a friend. If a legalization issue is not considered specifically religious, its resolution is less likely to alienate a disapproving religious group.

Since there are other ways polarization along religious lines may be caused, it is well to frame a second public discourse principle here: in public discourse, one should seek to frame any religious treatment of a sociopolitical issue in a way that avoids polarization along religious lines. All polarization is prima facie bad and we need further distinctions and principles to help us avoid it, but religious polarization is uniquely serious. A clash of Gods – or even of clerical authorities – easily becomes a battle to the death.

A third standard concerns differences in sociopolitical role: the public discourse of ordinary citizens is generally less constrained as to appropriate religious content than that of government officials, and among them the highest constraints tend to be on the judiciary. There are considerable differences even here: a preliminary discussion of a proposed local ordinance among citizens in the town hall is one thing; a citizen's formal testimony before the state legislature is another, and generally more constraining. A legislator's conversations on a Saturday radio show are, similarly, less constrained than the same person's speech in support of a bill that is about to be voted on in the legislature.

If we keep in mind the importance of avoiding coercion on religious grounds, we can formulate a related principle. Once again, I think the secular rationale principle is suggestive of an appropriate standard for public discourse that supports or suggests coercion. It supports what might be called a *principle of minimal coercive suggestion:* other things equal, the more likely one's public discourse is to be understood as supporting coercive laws or public policies, the greater the appropriate restraints on using religious language or otherwise making one's discourse religious (in any of the indicated ways). This principle helps to account for differences in the restraints appropriate for public officials setting forth their views in differing contexts.

If I am right in thinking that moderate discourse tends to reduce resentment and to enable cooperation more than authoritarian discourse, we might adopt the principle that especially though by no means exclusively in religious public discourse, moderate discourse is to be preferred. Commitment to the principles of secular rationale and motivation is a significant support of moderation in both tone and content. I hasten to add, however, that this commitment does not strictly require giving up the position that one's view – religious or secular – is better grounded than alternatives or even in some way epistemically privileged. It simply provides an incentive to have and offer adequate secular reason for support of coercion, and to use a voice for expressing such reasons, that can give other citizens a sense of being treated with respect, and of a range of common standards available for compromise. A civic voice is appropriate for this purpose. It should go without saying that there are counterpart restraints appropriate to those using wholly secular discourse; they should, for instance, also aim at expressing and preserving respect for fellow citizens regardless of the religious position on either side.

Referring back to the distinctions made in this section, we might propose something more general – call it *the public discourse standard* for citizens in a liberal democracy who speak publicly on matters in which religious and secular considerations bear: other things equal, public discourse on sociopolitical matters is ethically (and certainly from the point of view of civic virtue) less constrained as to religious content where that content is implicit rather than explicit, mixed rather than unmixed, secondarily rather than primarily religious, descriptive rather than persuasive, self-directed rather than audience-directed, and moderate rather than authoritarian. Meeting this standard can also significantly help in achieving an appropriate civic voice. To say, for instance, that we should protect the natural environment to make it possible for all citizens to enjoy green pastures and still waters may for many evoke the Twenty-third Psalm, and to say that a proposed development would deprive the foxes of their holes and birds of their nests may, for some, evoke Jesus's words about their natural places of refuge; but such implicitly religious allusions have an independent appeal to any sensitive listener and tend to be preferable, in the public discourse of a legislature in a liberal democracy, to an overt appeal to a divine command that we be stewards of the earth. And if that command is cited by a defender of the environment, it may be welcomed by non-believers as an honest statement of conviction when it is combined with secular arguments, but felt to be a sectarian ground they cannot share if offered as the sole reason for an environmental protection. In many such cases, moreover, voicing can be as important as content.

INSTITUTIONAL DIMENSIONS OF CIVIC VIRTUE

The kinds of considerations that call for civic virtue in individuals also apply to institutional conduct in a pluralistic democracy. This section will suggest how two of the principles of church-state separation proposed in this book are supported by extending to institutions the conception of civic virtue developed here for individuals. I have in mind especially churches and the clergy as individuals representing them, but will also consider secular institutions.

Civic Virtue in the Ecclesiastical Domain

If we take seriously the idea of institutional citizenship, and if we regard civic virtue in a liberal democracy as embodying a commitment to both liberty and equality, then we can see a case for institutional ideals that include the principle of ecclesiastical political neutrality, which ascribes to churches committed to being institutional citizens in such a society a prima facie obligation to abstain from supporting candidates for public office or pressing for laws or public policies that restrict human conduct. If this principle is plausible from the point of view of civic virtue, it is also plausible from the point of view of clerical virtue as having the spiritual good of the people of the church as its primary object. As emphasized in Chapter 2, political positions from the pulpit can dilute and undermine the spiritual mission of the church and produce factions in the congregation.

The restrictive force of the principle of ecclesiastical political neutrality should not be exaggerated. For instance, it does not require churches in general to abstain from taking moral positions on, for instance, the permissibility of abortion. There are, in addition, moral aspects of the question whether abortion should be legally permissible. But there are also political aspects of the question. One is what political party (if any) has the best program for instituting or enforcing the appropriate laws. Another is how this issue should be weighted in relation to other contested ones to yield an overall political choice of party or candidate. Civic virtue, in institutions as in individuals, is in part a matter of judiciously adhering to the inevitably somewhat elastic standards we are forced to live by. It is one thing for churches to defend moral positions in ways that guide parishioners in making political choices; it is another to endorse candidates or propose detailed public policies, say a specific welfare system as opposed to the compassionate treatment of the poor by individuals and governments.[33]

Since ideals of civic virtue apply to clergy as individuals as well as to churches as institutions, I suggest that even in making avowedly personal statements clergy who believe in freedom and democracy should follow an individual neutrality principle that complements the institutional principle of ecclesiastical political neutrality, which concerns their conduct as church representatives. This individual counterpart is the *principle of clerical political neutrality;* it says that clergy have a prima facie obligation to observe a distinction between their personal political views and their views *as* clergy, to prevent any political aims they may have from dominating their professional conduct, and to abstain from officially (as church leaders) supporting candidates for public office or pressing for laws or policies that would restrict human conduct.

This principle is quite consistent both with the clergy as individuals following the rationale and motivation principles – with all the freedom to use religious reasons that those principles provide for – and with the point that applying religious principles and insights to issues of law and public policy can be highly beneficial. Nonetheless, it is appropriate that clergy exercise restraint – *clerical virtue,* we might say – in dealing with political issues, particularly in public. If they do not, they invite peers who disagree to use religious leverage for opposite ends; and the public, quite possibly including their own congregations, may suffer. There is a significant risk of inducing political discord in parishes or denominations that might otherwise enjoy a harmonious unity.

Civic Virtue in Non-Religious Institutions

Because the special concern of this chapter is civic virtue in relation to achieving a good balance between religious commitments and the secular concerns of citizenship, I have emphasized clerical responsibilities under the heading of civic virtue. But to some degree, my points also hold for at least some other professions and to at least some other institutions besides churches. A brief exploration of some representative cases can both clarify civic virtue and provide a wider context for the use I make of the concept in defending the overall position of this book.

Educators, especially of the very young, share with clergy a certain moral and intellectual authority. There remains the important difference that the authority of educators as such is (often avowedly) secular and clearly fallible. Nonetheless, a principle of political neutrality applies, if to a lesser degree, to educators as well, again in the light of a distinction between public and private conduct. This distinction is not necessarily connected with religion, but religious motivation tends to be the greatest source of departures from neutrality. There is no sharp line between these, but there are distinct differences between, for example, moral criticism of a policy, such as the United States' "containment" policy in the Vietnam War, and political attack on its proponents.

To be sure, with educators there is a further distinction between private and public institutions, and the avowed purpose of a private educational institution could be in part political. This would weaken the prima facie obligation the principle expresses. We should not underemphasize, however, the plausible contrasting point that political purposes tend to be inimical to the core mission of an educational institution and that political neutrality tends to facilitate concentration on the work of learning.[34]

Insofar as institutions, particularly churches and others not maintained for profit, can be viewed as citizens, we may ask what constitutes responsible citizenship on their part and, correspondingly, what counts as civic virtue on the part of their officers in acting as such, say in abstaining from pollution and in donating to civic causes or political campaigns. With the obvious exception of political parties and other political organizations, there is good reason to think that political neutrality is a prima facie reasonable posture for a great many institutions, especially those that, like certain foundations, exist to serve a large segment of a pluralistic public. There may also be dangers of corruption from within, as with churches or educational institutions that become politically involved to the detriment of their proper business. With public institutions, such as state universities and public power companies, the prima facie obligation of neutrality is especially important.

One point that emerges from considering non-religious institutions is that some of my principles of the ethics of citizenship need not place significantly higher demands on religious institutions or clergy than on certain other institutions and their official representatives. In both kinds of cases, there are constraints imposed by the needs of good citizenship; and in both, virtue requires doing better than one might if one merely lived within one's rights. Civic virtue requires institutions to take account of public responsibilities, which, in a liberal democracy, include showing respect for individuals and other institutions. It also calls on their governing officials, as individuals, to concentrate on the central target of their task – the flourishing of the proper beneficiaries of their institutional work – even if this means constraining their pursuit of certain political ends.

Civic Virtue and Religious Commitment

A virtue is a feature of character with a significant capacity to influence conduct. A virtue supplies its possessor both with normative reason indicating what sort of thing should be done in a wide range of contexts and with motivation to do such things for the right kind of reason. Virtue is not a mere capacity for good deeds, but a settled tendency to do them for an appropriate reason. Civic virtue in particular, at least in the form appropriate to citizenship in liberal democracy, is constituted above all in relation to protection and promotion of the flourishing of civil society. This implies a disposition on the part of civically virtuous citizens to participate in sociopolitical decisions and a determination to do so with respect for the freedom and autonomy of others. It implies (within limits) a commitment to having, and a willingness to offer, publicly comprehensible, evidentially adequate reason for one's sociopolitical conduct, particularly when that conduct is in support of a law or public policy that would restrict the liberty of citizens.

Given the special character of religious reasons for sociopolitical conduct, civic virtue is best realized in individual citizens by a commitment that includes the principles of secular rationale and motivation, which require that one recognize a prima facie obligation to have and offer adequate secular reason for such conduct, and a related prima facie obligation not to act in certain coercive ways without being sufficiently motivated by such a reason. If these principles, together with the parallel neutrality principles I have defended, express justificational and aretaic requirements for civic virtue, they also contribute to a further element in such virtue: a civic voice. This is affected even more by our motivating reasons than by the content of the reasons we publicly give for our civic and political conduct; but both our offering secular reasons and our being motivated by them contributes to a civic voice.

The rationale and motivation principles hold not only for ordinary citizens but have some application to clergy and officials in religious institutions. For clergy committed to a liberal democracy, moreover, civic virtue seems to require a prima facie obligation of political neutrality. Such neutrality does not reduce the capacity for moral leadership, nor does it prevent clergy from employing religious discourse in their public statements. In part because the principles of secular rationale and motivation mainly concern reasons one has and is moved by, they leave both individuals and institutions free to use religious language, as well as to employ religious reasons, in a number of ways. Commitment to giving the secular an essential role in determination of law and public policy is compatible with a major role for religious considerations both in that task and in public discourse.

In the light of the account of civic virtue proposed here, conscientious adoption of the principles of civic virtue I have endorsed is unlikely to be an undue burden for reflective religious people, clergy or lay, provided they are committed to seeking something that, assuming Western theism, one might expect them to wish for: theo-ethical equilibrium. If adherence to these principles is in some cases a burden, that may be offset by the incalculably large contribution it can make to harmony between the religious and the non-religious and even among religious people whose visions of the good society are sharply different. There is no way to maintain a flourishing pluralistic democracy without some sacrifice or at least self-discipline on the part of nearly everyone. I have tried here to outline some of the minimal sacrifices highly consonant with civic virtue.

CHAPTER SEVEN

RELIGIOUS CONVICTION AND POLITICAL ACTIVISM

The overall theory developed in this book can be clarified and shown to be fruitful by application to some deeply troubling issues. The abortion question is among the most divisive and will be my main example, but there are many other issues that raise difficulties concerning the proper balance of religious and secular considerations in public policy decisions. I will not propose a stand on the moral or legal status of abortion; but I believe that my overall position on the balance between the religious and the secular provides a basis on which a free society can operate without undue strife despite irreconcilable religious differences among its citizens on abortion and other profound issues. If, as individuals or as occupants of government roles, we are guided by the principles defended in this book, and by appropriate ideals of civic virtue that reflect them, we can at least agree on a framework for accommodating civilized disagreement and on the kinds of reasons needed to justify governmental coercion. The two sets of separation principles I propose, those addressed to individual citizens and those addressed to governmental or other institutions, can strengthen that framework without undermining the respect and autonomy that religious people and institutions should have.

This is not to suggest that the problem of the moral status of abortion can be resolved in the foreseeable future. It is not even clear that we may hope that the problem will soon be less hotly contested. The problem has, moreover, spawned violence and political strife. But even if the controversy remains intense, it may be possible to reduce these widely deplored effects of the problem. Here and in relation to such issues as assisted suicide and biomedical research, I seek to make some contribution on the basis of the position developed in earlier chapters.

In the hope of reducing some of the violence surrounding abortion, I begin by trying to understand the case for such violence as necessary in order to prevent a heinous wrong. I then discuss that case in the context of some plausible principles that seem common to most of the parties to the abortion dispute. These explorations require considerable space; the abortion problem is highly complex, and it is important to see that the most prominent and apparently most plausible arguments concerning it leave us with a great need to establish a balance between religious and secular considerations, since neither kind alone will satisfy proponents of the other, nor is there even agreement among those moved chiefly by considerations of just one of the two kinds. In the light of this exploration of some influential arguments, I propose a framework for peaceful coexistence among those parties. The framework applies in similar ways to other divisive issues, for instance assisted suicide, animal rights, genetic research, and protection of the environment.

PREVENTION OF KILLING THE INNOCENT AS A RATIONALE FOR VIOLENCE

The two most common and most widely respected justifications of violence are self-defense, broadly construed, and protection of the innocent, also broadly construed.[1] In the case of abortion the latter is the most appropriate category in which to explore the possible rationale for preventive violence. It may seem odd to pursue this topic here, given the widespread rejection of violence even among those who conceive most abortions as murder. But first, there are probably quite a few people who believe, perhaps without acknowledging it, that there is a good rationale for violence if it is the only way to prevent abortion (or to protect innocent fetuses); second, many who reject the view that violence is warranted to prevent abortion accept one or more sets of premises that may seem to support this same belief; and third, there is much to be learned from considering the case for the position that violence is warranted where it is the only way to prevent certain kinds of abortion. Reflection on this case may teach us something about the possible justification of violence, about the proper grounds for legal or social coercion in a free and democratic society (a liberal democracy), and about the kind of respect citizens in such a society owe to one other.

It should help to begin with a hypothetical case that some people would tend to consider analogous to a possible response to abortion conceived as the killing of an innocent person. Imagine that I am walking along a country road and I see a man approach a toddler playing in her yard. Suddenly he pulls out a knife and stabs her in the leg. She screams in agony, and he quickly covers her mouth and pushes her to the ground. If I am armed with a gun I may now raise it and order him to stop. If he turns and sees me aiming at him but, ignoring my loud order to stop, still positions his knife to stab her, it would be the judgment of many reflective people that I may shoot him and, if I am not close enough to be confident of disabling him without killing him, may aim at his midsection with the knowledge that he will probably be killed. This would be a presumptive case of preventive violence, and I would be using the minimum force I can reasonably rely on to prevent the killing of an innocent person.

The case for my justification in killing the would-be murderer is that it is the only way to prevent his killing an innocent child. If one believes that from the moment of conception there is an unborn child and thus an innocent person inside the pregnant woman's body, then in some circumstances one may also believe that killing the would-be abortionist is the only way to prevent the killing of an innocent child – indeed, a child even more clearly innocent than a toddler.[2] The same holds for any abortion occurring when there is an unborn child in question, even if this is believed to occur only after, say, six weeks. But we can properly explore the issues in relation to the common position that conception is the crucial point at which a human person comes into being (this position is held not only by the Roman Catholic Church but also by many others).

There are, of course, some disanalogies. One is that in the would-be stabber case I alone can save the child. In the would-be (legal) abortion case, the pregnant woman herself can normally stop the procedure at the last minute, as can the physician or, probably, any of a number of people assisting or nearby.

A second disanalogy is best seen by reflecting on what at first sight is a likeness between the two cases. It may seem obvious that the physician intends to kill a child, just as the would-be stabber apparently too intends this. Intending to kill an innocent child is unequivocally evil. Many physicians performing abortions, however, would likely deny that there is a "child" in the womb, since the term's only normal uncontroversial use (in English as well as in at least a great many other languages) is in reference to a male or female "postborn" person.[3] They might point out that if a journalist reporting on atrocities in Kosovo listed twenty children killed but knew that two of this number represented fetuses, everyone would get the wrong impression. Moreover, no responsible news organizations would allow this way of counting without a special explanation – which is not to imply that the full information is not *important* by any reasonable lights.

One might reply that if, quite apart from standard linguistic usage, it is plain that the fetus *is* an innocent child, then in intending to kill it the physician intends to kill an innocent child, just as the would-be stabber apparently intends this. Abortion would then be a case not of culpable ignorance but of willful malice. Intention, however, does not work this way. It can be clearly true that my withholding a check will cause someone to default on a payment; but if I do not *believe* my act has this property, I can intend to perform it without intending to cause the default and without even envisaging any default. Now, most physicians performing an abortion will not believe – and will probably disbelieve[4] – that the fetus is a child or, on that or any other ground, that it is a person. Grounds for this position on personhood may be religious or secular or both (for reasons to be indicated in the next section).

It may be objected that it is not a mere contingent truth, but a necessary one, a truth that cannot be otherwise (perhaps because ordained by God or in any case part of the metaphysical character of reality) that the fetus (or conceptus if we are speaking of an abortion too early for proper application of the term 'fetus') is a person. Supposing this is true, it is still not enough to permit inferring that the physician intends to kill a child. Take the case of a right triangle's being equivalent to the kind of triangle obeying the Pythagorean theorem, the proposition that the square of the hypotenuse equals the sum of the squares of the other two sides. The notion of a right triangle is commonly introduced, and some of its identifying properties indicated, before this theorem is taught. One can thus believe that a figure on the page is a right triangle without believing (or even having the faintest thought) that it obeys that theorem; thus, one could plainly intend to draw such a triangle without intending to draw one that obeys the theorem. The general point here is that even if *A* not only entails *B* but is provably equivalent to *B*, it does not follow that intending *A* implies intending *B*.

Similarly, even if it is necessary (and even provable) that a person is a child of God and that a fetus is a person, a physician assisting in a suicide, like one performing an abortion, might not believe (and could disbelieve) that the expected death will be that of a child of God. Intentions are in this way very personal. We cannot read off others' intentions through our own descriptions of the objects of those intentions, even if these objects are necessarily as we believe them to be.

A defender of the use of violence to prevent abortions might now reply with two points. First, even if the would-be deed is not malicious, it is a heinous killing of an innocent person. Second, even if this did not justify violent prevention, that kind of action might be justified if one reasonable constraint is met, namely that the physician have had a chance to see some of the cogent arguments for the fetus's being an innocent child. Those who reject these arguments, the objection continues, are guilty of egregious moral error – a serious, culpable mistake – even if they do not thereby acquire the intention to kill an innocent child. And egregious moral error makes them sufficiently like the would-be stabber to warrant preventively obstructing them, or even killing them, if it is the only way to save the child.

It is of course controversial whether there is any error in rejecting the arguments for the *personhood* of the fetus – a useful characterization of the moral status virtually everyone would agree the fetus (or conceptus) has if it is an innocent child. But supposing these arguments are sound, the question is whether a *conscientious* if wrong-headed rejection of them is sufficient for a degree of moral guilt adequate to warrant, if not preventive killing, then coercive prohibition. Again, our initial example may help. Surely the defender of preventive killing will say that even if the would-be stabber conscientiously (though mistakenly) thinks that the toddler, if not immediately killed, will infect innocent people with a fatal incurable disease, or, for that matter, conscientiously (by his lights, at least) takes the toddler to be not a child but a witch, he should still be shot. This is plausible, but it differs greatly from what holds in the abortion case: here it is hard to see how anyone sane and intellectually competent could have such beliefs about the child, whereas the sanity and intellectual competence of many who reject the arguments for the personhood of the fetus are, I take it, beyond dispute.

I feel sure that defenders of preventive violence in abortion cases will tend to argue that even conscientious and competent rejection of the personhood of the fetus does not offset a kind of negative status on the part of those who perform abortions, whether it is precisely moral guilt or not. They might consider this rejection a culpable failure to recognize moral or religious truths – or both – and might regard it as still making preventive killing a morally possible option at least where it is the last resort. Some of these people hold, as indeed some opponents of abortion who reject preventive violence hold, that it is quite clear that from the beginning of a pregnancy there is a person – an unborn child – in the womb. If it is pointed out that the physician acts at the request, sometimes the extensively considered request, of the pregnant woman, this will only arouse a sense of compounded moral guilt: the woman herself should also realize that she is requesting the killing of her own child.

For the sake of argument let us for the moment grant these points to proponents of preventive violence in abortion cases. What follows? One important conclusion does not: the points do not entail that those who conscientiously approve of abortion can be accused of *murder.* For murder requires a range of intentions or aims – paradigmatically an intention to kill a *person* – and it is plain that one cannot have those intentions toward what one believes is not a person.[5] The point of stressing this is not to suggest that the case for preventive violence in abortion cases would succeed only if the term 'murder' applies to typical abortions; it is to reduce the inflammatory language in which the discussion is sometimes couched and often conceptualized. Murderers are not only dangerous to innocent people – that applies to such common folk as drunk drivers – murderers are heinous and often clever criminals who must be both stopped and punished, even if they must sometimes be stopped by conscientious citizens rather than law enforcement officers.

If we can eliminate the notion of murder from the candidates to describe the kinds of abortion at issue, then even if we continue to use expressions implying culpability, we may remove some significant barriers to mutual understanding and perhaps open up some paths to partial resolution at least at the level of law and public policy. If abortion is conceived as murder, its permissibility is not even likely to seem a topic for discussion in a civilized society. If it is not at least that, polarization may worsen. Moreover, for those to whom religious grounds are the basis for taking the fetus to be a person, the urgency of preventing murder in the matter of abortion will surely seem a clear case in which any prima facie obligation not to restrict liberty without adequate secular reason is overridden.

Far more could be said about the analogies and disanalogies between our two cases of preventive violence, as well as about their bearing on assisted suicide and other contemporary issues involving religious and political considerations, but it may be more useful to proceed to the kinds of considerations that underlie the belief that personhood comes with conception. For it seems to be common ground to people on both sides of the abortion question that a central issue, probably *the* central issue, is the force of these considerations and the sense, if any, in which rejecting them is sufficient for a kind of moral guilt or at least for justification of certain preventive measures.

SOME ARGUMENTS FOR PERSONHOOD AT CONCEPTION

The case for personhood at conception can be made from many points of view, but the literature shows a tendency to give weight to two quite different kinds of considerations, which are often but not always distinguished: secular and theological (or theologico-moral) considerations. My purposes here do not require a comprehensive survey of these considerations, in part because I do not take a position on the morality of abortion itself. It should suffice to examine what seem the most widely influential arguments, beginning with the secular ones.

Secular Arguments

Among the secular arguments, the *genetic argument,* as we might call it, is perhaps the one that appears most scientific: its crucial premise is that (1) at conception there is all of the genetic information required for the development of the conceptus into an adult human being whose personhood is obvious. It might be added, as a second premise, that (2) this genetic code is realized by a natural process of development from conception onward. The conclusion is that (3) the conceptus is a person; loosely, the fetus is a person from conception onward.[6]

A second argument is implicit in a very common kind of reasoning: from the premise that human life begins at conception to the conclusion that personhood is first instantiated in our species "when life begins," namely at the first point at which there is human life in the womb. Call this the *human life argument.*[7] The reasoning here apparently represents an argument from the premise that there is biological human life at conception to the conclusion that personhood begins at conception, that is (roughly), there is at conception a human being that, like you and me, has a "right to life." More explicitly, the premise is that (1) at conception there is a being – the conceptus – that is human, clearly belonging to our species; and the conclusion is that (2) at conception, there is a human being. It is apparently presupposed that everyone understands a human being (or should understand it) to be a person.

The third argument is a *wedge argument* (also, perhaps tendentiously, called a slippery slope argument). This is simply the three-stage argument that since (1) there is a continuous process from conception to childhood (or to any period of life you like at which it is clear that there is a person), it follows that (2) there can be no non-arbitrary line drawn along the way; and, by (2) understood in accordance with (1), it follows that (3) if personhood is reached by this continuous process at any point on the postborn end, it exists at any point on the preborn end. Clearly, (4) it is reached on the postborn end; hence, (5) personhood exists at any point on the preborn end.[8]

Religious Arguments

The religious arguments I want to consider are by comparison more straightforward. The most important is perhaps the *ensoulment argument:* since (1) ensoulment occurs at conception, and (2) a person is an embodied soul, it follows that (3) the conceptus (which is an ensouled "body") is a person. It is assumed that the "body" that is ensouled need not look like the normal postborn human body. It could be held instead that a person simply *is* a soul and that that soul is embodied at conception. In that case the notion of killing entailed by abortion would not be so straightforward, since there are probably no clear criteria for killing a soul and in any case none that are uncontroversially acceptable. But a prohibitive case against abortion could probably still be mounted with similar moral force.[9]

This ensoulment idea *could* be combined with an atheistic metaphysics – say, with the view that a person is the biological embodiment of a soul, conceived as an entity present at conception, the point at which the biological program for the creature's development is first physically realized. But we need not consider that view separately; some of what is said below applies to it, and by comparison it is not as well motivated philosophically.[10]

The second religious argument we might note – one more often presupposed than stated, I think – is what we might call the *divine gift argument:* this simply proceeds from the premise that (1) children are gifts from God that are received at conception, to the conclusion that (2) personhood begins, at conception, with the gift of the preborn child. This argument has the advantage of bringing out that from many religious points of view, abortion, even beyond being the killing of a child, is destruction of a gift from God. Even if the fetus is not considered a person (or not taken to be a person "from conception"), a similar argument can be constructed to oppose abortion as destroying a divine gift; and the same basic premise concerning God's giving life can be used in opposition to suicide and assisting in it and to various forms of non-suicidal euthanasia.

Difficulties and Complexities of the Arguments

A great deal can be (and has been) said about these arguments or variants of them. Fortunately, we do not need a full-dress appraisal here. Our main task is simply to say enough to bring out how those who conscientiously disagree on the soundness of the arguments should regard each other from the moral and the sociopolitical point of view. The latter viewpoint, at least, includes the perspective from which we can properly decide what conduct is legally prohibited. I begin with the secular arguments.

The genetic argument certainly shows that there is something important about the conceptus. This is sometimes put by saying that it is at least a *potential person*. I think this important conclusion should be granted. But however clearly it may show (at least together with obvious facts about the natural development of pregnancy) that abortion is not to be undertaken without weighty reasons, it does not show that it may be prohibited where pregnancy is due to rape or incest or threatens the health of the pregnant woman or, if carried to term, imposes serious hardship on the woman (for instance, a highly confining, very painful pregnancy and the need for a caesarian section). For there is good reason to think that whatever the rights of a potential person of this kind, those of an actual person tend to take priority in any case of conflict.[11]

Regarding the question whether the genetic argument establishes the personhood of the conceptus, we should note some apparently close analogies which suggest that the argument fails to show that. Consider that an implanted, germinating acorn at the beginning of the natural process that leads to the growth of an oak tree is not itself an oak tree.

Here we have a kind of biological implantation or even fertilization, all the relevant genetic material, the beginning of a natural, continuous process leading to what is unmistakably an oak tree, and perhaps even a slow-motion analogue of birth.[12]

The human life argument can be illuminated by some of these same considerations. The implanted, germinating acorn is oaken, as opposed to maple or ash; and clearly it is alive, as opposed to inanimate. It also has the kind of developmental tendencies we assume are "natural" for the conceptus. Its germination (or implantation with a "take," in the sense of a biological initiation of the process of development) is thus the point at which oaken life begins. But this seems quite insufficient for its being, at that point, an oak tree.

One may object that whereas an oak tree is not just an oaken being, a person is just a human being. Supposing this is so, it may be because in the phrase 'human being' the whole is as it were more than the sum of its parts: in the morally relevant sense of 'human being', not just anything to which the separate terms apply qualifies. If human beings are equivalent to persons, one might even expect this to be so given the complexity of the notion of a person. If it is so, however, we cannot argue validly from the premise that the conceptus is human and is a being to the conclusion that it is a human being, any more than we can argue from the premise that someone is a mother and is expectant (awaiting the return of her great-granddaughter, say) to the conclusion that she is an expectant mother, in the common, integrated sense of that phrase implying the expectation of giving birth to a baby.

There is also some question whether, without argument, the conceptus may be called a "being" – at least in any sense rich enough to yield the conclusion that if it is human (in belonging to the human species) then it is a person. It is difficult to avoid the conclusion here that rational reliance on the human life argument will not survive the recognition of the possibility that it is equivocal. The argument seems to trade on the clear applicability of 'human' to many living things, such as hearts, simply on the basis of their biological species; but in this case the fact that they may perhaps be considered to be both beings, say, as complex living entities, and human plainly does not entail that they are human beings in the integrated sense of 'persons'.

The wedge argument is also clarified by the analogy to the acorn, for oaken development could be as smooth and natural as human development. But as with the human life argument, there is also the general consideration that the *kind* of argument we are talking about is not valid: there are many cases in which we cannot draw a non-arbitrary line, yet there are clear differences of kind on the continuum. The gradual shadings that can change a colored object from red to orange illustrate this point. A series of imperceptible changes ultimately yields a major contrast and, in some sense, a difference of kind.

Let me add, however, that on reflection we may find it peculiar that *birth* is not more widely taken as a non-arbitrary – which is not to say self-evident or even uncontroversial – dividing line. Perhaps because, historically, men have dominated the discussion of the abortion issue, the momentousness of birth, psychologically, interpersonally, and biologically, is not often mentioned in discussions of abortion.[13] This is the more striking given the (so far) almost entirely unselfconscious commonality of counting the number of people killed in accidents or otherwise as if persons were postborn human beings. The existence of the fetus inside the woman's body, the union of bloodstreams, the far-reaching effects that pregnancy has on her, the labor and agony of giving birth – these are no minor facts of human life. Granted, it is important that the fetus just before birth looks essentially as it does just afterward and normally would survive even if born considerably earlier; but surely appearance is not a decisive consideration.

As to survivability upon removal from the womb, it is entirely relative to our medical technology and can in principle go back to conception. It is at best doubtful that moral status should depend on our technology in the way it would if such survivability were sufficient for personhood. We should resist letting the technological tail wag the ethical dog. Even apart from the importance of the changes that come with birth, however, the kind of reasoning exhibited by the wedge argument is not sound.

The ensoulment argument is an entirely different matter. There are those who hold that the Cartesian view of personhood it presupposes is incoherent, but I do not think the alleged incoherence has been shown. If there is ultimately an incoherence, cogently establishing that has long escaped brilliant philosophers, and in any case the alleged incoherence is surely not a basis for claiming that those who hold the ensoulment view of personhood are guilty of an unconscientious appraisal of the data. This point must be balanced, however, by the admission that it certainly need not be unconscientious to conclude that the relevant notion of a person is not ultimately coherent, or at least to reject it as mistaken. These two points taken together suggest that the issue is one on which each side should respect the other as holding a prima facie defensible if inconclusively argued view.

Fortunately, there is no need for an excursion into the philosophy of mind here. The most important single point to be made is that even among the religious people who hold an embodied soul conception of the person, there is disagreement over when ensoulment occurs. If, as some have thought, it occurs after at least many weeks of pregnancy, then on the ensoulment view, abortions before that time do not entail killing a person. Differences concerning the time of ensoulment might also divide adherents of a secular version of the ensoulment conception of persons.

It is noteworthy that even in the history of the Roman Catholic Church there have been different times officially regarded as the points at which ensoulment occurs, say at ninety days versus conception.[14] Even within Christianity, moreover, there seems to be sufficient conscientious, informed disagreement about what the scriptures imply on this matter to make it impossible for a proponent of any one biblically implied point in human development as the time of ensoulment to regard all proponents of different points as guilty of any more than the kind of unfortunate error that even fully conscientious people sometimes make.

These considerations help to put the divine gift argument in perspective. Suppose for the sake of argument that ensoulment occurs either at conception or not later than birth and that it marks the beginning of childhood. Then God's gift of a child can be located at various points in human development depending on one's theology or philosophy of mind or both. To be sure, even if the God-given gift cannot be said to be a *child* until well into the pregnancy (or until birth for that matter), it is arguable that the conceptus is in any event a gift from God not to be tampered with. This is a point most theists will respect even if they give it different interpretations.[15] But the obligation not to tamper is still differentially strong depending on whether it is a person who would be harmed; and at least if it is not a person, the obligation would seem to be a prima facie one that is overridable for weighty reasons of the kinds that can in many instances be offered to justify abortions.

One can imagine some religious people holding that if the early fetus is not a person and has mental and physical defects that would lead to a terrible and short life without the normal capacity to relate to others, then abortion is more, or more nearly, in line with God's plan than carrying the fetus to term. This is particularly likely if they believe in afterlife and take it that God's plan for human beings includes a use of it that compensates for unrequited losses on earth. Again, there is no one rational way, and apparently not just one biblical way, of determining in every case what is or is not in accord with God's plan.

It may also be instructive to recall that even on the Roman Catholic view, abortion may be permissible under the *principle of double effect* – which for illustrative purposes I will take as roughly the principle that if an action has two effects, one good and one bad, we may perform it in order to bring about the good effect provided the bad effect is neither our (intended) means nor our (desired) end in doing the deed, and the good effect is sufficiently good to warrant permitting the bad one. If an appendectomy or tumor removal is urgent enough to warrant killing the fetus, what about protecting the pregnant woman's mental health? A physician who took doing that to be imperative perhaps would or could (by the double effect standard) do the abortion under a description like 'bringing about by one's medical action, the regretted consequence that the fetus will be killed, specifically, as a result of one's removing the tumor in order to protect the patient's health'. Might such a physician also argue that, in the case in which the development of the pregnancy will harm the patient's mental and emotional condition, the death of the fetus as a result of removing it is a regretted effect of adopting (as a strong medical commitment) a policy of protecting her mental and emotional health? This may very well be an inadmissible application of the principle of double effect. The main point here is that even within a single religious tradition there is room for argument about both the exact nature of the prohibited acts and the scope of the prohibition.[16]

Before concluding this brief appraisal of representative arguments for the personhood of the fetus, I want to consider the group as a whole. When there are multiple arguments for a view, their cumulative psychological effect may be great, sometimes disproportionately to their joint cogency. In any case, those who find each at least somewhat plausible may argue that even if none is individually cogent the set taken together is. Imagine that each of the premise sets of the five arguments is independent of the other sets and provides a probability (as some kind of evidential weight) of .2 to their common conclusion. Then the probability of the conclusion would seem to be far higher – perhaps 1 minus the likelihood that all the premise sets are misleading, that is, are true despite the conclusion's being false. This overall probability might be calculated (on analogy with that of getting at least one head on five independent tosses of a five-sided die) as .8 to the fifth power. This procedure yields an overall probability of about two-thirds (1 minus .32768) to the conclusion – a fairly high "confidence level" – and we can increase it dramatically if we can find a few more equally plausible independent arguments.

This reasoning in support of the case for personhood at conception will not do. For one thing, there is no justification for assigning numerical probabilities in such cases; we scarcely have a rational procedure for assigning even a probability estimate for invalid arguments of the kind we are imagining, each of which is logically inconclusive (I am not implying here that all of the arguments for the personhood of the fetus are defective on purely logical, as opposed to content, grounds, nor are they). Second, those who reject the arguments would likely insist that if there were a method for assigning even approximate probabilities, it would yield about the same probability as that of the conclusion taken apart from the premises, which they might hold to be close to zero. Third, the kind of independence in question is not relevantly like that of different tosses of a fair coin, so that combining the arguments might not yield the overall probability in the way described. For one thing, even if two premise sets are logically independent, one may *evidentially* depend on the other or on some common assumption, in a relevant way, say because two or more evidentially depend on the existence of God.

There is also an opposing consideration to be reckoned with once we start combining individually inconclusive arguments. The clear failure of many different arguments each constructed in a serious effort to establish an enduringly controversial view may be some reason to suspect that their common conclusion is false.

The various points I have made in appraising the representative secular and religious arguments for the personhood of the conceptus and thereby against (most categories of) abortion are certainly limited. But they may serve to indicate how problematic the religious and secular arguments to this effect are: the secular ones for any rational person, the religious ones for at least a large number of conscientious theists as well as for perhaps most non-religious rational people. If the points do indicate this, it may now be fruitful to ask whether the arguments can play the role they should if violence or other coercive efforts to prevent abortion are to be justified.

THE RESTRICTION OF ABORTION AND THE PRESUMPTION OF INNOCENCE

So far, I have been mainly exploring the moral status of abortion by considering what seem the most widely influential arguments for the personhood of the fetus from conception onward. A further issue is the bearing of the moral status of abortion on its proper legal treatment in a liberal democracy (a free and democratic society). If, for instance, its moral status is unclear or, in a certain way, controversial, or both, then there may be great difficulty deciding whether it should be legally prohibited.[17]

Two Dimensions of the Presumption of Innocence

In connection with both the moral and the sociopolitical issues we face here, it is fruitful to consider the standard presumption of innocence operating in a liberal democracy: the presumption that a person is not to be convicted unless proven guilty. This presumption is not merely an element in the liberal tradition; it can be defended as a requirement of justice, and – particularly relevant to this book – it is likely to receive strong support from any plausible approach, such as the seven discussed in Chapter 1, to grounding a liberal democracy. I think it turns out that this presumption of innocence can be crucial for justifying legal coercion in general as well as legal punishment, and understanding it may be important even in cases where it is clear that preventive violence is warranted.

To apply these points to the abortion issue, let me begin with the question of how the anti-abortion arguments just considered bear on the presumption of innocence, construed as pertinent to determining both moral and legal guilt. First, recall the would-be stabber. Since it is obvious that he intends to kill or wound an innocent person, the question of his possible moral innocence does not come up: even an innocent person may in some cases be justifiedly killed as a last resort to save another innocent one. Now let us vary the case. Suppose I had seen the first stabbing from a great distance and without being able to tell exactly what the man does, so that he may for all I can tell be disciplining his own child. I rush to the bleeding child, and then see a man running away from the scene. I may demand that he stop. But if he does not, I may not simply shoot him: he may not hear me or may be running for help (having regretted what he did); and for all I know, he did not inflict the wound, he may be able to get help fast, and he thinks that stopping to explain things to me would cost vital moments. In short, there is reasonable doubt regarding his guilt or innocence, and serious though the crime I *think* he has committed is I should not kill or seriously harm him. Reasonable doubt of various sorts can also undermine the permissibility even of self-defensive violence (though in this particular case there may no longer be any danger to oneself), but it does so more clearly in the case of preventive violence toward someone else, particularly if it is not for the sake of a person one has a special obligation to protect, such as one's own child.

If we now ask how the presumption of innocence illustrated by this example is relevant in the abortion case, we find that there are two dimensions of its bearing. In one dimension the issue is the strength of the presumption that the agent in question is morally innocent of doing a wrong, say killing a child. In that case something like malicious intent or perhaps gross negligence must be shown to override the presumption of innocence. The issue in the second dimension is whether the *act* in question, here abortion, is itself a wrong. In the first case, then, the question is the *evidential presumption of innocence:* the presumption that the *agent* is morally innocent of the act in question unless shown to be guilty. This is the usual sense of 'presumption of innocence'. In the second case the question is what I propose to call the *constitutive presumption of innocence:* the presumption that the relevant *act* is innocent, that is, not a crime (or a moral wrong).

Both the evidential and the constitutive presumptions must be satisfied for a just conclusion that someone culpably committed a wrong or a crime; both are for this reason crucial for understanding the basis of just moral criticism and, in a free and democratic society, just punishment for crime. Ordinarily, however, the presumption of innocence comes up only where there is already agreement that the deed someone is accused of is a wrong or a crime, and here the evidential presumption of innocence is taken to be the only relevant one. I am considering both presumptions in this context largely because there is no such agreement in the case of abortion, as with many other issues. To see the bearing of both presumptions on the abortion issue, it may be best to begin with the application of the evidential presumption and assume that abortion is the wrong it is often taken to be: killing a person.

One important point has already been argued: that there is no good ground for maintaining that a conscientious (or even simply representative) physician planning to do an abortion *intends* to kill a person. This point holds even if there are decisive arguments that the conceptus or fetus in fact is a person, provided the physician does not believe (or tend to believe) that conclusion.[18] But now we come to the constitutive presumption of innocence – concerning whether the act itself may be properly presumed to be innocent; this question is independent of what those who perform it happen to believe about it. Let us ask, then, whether there is still some kind of moral deficiency – beyond simply mistaking the character of the conceptus or fetus – such as a willful or corrupt rejection of a public and morally compelling case for its personhood.

Our main question, as applied to physicians doing abortions, is whether, even if morally innocent of intending to kill a person, they are killing one and so lack de facto innocence (and presumably also moral innocence), and do not satisfy the constitutive presumption of innocence, on the ground that it *is,* and can be shown to be, a person whom the abortion will kill, in which case preventive violence would seem warranted. This question brings us back to the question of the moral status of the fetus.

The Presumption of Innocence and the Status of Abortion

In view of the difficulties facing the five representative arguments we considered, it seems reasonable to conclude that the moral status of the fetus, and especially the conceptus, is a clear case of a question on which conscientious reasonable people can disagree. It may also be an example of an issue for which there simply is no determinate answer in terms of purely rational considerations (roughly, those accessible to any rational person).[19]

This conclusion does not establish that there *cannot* be considerations showing that the fetus is a person and hence that, even if abortion is not murder in a sense implying intention to kill a person, it nonetheless is killing one. Nothing I have said entails that religious considerations, such as a religious argument, cannot establish something conclusively, even if it may not be in terms accessible to every rational person. Surely some religious proponents of the ensoulment or divine gift argument believe that religious considerations can be conclusive. Let us explore this.

We must distinguish between considerations that establish something in the completely objective *logical* sense of entailing its truth and those that establish it in the much more common *evidential* sense (roughly speaking) of implying it from indications accessible to attentive rational persons of normal human intellectual powers. God's will, say God's willing that something be so, might establish a truth in the first sense (since of necessity what God as an omnipotent being wills to be so *is* so) but not the second sense, somewhat in the way the presence of chemical wastes in outer space might establish the vast extent of pollution even if no one is in a position to find them. One can grant that religious considerations such as the directives of God's will may establish the personhood of the fetus in the first sense and deny that they do so in the second. To support this denial, one might point to the enduring disagreement among the religious – even within religions, such as Christianity and Judaism – as evidence that whatever the objective truth about God's will, God has left some ambiguity in the evidences of it accessible to us.

Whether this enduring disagreement on the status of the fetus, even among highly rational religious people, implies a divine intention that one rely on secular considerations in the relevant matter is a theological question that is bound to be controversial. But even if one answers it negatively, one may still reasonably suppose that to achieve the best possible resolution one should seek theo-ethical equilibrium. The results will differ for different people, but my point here is only that with the abortion issue even devoutly religious people may find good reasons to consider secular as well as religious grounds for a moral or sociopolitical position.

In the light of all this, let us ask whether the constitutive presumption of innocence can be satisfied by at least a wide range of abortions given the existence of people who reflectively consider both the secular and the religious arguments for personhood from conception and reject them. Do even the religious who accept at least some of the arguments still want to maintain that there is no room for reasonable doubt about personhood and that the act of abortion cannot satisfy the presumption of innocence? I believe a great many do not. A great many would on reflection grant, I think, that the reason for their belief that personhood begins at conception may be less what the arguments for this show than a confidence in authority, say papal or clerical authority, or a sense of intuition on the matter, perhaps a sense of intuition taken to be religiously inspired.

I do not propose to argue that these authoritative and intuitive sources are in general unreliable, though it is noteworthy that their deliverances have often been known to change either historically or, even in a short time, in the life of some individuals. Instead, I want to raise the question of how the stance we are considering – that the arguments and grounds we have been discussing (some of which are religious) show that abortion is killing a person – might be viewed in the light of the presumption of innocence in both senses.

Standards for Criminal Conviction and Standards for Legal Prohibition

Consider first the evidential sense of the presumption of innocence. Would any of us be content to allow that the accused in a criminal trial might fail to merit the presumption because there is – relative to grounds as contestable as those brought against abortion by arguments of the kinds we have considered – no reasonable doubt of guilt? And if the grounds are wholly religious, including the non-argumental kinds of grounds noted – authority and apparent intuition – would that satisfy us? Even if the charge is murder and the accused, if guilty, is likely to be dangerous, supporting a verdict of guilty that depends on the kinds of arguments and grounds we have considered would not be acceptable to most reflective people. This applies to those of us who are religious, as well as to others. There is, for one thing, the repugnant possibility that will occur to us if we apply the do-unto-others rule: being found guilty by the arguments, intuitions, and authority that depend on some *other* religion that we completely reject.

If we may accept these points about the kind of grounds needed to override the evidential presumption of innocence, there is good reason to think that in a free and democratic society grounds of a similar kind should be required, at least in the matter of legal permissibility, to override the constitutive presumption – the presumption that, by treating actions as innocent (permissible) unless appropriately proven to be wrong, in effect corresponds to our normal rights of liberty, moral and sociopolitical. It must be granted that when the evidential presumption concerning an action is overridden, the agent in question is liable to punishment, whereas when the constitutive presumption is overridden it is only would-be agents who are affected (and even then in doing the thing in question they are liable only to accusation, which will lead to punishment only if the evidential presumption is also overridden). But notice how many more agents may be affected in the second case – at least everyone in the society in question who may want to engage in the prohibited conduct.

We should also ask whether it is reasonable, at least in regard to establishing just laws, to uphold a higher standard for individual guilt upon accusation than for legal prohibition of an action in the first place, especially if many believe the action permissible and want to engage in it. I do not see that it is, though this is difficult to show. If we add that the main point at issue here is in any case not the appropriate amount of evidence but the proper *kind*, then we should ask whether suitable grounds for overturning the constitutive presumption can depend on religious considerations, even assuming their evidential strength is adequate. In a free and democratic society, particularly one that is religiously pluralistic, it seems that (in legal matters) both kinds of presumption should be overridable only where, whatever other evidences there may be, there is adequately strong secular evidence. This protects all citizens both from restriction of liberty and from legal punishment without cogent evidence of a kind they can accept by virtue of being rational citizens; and it has the additional merit of protecting the liberty of the religious from biases stemming from a religion other than their own.

My suggestion, then, is that if we sufficiently appreciate how reflective people wish to be treated under the evidential presumption of innocence, and if we properly connect that presumption with the constitutive one as a significantly similar protection of our liberty, we can see a double standard sometimes operating in the abortion case and perhaps in other cases where religious convictions bear strongly. I have mentioned assisted suicide as one, but we might consider whether the point also holds for certain controversies involving sexual conduct, school curricula, and government support of private education. There is a readiness to convict (or preventively coerce) on the basis of overall grounds one would reject as insufficient for one's own conviction (or coercion) if one should be on trial, especially for killing a person. The caution here concerning appropriate standards for conviction (or coercion) applies both to jurors and, for some of the same reasons, to judges.[20]

Some people might reply that they would be willing to be judged similarly in a criminal trial: religiously inspired arguments simply will not go wrong here, at least no more than certain other permissible kinds, such as arguments based on intuition, and they are especially unlikely to go wrong when supported by plausible, if contestable, secular arguments.

This claim of parity is difficult to assess without a careful, partly empirical study, and it could be correct. But reliability is not the only consideration. We may quite properly care about the route by which we get to a destination, not just about whether we in fact get there. In any case, there is something repugnant about being convicted (or having one's liberty restricted) on the basis of someone else's religious attitudes or views, even if they are only a significant part and not the whole of the ground of the prosecutor's (or coercer's) case; or at least this is a feeling that tends to be shared both by those who are religious – especially if they are in a religious minority in their society – and those who simply respect liberty, whether or not they are religious.

It may be objected that there is no reason to think that in general differences of religious orientation should affect one's sense of the evidence of ordinary crime, and hence there is no need to require that secular considerations have a crucial role. I see no good ground for any conclusion of that scope. Certainly if we agree that (as seems plain) religious considerations can influence what we take to *constitute* a crime and many other aspects of our thinking, we might plausibly expect that they will often affect our sense of the quality of the *evidence* for such a crime, particularly if they are themselves among our main kinds of evidence. Imagine, for instance, trying someone for violating the anti-establishment requirements of the Constitution or, on the other hand, for unduly restricting religious liberty. If religious convictions about what counts as genuine religion or as an important religious liberty figure in determining innocence or guilt, it is easy to see how biases can adversely affect the fairness of the procedure. A pubic school teacher's hostility to one's religious position can be unwarrantedly conceived as preaching a "secular religion"; a restriction of one's religiously claimed freedom to refuse life-saving medical treatment for one's minor children can be seen as an unwarranted violation of the free exercise of one's religion. As examples like these indicate, it is salutary to bear in mind that in any system of appraising evidence, biases are a problem to be eliminated; and many religious people are acquainted with some biases against them from other religious perspectives.

I conclude, then, that citizens within the framework of a liberal democracy have a right to be judged as guilty or not guilty of crimes, if not by a religiously neutral jury of their peers, then at least by standards neutral among religions and even neutral with respect to religion.[21] This applies, if with less urgency, to trials for lesser crimes than murder. The considerations supporting this neutrality standard seem to me to support, in the ways I have described, a similar neutrality regarding what counts as a crime in the legal sense, though in that case there may be less reason to speak of a right to neutrality of judgment as opposed to its desirability.[22]

Both points are highly recommended by reflection on the do-unto-others rule. But I take these conclusions to be controversial and will not argue them further here. What I prefer to do now is argue that the principles of citizenship defended in this book may provide scope for both the moral autonomy and the religious freedom of all concerned in the abortion debate and other major issues that may lead to violence or coercion. I begin with the question whether at least in cases like abortion we should prefer weaker principles.

The Indeterminacy Question for Some Major Moral Issues

Particularly because conscientious rational persons persistently disagree on the morality of abortion, it may seem that here, even if not in general, the principle of secular rationale is too demanding. The strongest case for a weaker principle of similar scope is probably one proposed by Kent Greenawalt. As he put it at one point,

> Legislation must be justified in terms of secular objectives, but when people reasonably think that shared premises of justice and criteria for determining truth cannot resolve critical questions of fact, fundamental questions of value, or the weighing of competing benefits and harms, they do properly rely on religious convictions that help them answer these questions.[23]

We can interpret such a standard more or less strictly depending on our criteria for "reasonably" considering a question secularly unresolvable. It may be that in general we could not reasonably draw this conclusion without in effect at least trying to apply the principle of secular rationale by seeking an adequate secular reason. I propose to bypass this problem and grant for the sake of argument that some issues (including some "critical questions of fact") cannot be settled by secular reason and may be justifiedly believed to be indeterminate in that sense. Since the notion of a person is arguably a basis for ascribing such indeterminacy, let us assume for the sake of argument that the abortion and euthanasia issues are of this sort – the former mainly because secular reason cannot settle when, in human development, we first have a person, the latter partly because it cannot settle when, owing to declining or impaired mental condition, we cease to have one.

If we restrict Greenawalt's standard to cases that a vast majority of citizens reasonably agree are indeterminate in this way, it is surely plausible, and I have much sympathy with it (I might indeed hold a qualified version of it if I became convinced that the principle of secular rationale is too strong). But for several reasons I prefer not to adopt it even for cases like abortion. One problem is that there are no clear criteria for indeterminacy, and we would thus be thrown back on our best criteria for reasonably believing it exists. This is a serious difficulty in itself; but even apart from it, adopting the principle would create incentives for some religious citizens – and others who do not have adequate secular reason for supporting coercive laws or public policies – to deem an issue indeterminate prematurely or even uncritically.

More important still, I believe that in cases of reasonably posited indeterminacy, the default position of liberal democracy is just what its core emphasis on liberty would suggest: freedom. I have tried in this book to indicate why, given the uncontroversially good secular reasons for upholding human dignity – as including both equal basic liberty and basic equality of political power – this position is acceptable. If this rather strong liberal position is sometimes burdensome for those who cannot conscientiously accept a liberty it supports, I would again stress how they themselves wish to be treated by those who disagree with them for religious reasons, particularly where their religious conduct might be restricted.

For those who cannot be persuaded to adopt the principles I have proposed, I would reiterate that if the points made here and my various arguments in earlier chapters are not compelling to them, they have a moral right to adhere only to a less demanding principle such as Greenawalt's. This acknowledgment is by no means an indication of approval. As I have stressed, one can be justly criticizable even when acting within one's rights; and although I recognize the right in question, I have been arguing for a prima facie obligation to restrict its exercise.

There is, however, one way religious citizens and others may avoid invoking that right where they can find no adequate secular reason to restrict liberty that they cannot forbear opposing by coercive measures. It is persuasion. Persuasion is a non-coercive way to change human conduct, one that there is reason to think should be highly effective where its object is backed by truth. Persuasion is a main topic of the next section.

VIOLENCE AND COERCION VERSUS CIVILIZED DISAGREEMENT AND PERSUASION

I hope that enough has been said to make it clear (for anyone in doubt about the point) that the moral status of the conceptus is the kind of issue on which reasonable people can disagree even in the light of what appear to be all the available relevant arguments, but that nonetheless some people can be expected to continue to take it to be quite evident that personhood begins at conception. If this is so, there is some urgency about the question whether there is any set of principles that might reduce the violence of the dispute – and indeed might help with other disputes involving church-state issues or other sources of apparently irresoluble disagreement that may lead to violence.

In suggesting that the religious and the non-religious alike should be able to see the benefits of the presumption of innocence as a protection of citizens – and certainly as an essential element in liberal democracy – and in arguing that at least in a liberal democracy this presumption should be understood in secular terms, I have, as in earlier chapters, been taking a kind of separation of religious and secular considerations to be a rational strategy for citizens in general, largely irrespective of religious affiliation. Let us consider the abortion question, and by implication other troublesome sociopolitical issues, in relation to that separation as partially expressed in principles like those of secular rationale and secular motivation.

First, if the principle of secular rationale is a good one for a liberal democracy, it is also reasonable as applied to the use, in such a society, of coercive violence for moral ends. Surely coercive violence for moral ends should meet at least as high a standard of justification as restrictions of liberty in general, which do or should have similar ends, as in the case of coercive laws. Second, as our discussion brings out, coercive violence requires – not surprisingly, since commonly it both curtails liberty more than does legal pressure and also harms others – a stronger principle along the same lines. It is stronger both in implying a greater prima facie obligation and in requiring a stronger evidential condition. Call this the *principle of defensive violence;* it says that one has a prima facie obligation not to engage in defensive violence – either self-defensive or other-protective – unless there is an adequate secular basis strong enough to preclude reasonable doubt that the person(s) in question will otherwise commit a sufficiently serious wrong.[24] There is no brief way to give an adequate characterization of sufficiently serious wrong, but normally it should be clear that the wrong to be prevented is serious enough to warrant any harm done by the violence.

Four further clarifications are needed. First, this principle does not imply that where the condition is satisfied one *has* a prima facie obligation to do violence, only that one is not then prima facie obligated not to. Second, although the obligation in question is overridable, I doubt that there is in general a moral right to depart from the principle itself, as I allow there generally is in the case of the rationale and motivation principles, which I present as principles of civic virtue rather than of stricter civic obligation. Third, it is not implied (any more than in the case of my other principles) that no secular reasons can appropriately be ruled out or that no religious reasons can play an evidential or motivational role; many of each kind may be eliminated by the adequacy requirement, but religious reasons need not be ruled out by this requirement. Fourth, the principle is also defensible as a constraint on most cases of violence to persons, and in part for that reason it applies to political violence, such as systematic violence that is illegal under abortion laws, as well as to other kinds that are aimed at changing policy as well as defending or punishing someone.[25] The presence of reasonable doubt that preventing murder (or any unjustified killing of a person) requires violence would be an example. The important question for this chapter is whether there is an adequate secular basis for violence in the case of abortion or other hotly contested sociopolitical issues, particularly if their moral status is arguably undecidable by secular reason.

It should be reiterated that both the principle of secular rationale and the principle of secular motivation allow that religious reasons may be evidentially and motivationally *sufficient.* The principles require having secular reasons with a certain cogency, but do not deny the possibility of religious reasons' being cogent. The principles do not, then, slight religious considerations in a way they may initially appear to. The principles even allow (as I have stressed) that people following them judge the religious reasons to be more important than the secular ones. The aim is not to eliminate the religious as a factor; it is to include the secular in a certain role crucial for civic harmony and, for the many who are moved by religious considerations, to create an integration of secular and religious evidences and incentives.

The reasoning underlying the principle of secular rationale applies to coercive civil disobedience as well, such as sit-ins or demonstrations that effectively prevent some people from using a facility, say a clinic or office. If one does not have an adequate secular rationale for disapproving of certain conduct, then one lacks a good basis for supporting its legal prohibition. Hence, civil disobedience of a kind that is coercive or aimed at forcibly undermining the law, as some sit-ins do, is not appropriate.

Persuasion of the wrongfulness of the relevant conduct, leading to voluntary rejection of it, is of course an entirely different matter. And the religious should be the last to abandon this – or providing prominent moral examples – as ways of combating wrongdoing. For if something is genuinely wrong by divinely grounded standards, one would expect people to be capable – at least with help from those who realize this – of seeing the point themselves. It may be, of course, that God has reasons for not making certain truths evident to all. That, too, bears reflection and should contribute to humility on all sides.

It must not be assumed, however, that in moral matters a religiously privileged status is needed to discern what God requires. That view is rejected by Thomas Aquinas and much of the natural law tradition. As argued in Chapter 5, moreover, on the assumption that God is omniscient and omnibenevolent, any cogent argument, including an utterly non-religious one, for a moral principle *is* in effect a good argument for God's knowing that conclusion. It can thus serve as a good argument for our urging or requiring conformity to it. Indeed, I have argued that it is reasonable to think that God should be expected to have brought it about that there *are* non-theological ways of discerning moral standards, since otherwise people who already suffer the great loss of failing to believe in God would in addition be unable on their own to discover proper standards even for their secular lives. These and related considerations from philosophical theology support my thesis (in Chapter 5) that ideally, religious citizens should try to achieve theo-ethical equilibrium.

It is possible, to be sure, that a person who believes, on authority or through religious experience or from a reading of scripture, that God commands or prohibits a certain kind of action, has no understanding of why this kind of action should be divinely commanded or prohibited. This might hold for persons of little education, particularly on matters where the available arguments, if there are any, are difficult to grasp. The principles of secular rationale and secular motivation do not deny such a person a right to act nonviolently, even publicly, in favor of the commanded conduct, but this acknowledgment must be balanced by two points. First (as noted in Chapter 6), we can act wrongly – *countervirtuously,* one might say – even when we are within our rights; second, the principles also suggest an obligation to seek secular grounds for the policy restricting freedom, and this is not an unduly burdensome requirement. Moreover, if religious authorities are the source of such a person's belief, we may certainly ask that the relevant people, such as clergy, should themselves try to provide a readily intelligible secular rationale if they are promoting public policies that restrict liberty.

This may be assumed to be what clergy would reasonably wish regarding their counterparts among officials of other faiths who promote practices incompatible with their own. The kind of commitment to secular reason that I propose may constrain the use of some of one's own religious arguments, but it can also protect one from coercion or pressure brought by conflicting religious arguments from others.

The rationale and defensive violence principles do not, then, rule out a major role for religious considerations, even in public political advocacy; the principles simply provide a measure of protection against the undue influence of those considerations where they should be constrained. In particular, where moral or religious conviction would lead to violence against those of opposing viewpoints or even to peaceful but coercive legislation, these principles require that one have grounds of a kind that put beyond reasonable doubt the basis on which the violence is to be justified. This is a comment on what counts as adequate reason in interpreting the rationale, motivation, and violence principles, and the standard of adequacy naturally rises as the relevant restrictions of liberty, or the degrees of violence, intensify.

Even if one has adequate grounds for political violence, in a free and democratic society violence should be resorted to only when other avenues of redress have been properly ruled out. If any legal standard permitting violence is to be properly applied to all citizens in a religiously and culturally diverse society, it should be justifiable from an appropriately neutral point of view. The standard should also be one that can be respected from all of the diverse perspectives. However much weight we give religious considerations in determining what range of conduct should be prohibited by law or by other coercive measures, then, there should also be adequate secular standards for appraising laws and coercive policies, and conscientious citizens who would like to support a coercive law or policy have a prima facie obligation to forbear from doing so unless they have evidentially adequate secular reasons.

Nothing said here will settle the question of the morality of abortion or assisted suicide or other complex issues facing contemporary democratic societies. I have not even presumed to suggest appropriate legal restrictions on abortion or other controversial practices. But if the main points of this chapter are sound, we can at least see in fairly detailed outline both that the legal issues need not depend on resolution of the moral issues and on what basis the moral issues may be resolved. Any resolution will doubtless be imperfect and must be subject to critical review. But justice can be best served, and liberty best protected, if we adopt the framework for integrating religious and sociopolitical considerations that is constituted by such standards as the principles of secular rationale and secular motivation.

CONCLUSION: ETHICS, RELIGION, AND DEMOCRACY

In concluding this book I want to start with a short redescription of its task. The overall problem it addresses is how, in a liberal democracy – a free and democratic society – a proper balance may be achieved between church and state and between religious and political considerations. The problem is particularly urgent today, and I hope that this book will help both individuals and institutions to arrive at sound and well-reasoned positions on how they should approach it. I have sought to speak not only to individuals whose interest in politics, religion, or philosophy is mainly intellectual, but also to conscientious activists; and not only to clergy and churches but to educators, journalists, legislators, judges, writers, and others who are in positions of authority or can influence some segment of the life of a free democracy.

Despite the diversity among major religious groups, they tend to share a wide range of specific concerns about the present direction of Western culture. Many believe, for instance, that there is too much violence and indiscriminate sex in the media, especially on television and the Internet; a pervasive self-centeredness that affects the tone of life and, in particular, conduct toward the poor and the unfortunate; a marginalization of religion, and, especially in the United States and other Western nations, of Christianity; an aggressively secular atmosphere in many educational institutions, private as well as public; and far too much permissiveness toward abortion and other forms of killing.[1] I have explored how these and similar concerns should be pursued in liberal democracies characterized by great diversity both in and outside religious communities.

In Chapter 1, I articulate what may be the leading conceptions of the basis of a liberal democracy: instrumentalist, utilitarian, Kantian, virtue-theoretic, communitarian, theological, and intuitionist. I do not defend any one account, or even any integrated combination of accounts, of the basis of liberal democracy, though at various points I have noted reasons for preferring a moral framework over, say, an instrumentalist or a purely religious one. My primary aim is to show that certain sociopolitical ideals are common to all of the plausible accounts of what grounds liberal democracy. Liberty and basic political equality are central among these ideals of free democracy, and some form of separation of church and state is essential to fulfilling the ideals. So is a commitment to rational public discussion and shared, rational decision making concerning laws and public policies. These liberal-democratic ideals provide a rationale for my principles of separation of church and state and, in individual conduct, of the religious and the secular. If the ideals do not constitute an "ultimate" foundation for the principles, they enable us to see why those principles represent reasonable commitments for liberal democracy and how one might frame a moral or other deep grounding for the principles.

Chapter 2 pursues the question of separation of church and state at the institutional level. In broad terms, I argue that government should not interfere with churches (religious institutions) nor churches with government. More specifically, I propose a set of principles for both sets of institutions: the libertarian, equalitarian, and neutrality principles for government, and the principle of ecclesiastical political neutrality for churches. The latter is one among other principles of institutional ethics that I propose; it partly defines a standard of institutional citizenship in a pluralistic democracy. In defending it I assume – what is sometimes not adequately borne in mind in discussions of sociopolitical standards – that institutions are *agents* whose acts are determined by individuals, and they, like individual citizens, should be held to appropriate standards of conduct. All of these institutional principles serve to protect religious and other liberties, particularly the liberties of religious minorities and non-religious citizens. Even a majority religion is likely to benefit from adherence to the principles. If the operation of government is too closely connected to institutional religion, government may dominate religion or vice versa; and even apart from that liability, where clergy become preoccupied with politics, churches may be corrupted from within.

The main task of Chapter 3 is to indicate, in the light of the partial theory of liberal democracy developed in Chapter 1 and of the account of separation of church and state defended in Chapter 2, what kind of basis is required for warranted governmental coercion of citizens in such a society. In exploring this basis I argue that a liberal democracy need not be entirely neutral with respect to secular, as opposed to religious, conceptions of the good and that indeed such neutrality is impossible given the need for compulsory education and for an account of the kinds of harms that warrant restrictions of liberty. Education is essential for liberal democracy: negatively, to prevent the ignorance that paves the way for a manipulated population and a multitude of material evils; positively, as a protection of basic political equality and an essential preparation for the exercise of liberty in autonomous citizenship. Liberty cannot be unrestricted, and democratic societies need an account of the conditions that warrant its limitation; this requires countenancing both a variety of harms and, at least by implication, the positive values that are served by any good plan for their systematic avoidance.

By way of indicating a basis for limitations of freedom in a liberal democracy, Chapter 3 also suggests a surrogacy model of justified coercion as both plausible in itself and perhaps the only good basis for justifying restrictions of liberty, a basis that rational citizens need not resent. This model depends on moral notions and is, in that limited sense, not entirely neutral with respect to conceptions of the good, but it does not presuppose any particular ethical theory or any value that cannot be presumed to be shared by citizens who are fully rational and adequately informed about the basis of the coercive measure in question. I argue, moreover, that the kinds of governmental restrictions of liberty that are acceptable in liberal democracies must be justified by secular reasons, even if there are good religiously based arguments toward the same end. This does not imply that religious arguments have no role in governing such a society; it is rather a constraint on their proper use. To clarify that use, I indicate the diversity of religious arguments. These must be viewed in relation not only to their content but also to their evidential, motivational, and historical bases, and I describe a number of their uses. The account of restrictions of governmental coercion and the related account of the kinds and uses of religious arguments paves the way for the individual separation principles developed and applied in the remaining chapters.

In Chapter 4, I seek to show how the same kind of basis of liberal democracy that restricts governmental coercion and supports institutional separation of church and state is also crucial for a different kind of separation principle: the kind governing the sorts of reasons conscientious citizens may use in guiding their political conduct, especially their actions affecting those with differing religious outlooks. The principle of secular rationale, the most important of the set, says that for a wide range of their political conduct (though not all of it), citizens have a prima facie obligation to have, and to be willing to offer, an (evidentially) adequate secular reason. This applies to advocacy and not to free expression; it is directed particularly to advocacy or support of laws or public policies that would restrict the liberty of others.

A major ground for the principle of secular rationale is that adequate secular reasons (though by no means intrinsically better than religious ones) tend to be acceptable to people of differing religious convictions, and a commitment to having them as a basis for coercion tends to reduce the chance that a majority representing one religion or denomination will abridge the rights – including the religious liberties – of another religion or denomination. Such reasons at least can be acceptable to rational persons who are adequately informed by relevant facts; and it seems to be only when reasons of this kind justify coercive legislation that it cannot be reasonably resented by citizens as such, considered apart from their special religious or personal commitments.

Just as a democratic state should have adequate secular reason for, say, forcing people to fight wars, individual citizens who want policies that, for instance, compel biology teachers to include creationism in their courses should have adequate secular reason, such as the explanatory plausibility of creationism, for supporting those policies. These considerations also lead to the principle of secular motivation, which adds to the rationale principle that, in the same range of cases, citizens should be sufficiently motivated by adequate secular reason and should not coerce others unless their motivation meets this standard. This motivation principle expresses a requirement of civic virtue. In explaining and applying these principles, I indicate what counts as a secular reason, why religious considerations, as opposed, say, to selfish or economic or aesthetic influences, are of special concern, and how the principles may be followed by religious citizens without unduly burdening their practice of their religion.

Chapter 5 introduces the notion of theo-ethical equilibrium: a kind of integration between a religious outlook and secularly grounded moral or political principles, the kind of integration that results from getting these several elements in reflective equilibrium. Appealing to some widely accepted elements in – but by no means limited to – the theologies of Western religions, particularly Christianity, Judaism, and Islam, I argue both that there is reason to expect such equilibrium to be achievable regarding major sociopolitical principles and, secondly, that in a free democracy conscientious religious citizens should try to achieve this equilibrium in their outlook and attitudes toward laws and public policies – especially the coercive ones – which they support. This first point seems most clearly applicable to Thomas Aquinas and the natural law tradition, but I think the point also holds for other theological traditions.

I also provide (in Chapter 5) some reason to think that for many of the sociopolitical principles needed for harmonious life in a pluralistic democracy, theo-ethical equilibrium should be expected and can be achieved (at least in many biblical traditions); and further, that some of the most divisive ideas – historically as well as in the current climate – are ideas that apparently cannot be brought into this equilibrium. This resistance to assimilation into such an equilibrium does not entail error, but it is often a good reason to suspect error or other serious inadequacy. No formula can determine where adjustments should be made if theo-ethical equilibrium cannot be reached. Reasonable adjustments may lie on the secular as well as on the religious side. But there is reason to hope that conscientious religious citizens and clergy alike can in the end better achieve their ideals in both domains by seeking to integrate the two sets of considerations in the ways I have described.

The primary task of Chapter 6 is to set out an account of civic virtue as an ideal for citizenship. I connect the ideal with the various plausible foundations of liberalism described in Chapter 1 and then proceed to argue that civic virtue in a pluralistic democracy is partly constituted by internalization of the kinds of principles of separation of church and state and of religion and politics defended in Chapters 2 to 4. I also argue that civic virtue is not just a matter of what we do and say, but also of how and why we do it and say it. In our public political conduct, we have a civic voice, and it takes its character from what motivates us more than from the content of what we say. The effect of what we say, moreover, often depends on our perceived voice in saying it.

Civic virtue calls on us, particularly in advocacy of laws or policies that restrict liberty, to seek premises that appeal to people of all kinds – religious and non-religious, political and non-political, activists and sideliners. When we find such premises and are sufficiently motivated by them, we are on the way to fulfilling one ideal of civic virtue: we are at least likely to have an appropriate voice, and if our premises include evidentially adequate secular reason for the position we support, we can also justify that position in terms that do not depend on sectarian positions. Doing this does not, however, prevent us from bringing religious considerations into public discourse in many ways. Indeed, a commitment to my principles can give one greater freedom to invoke religious considerations in an appropriate way and to express them, at least some of the time, with a civic voice. The principles require neither that religion be "privatized" nor that religious adherents of them must split themselves into secular and religious personae. They require a balance that can generally be achieved by conscientious citizens and is an important element in civic virtue.

Chapter 7 brings the theory developed in the book to bear on the deeply troubling issue of abortion and other such issues, for instance assisted suicide. I propose no stand on the moral or the proper legal status of abortion or assisted suicide. Instead, I argue that my overall position on separation of church and state provides a distinctive basis on which a free society can progress without undue strife even when there are irreconcilable religious differences among its citizens on this and other profound issues. If we are guided by appropriate ideals of civic virtue, we can at least agree on a framework in which civilized disagreement is to take place and on the kinds of reasons that must support a view before it can properly acquire coercive power. To be sure, there is a right, in a liberal democracy, to vote on virtually any basis one conscientiously adheres to; but there are exercises of that right which conscientious citizens ought to avoid. My concern is with the best standards we can hope to bring to its exercise, and I have tried to set forth a framework for discussion that maximizes the chance that in free and democratic societies education and persuasion can replace coercion where improper conduct cannot be legally prohibited.

In viewing this book as a whole, it might be natural to regard it as taking reason, in a form implying commitment to certain basic moral standards, as our only resource for reconciling the constraints of citizenship in a liberal democracy with the freedom of religion that is a deep commitment of such a society. This is not quite accurate. For one thing, we might take a non-moral, instrumentalist view and arrive at the kinds of principles I defend, not as I do, but by proceeding through instrumentally rational but morally neutral considerations based on our shared desires to live in some kind of harmony. This would be a pragmatic route to the principles. We might also proceed from certain theological assumptions about the purpose of government and the appropriate structure of a just state. This would be a religious route to the principles. If, however, the principles can be grounded by non-moral reason or by a theology taken to be more basic than moral standards, they can also be grounded – and I think are best grounded – from a moral perspective, such as a Kantian or intuitionist position or some integration of diverse moral standards.[2]

This is not in the least to suggest that sound ethical standards may not themselves be derivable from more general rational considerations. The point is that defending the principles set out in this book does not depend on such a derivation, either of the principles themselves or of any moral or theological view that can ground them directly. I leave open that there may be a highly plausible comprehensive theory of rationality that has such results, but my main points in this book do not depend on it.[3]

If I have seemed to trust reason too much, as against faith and intuition and tradition – different people will have different favorites here – I would reject the contrast as misleading. Reason without intuition is at best too formal to guide everyday life; faith requires reason to interpret its objects and human life in general; and the traditions most worthy of our attention surely reflect reason in major ways or at least depend on it for their interpretation. In any case, as argued in Chapter 5 in criticizing the idea that reason is corrupt, I do not see how we can proceed in moral, political, and even religious matters without trusting reason to a high degree. If, as I believe, we may trust it, this is in part because at its best reason can be used in self-correction, because it does not license self-pride, and because it must be recognized as embodied as much in others as in oneself.

A liberal view may be criticized not only as too sanguine about reason, but as too individualist. I grant that I have been individualist in taking the flourishing of individual human beings as the single most important proper concern of government. Here, I think, ethics and at least much of the world's religious tradition are at one. The differences among religious traditions over what constitutes flourishing are certainly important, but there is also substantial overlap, as is apparent in their almost universal concern with relieving poverty and disease and their common endorsement of some version of at least much of the ethical content of the Ten Commandments. This surely holds for Christianity, Judaism, and Islam. Neither in liberal politics nor in that rich array of religious traditions may individuals be treated as mere means to the welfare of the State or the Community or even Others taken in the abstract. I doubt that anyone will reflectively reject this kind of priority of the individual in judging the success of government.[4]

It is in part because individuals are non-negotiably important in a free democracy that I have been so concerned with the proper basis of coercion in such a society. My framework of separation principles is meant to preserve the liberty and dignity of individuals and to do so with minimal burdens on those the principles constrain. Citizens who feel constrained by the principles or, more loosely, by the related demands of civic virtue, should never forget the power of example and persuasion. What cannot or should not be achieved by coercion may well be possible by powerful example and persuasive discourse. And in the religious, for whom God's knowledge of the heart is more important than our sheer behavioral record in changing the world, this is doubly important. If we do our best within the limits that we cannot escape, then morally – and perhaps religiously in some deep sense – we are in good standing. And if some of those limits are required by respect for religious liberty, then for many theologies there is much reason to think we are also doing what is religiously right. I hope that my framework of standards of civic virtue will help in making us wiser and better in both domains. I am confident that there need not be any ultimate incompatibility between religious commitment and secular reason.

NOTES

1. The Plurality of Paths to Liberal Democracy

1. Immanuel Kant, "Perpetual Peace," in *Perpetual Peace and Other Essays,* trans. Ted Humphrey (Indianapolis: Hackett, 1983), p. 133.
2. This tension within liberal democracy has sometimes been associated with a contrast between the English democratic tradition, emphasizing liberty, and the French democratic tradition, emphasizing equality. For discussion of the origin and extent of this difference, see George Sabine, "The Two Democratic Traditions," *Philosophical Review* 61 (1952). John Rawls's *A Theory of Justice* (Cambridge, MA: Harvard University Press, 1971) may be seen as in part an attempt to reconcile these two elements – the libertarian and equalitarian – in the foundations of democracy. For related discussion of aspects of the history of liberal-democratic theory see Charles L. Griswold, Jr., *Adam Smith and the Virtues of Enlightenment* (Cambridge University Press, 1999), esp. Ch. 7.
3. For a characterization and defense of a minimal state, see Robert Nozick, *Anarchy, State, and Utopia* (New York: Basic Books, 1974). A contrasting conception of the foundations of democracy (one extensively criticized by Nozick) is found in Rawls, *Theory of Justice.* For detailed discussion of the workings of democracy conceived along non-minimalist, Rawlsian lines see Amy Gutmann and Dennis Thompson, *Democracy and Disagreement* (Cambridge, MA: Harvard University Press, 1996); and for some difficulties confronting such a democracy that are particularly relevant to this book, see Fred D'Agostino, *Free Public Reason* (Oxford: Oxford University Press, 1996).
4. Autonomy and freedom are both elusive and complex notions that cannot be explicated in detail here. I have offered accounts of them, respectively, with many references to relevant literature, in "Autonomy, Reason, and Desire," in my *Moral Knowledge and Ethical Character* (Oxford: Oxford University Press, 1997), and in Chs. 7 and 10 of *Action, Intention, and Reason* (Ithaca: Cornell University Press, 1993).
5. For detailed discussion of proceduralist versus constitutional conceptions see Gutmann and Thompson, *Democracy and Disagreement.*

6. The books cited above by Rawls, D'Agostino, and Gutmann and Thompson are among the multitude of works that cover some of this ground in ways relevant to this book. See also Thomas Nagel, *Equality and Partiality* (Oxford: Oxford University Press, 1991); John Rawls, *Political Liberalism* (New York: Columbia University Press, 1993), and Gerald F. Gaus, *Justificatory Liberalism* (Oxford: Oxford University Press, 1996).
7. Both rationality and freedom admit of degrees, and there is no need to try to specify an exact degree here; but with the former it should be made explicit that we are not talking about merely rational beings but about people who have at least the reasoning capacity of normal adults with a good high school education. A case for democracy should be intelligible to people of this sort even if they cannot be expected to make the case themselves and even if the case has more force for those with more education and a greater capacity to reason.
8. For a discussion of problems facing standard accounts of political obligation see A. John Simmons, *Moral Principles and Political Obligation* (Ithaca: Cornell University Press, 1979).
9. One could delete this clause on the ground that there is no morally neutral way to specify what counts as an available alternative; in that case failures to maximize due to overlooking an alternative may always yield objectively wrong action, but may or may not deserve disapproval, depending on one's theory of *excuses*. One other interpretive point is appropriate here: a case can be made that Mill is best read as a rule-utilitarian, but I leave this aside, partly on the ground that one can take the formulation in the text as basic and still hold that the good is best promoted by people's *internalizing* not the formulation itself but a set of standards of the sort a rule-utilitarian would take to be basic.
10. J. S. Mill, "Representative Government," in *Utilitarianism, Liberty, and Representative Government*, ed. A. D. Lindsay (New York: Dutton, 1951), p. 262.
11. It might be noted that the material success of many liberal democracies could be largely due to their capitalism. If that is so, it might still be argued that capitalism itself does not thrive apart from liberal democracy (a point consistent with arguing that the former poses some threats to the latter).
12. The priority of the worse off figures in Rawls's conception of justice in *Theory of Justice;* and Bernard Gert, in *Morality – Its Nature and Justification* (Oxford: Oxford University Press, 1998), stresses the greater importance, in the content of basic moral standards in general, of evil as opposed to good. One of the defects of utilitarianism, according to Rawls, is that despite its association with liberty of action and thought "utilitarianism is not individualistic . . . in that, by conflating all systems of desire, it applies to society the principle of choice for one" (*Theory of Justice*, p. 29). Among the proponents of utilitarianism who have defended the view in detail in the light of the kinds of criticisms Rawls and others have brought against it is Robert E. Goodin. See his *Utilitarianism as a Public Philosophy* (Cambridge University Press, 1995).

13. Rawls's difference principle in a *Theory of Justice* can be conceived as taking (or well fitted to take) suffering more seriously than happiness.
14. David Hume, *A Treatise of Human Nature* (Oxford: Clarendon Press, 1888), p. 415.
15. Ibid., pp. 483–4 (italics in original).
16. See a *Theory of Justice*, esp. sect. 25, for Rawls's statement of the conception of rationality he is using. His point that rational persons do not suffer from envy is not (as I note later in the text) instrumentalist (since envy might be a basic "passion" in some people).
17. See *A Theory of Justice*, p. 60, for the two principles. I use an early formulation since the complexities of the final one (pp. 302–3) are not relevant here. I cannot take time to consider any of the vast literature on the interpretation and justification of these principles, but it is obvious that they raise myriad questions.
18. See Rawls, *Theory of Justice*, pp. 143–4, where envy is discussed.
19. Rawls's political liberalism overall is, however, controversial, even conceived (in the way he prefers) as political and not metaphysical. See, e.g., *Pacific Philosophical Quarterly* 75, 3–4 (1994), a double issue on his *Political Liberalism*. Jean Hampton's "The Common Faith of Liberalism" (pp. 186–216 of this issue) is a notable challenge to Rawls's claim to have freed his liberalism of certain presuppositions of Enlightenment liberalism. Also relevant to this point is David Estlund, "The Insularity of the Reasonable: Why Political Liberalism Must Admit the Truth," *Ethics* 108, 2 (1998), pp. 252–75, which makes a plausible case for the view that a liberal theory must consider its basic principle true, not just reasonably acceptable. This paper also discusses in some detail another view relevant here, Joseph Raz's in "Facing Diversity: The Case of Epistemic Abstinence," *Philosophy & Public Affairs* 19 (1990), pp. 3–46. In this book I do not discuss the overall epistemological commitments of liberal democracy, but it will be clear that I see no bar to its presupposing certain normative truths.
20. Rawls, *Theory of Justice*, p. 62.
21. See the *Groundwork* on the character of good will and for Kant's view of the intrinsic end formulation.
22. Kant, *Groundwork*, sec. 433.
23. Ibid., sec. 429.
24. Among the major proponents of the centrality of rights in liberal democracy is Ronald Dworkin. See esp. his seminal work, *Taking Rights Seriously* (Cambridge, MA: Harvard University Press, 1977).
25. See the *Groundwork*, sec. 422 for the suicide example. To be fair, Kant was not considering (and did not there seem aware of) cases in which one might have a military obligation to commit suicide lest an enemy extract deadly information, nor even a case in which one's life has already been artificially prolonged and one is being threatened with further interventions.
26. See, e.g., G. E. M. Anscombe, "Modern Moral Philosophy," an influential essay originally published in *Philosophy* (1958) and reprinted in Roger Crisp

and Michael Slote, eds., *Virtue Ethics* (Oxford: Oxford University Press, 1997); Philippa Foot, *Virtues and Vices* (Oxford: Oxford University Press, 1997); and Alasdair MacIntyre, *After Virtue* (Notre Dame: University of Notre Dame Press, 1981 and 1984), and *Whose Justice? Which Rationality?* (Notre Dame: University of Notre Dame Press, 1988). The collection by Crisp and Slote contains valuable discussion by them as well as a wide range of recent papers.

27. The translation is by F. M. Cornford (Oxford: Oxford University Press, 1941). Comparing the passages quoted here and below with their counterparts in the translation by G. M. A. Grube does not appear to make a significant difference for the points I am making.
28. *Nicomachean Ethics* 1094b (trans. Terence Irwin).
29. For discussion of this issue and references to relevant literature, see my "Acting from Virtue," in my *Moral Knowledge.*
30. Alasdair MacIntyre has emphasized the lack of moral agreement in contemporary society and the importance of communities in overcoming fragmentation. See his *After Virtue* (1984).
31. Michael Sandel expresses what seems a version of the strong view when he says, "For a society to be a community in this strong sense [in which 'community' describes "its basic structure"], community must be constitutive of the shared self-understandings of the participants and embodied in their institutional arrangements, not simply an attribute of certain participants' plans of life." See *Liberalism and the Limits of Justice* (Cambridge University Press, 1982), p. 173. For revisions of his view and other valuable discussion relevant to communitarian ideals and democracy see the second edition of this book (Cambridge University Press, 1998).
32. See Aquinas, *Summa theologica,* Question 90, "Of the Essence of Law," Article 2.
33. John Haldane, e.g., says, "Although the notion of the right Rawls seeks is a commonly shared one, he conspicuously eschews any theory of the common good." See "The Individual, the State, and the Common Good," in Ellen Frankel Paul, Fred D. Miller, Jr., and Jeffrey Paul, eds., *The Communitarian Challenge to Liberalism* (Cambridge University Press, 1996), p. 69. This essay develops a concept of community as in part a "fellowship" constituted by an agreement about the common good. However, Haldane shares with many liberals the view that we cannot expect to form a contemporary society in which all citizens have the same political orientation and concedes that "we are all liberals now, or should be; and the acknowledgement of this presents a challenge to advocates of . . . comprehensive doctrines to show how they can endorse commonly held liberal values. Secular perfectionists like Joseph Raz do so by arguing that personal political freedom is an aspect of the good life . . . and something similar is being developed by American Catholic writers influenced by the likes of Maritain and [John Courtney] Murray" (p. 79). A related critique of liberal society has been given by G. H. von Wright; for a brief account of it see Mikko Salmela, "G. H. von Wright's Critique of Liberal Society," in Sirkku

Hellsten, Marjaana Koperi, and Olli Loukela, eds., *Taking the Liberal Challenge Seriously* (Aldershott, England: Ashgate, 1997).

34. For helpful discussion of communitarianism and relevant commentary on selected major literature, see Jean Hampton, *Political Philosophy* (Boulder: Westview Press, 1998), esp. Ch. 5.
35. Thomas Aquinas's *Treatise on Law* is a widely known example.
36. For detailed discussion of fundamentalism as pertinent to this book, see Daniel O. Conkle, "Secular Fundamentalism, Religious Fundamentalism, and the Search for Truth in Contemporary America," *Journal of Law and Religion* 12, 2 (1995–6).
37. See W. D. Ross, *The Right and the Good* (Oxford: Oxford University Press, 1930), p. 21.
38. I explicate this sense in "Moderate Intuitionism and the Epistemology of Moral Judgment," *Ethical Theory and Moral Practice* 1, 1 (1998).
39. Ross appeals to practical wisdom here and argues (Ch. 2) that no alternative theory, such as utilitarianism or Kantianism, is in a position to do better.
40. I have argued for this in "Moderate Intuitionism."
41. This last project I attempt in outline in Ch. 12 of *Moral Knowledge.*
42. Indeed, Ross called Kant an intuitionist. See W. D. Ross, *Foundations of Ethics* (Oxford: Oxford University Press, 1939), p. 189.
43. *On Liberty,* Introductory Chapter. Mill adds that he takes this principle to be defensible on the basis of considerations of utility; that is a controversial view that we need not assess, but from the treatment of utilitarianism above (and from other elements in this and later chapters) one can see some of the resources Mill might use.
44. There are exceptions concerning public health as well, but these are likely to be appealing at least if one thinks of them as preventing others' religious practices from harming one. The prohibition of peyote in certain Native American rituals is an interesting case here. It is significant that in the end religious freedom prevailed.

2. The Separation of Church and State

1. For one kind of minimalist view – a neutrality conception – see Charles E. Larmore, *Patterns of Moral Complexity* (Cambridge University Press, 1987). My neutrality condition is less demanding than his.
2. In describing and supporting these three principles, I draw on – and in places greatly abbreviate – a section of my "The Separation of Church and State and the Obligations of Citizenship," *Philosophy & Public Affairs* 18, 3 (1989), pp. 259–96.
3. Great Britain is an interesting case here, and it surely shows that some degree of establishment is compatible with a high (though by no means maximal) degree of liberal democracy. There are many kinds and degrees of establishment, but detailing them would take more space than I have here. It is noteworthy in this context that "In 1988, when British Muslims peti-

tioned their government to ban Salmon Rushdie's *Satanic Verses,* they discovered that the existing blasphemy law did not prohibit insults to the Prophet Muhammad. It protected only Christianity." See Peter van der Veer and Hartmut Lehmann, "The Moral State: Religion, Nation, and Empire in Victorian Britain and British India," in their *Nation and Religion: Perspectives on Europe and Asia* (Princeton: Princeton University Press, 1999), p. 15.

4. This restriction does not rule out teaching children moral principles that are commonly part of one or more religious traditions – a point that is not always appreciated, sometimes with the unfortunate effect that schoolteachers are reluctant to teach moral principles.
5. Douglas Laycock puts very well some of the founders' motivation for the First Amendment to the U.S. Constitution. Pointing out that they noted how (1) governmental attempts to suppress religion had caused vast suffering in Europe and England, that (2) religious beliefs are often extraordinarily important to individuals, and that (3) beliefs "at the heart of religion – beliefs about theology, liturgy, and church governance – are of little importance to civil government," he says that "these three propositions argue for separating the coercive power of government from all questions of religion, so that *no religion can invoke government's coercive power and no government can coerce any religious act or belief.*" See "Religious Liberty as Liberty," *Journal of Contemporary Legal Issues* 7 (1996), pp. 317–19 (italics added).
6. These features are stressed by William P. Alston in *Philosophy of Language* (Englewood Cliffs, NJ: Prentice-Hall, 1964), p. 88, where 'religion' is cited as exemplifying "combination of conditions vagueness" (I have abbreviated and slightly revised his list). This characterization does not entail that a religion must be theistic, but theistic religions are my main concern (even in non-theistic religions, the relevant moral code tends to be given a somewhat similar privileged status in relation to appropriate items on this list, such as the world view, the sacred and profane, and certain rituals, such as marriage). It is noteworthy that in *United States v Seeger* 380 US 163 (1965) the Supreme Court ruled that religious belief need not be theistic; but, for reasons that will become increasingly apparent in this chapter and the next, theistic religions raise the most important church-state issues at least for societies like those in the Western world. For discussion of the significance of *Seeger* in relation to church-state aspects of the foundations of liberalism see Abner S. Greene, "Uncommon Ground," a review essay on John Rawls's *Political Liberalism* and on Ronald Dworkin's *Life's Dominion,* in *George Washington Law Review* 62, 4 (1994), pp. 646–73.
7. For discussion of the extent to which justice should accommodate natural inequalities, see Thomas Nagel, "Nature and Justice," presented at Oxford University as the H. L. A. Hart lecture in 1996.
8. Nicholas Wolterstorff defends the weaker standard of neutrality as sufficient for liberal democracy in "The Role of Religion in Decision and Discussion of Political Issues," in Robert Audi and Nicholas Wolterstorff, *Religion in the Public Square: The Place of Religious Convictions in Political Debate*

(Lanham, MD: Rowman and Littlefield, 1997). I reply in part to his case in "Wolterstorff on Religion, Politics, and the Liberal State," ibid.

9. Conscientious objector status is debatable. Is allowing it only for religious reasons inadmissible preferential treatment, or is it required in recognition of religious freedom? Even if the latter holds, it is arguable that freedom of religion is being unwarrantedly preferred over freedom of secular conscience. For discussion of the nature of governmental neutrality and a case for it as essential in a liberal democracy see Larmore's *Patterns of Moral Complexity*, esp. Ch. 3. A different case for governmental neutrality, with a partial account of the liberal basis of impartiality toward religion, is given by Thomas Nagel in "Moral Conflict and Political Legitimacy," *Philosophy & Public Affairs* 16, 3 (1987), pp. 215–40.
10. On the constitutionality of public institutions' having or requiring the Pledge, with discussion of the church-state implications of the issue, see Abner S. Greene, "The Pledge of Allegiance Problem," *Fordham Law Review* 64, 2 (1995), pp. 451–90.
11. The Declaration of Principles of the Seventh-Day Adventist Church seems to reflect a similar concern about religious domination by a majority and is in any case both neutralist and strongly separationist. It reads, in part, "Religious liberty entails freedom of conscience: to worship *or not to worship* . . . in exercising these rights, however, one must respect the equivalent rights of others . . . Attempts to unite church and state are opposed to the interests of each, *subversive of human rights and potentially persecuting* . . ." Quoted in *Liberty* 94, 2 (1999), a bimonthly magazine of the Church's North American branch, p. 3 (italics added).
12. It might be argued that, as William P. Marshall suggests, religion is a mode of ideology and indeed religion and non-religious ideologies are "functionally equivalent"; but I take it that particularly where an ideology is avowedly anti-religious, the sociopolitical doctrines that mark it do not make it a religion even when it is comprehensive in its applications to human life. See his "Why Not Equality?" *Indiana Law Journal* 75 (2000).
13. The language of this sentence will remind some readers of the much-discussed "Lemon test" for the propriety of legislation: "First, the statute must have a secular legislative purpose; second, its principal or primary effect must be one that neither advances nor inhibits religion; finally, the statute must not foster 'an excessive entanglement with religion.'" See *Lemon v Kurtzmann* 403 US 602 (1971). The first two clauses are deservedly controversial. This book addresses some of the relevant issues, such as a possible voucher system for public education, in less vague terms (though some vagueness is inevitable on such matters). For an indication of how difficult avoidance of entanglement can be, with special application to enforcement of kosher laws and orthodox Jewish divorce law, see Kent Greenawalt, "Religious Law and Civil Law: Using Secular Law to Assure Observance of Practices with Religious Significance," *Southern California Law Review* 71, 4 (1998), pp. 781–847.
14. The governmental neutrality described here has certain costs. As Daniel O.

Conkle brings out, neutrality "carries substantial risks for religious liberty . . . it limits the practice of religiously motivated conduct." The free exercise of religion may, e.g., require rituals which, like use of peyote by a certain Indian tribe, are illegal or may dictate hiring preferences considered discriminatory; and in order to treat the religious no better than other citizens, government may impose restrictions that in the end are unwarranted. See "The Path of American Religious Liberty: From the Original Theology to Formal Neutrality and an Uncertain Future," *Indiana Law Journal* 75 (2000).

15. The notion of institutional citizenship needs explication, but I think it is significantly analogous to individual citizenship, though unlike an individual citizen a church has its own citizens – indeed, citizens forming a *community* rather than a mere group. There is a challenge here which the notion of institutional citizenship can meet only in part: according to Gerald Frug, as interpreted by Jean Bethke Elshtain, "American liberal thought and practice have no robust way to thematize entities intermediate between the state and the individual." See Jean Bethke Elshtain, "Catholic Social Thought, the City, and Liberal America," in Kenneth L. Grasso, Gerard V. Bradley, and Robert P. Hunt, eds., *Catholicism, Liberalism, and Communitarianism* (Lanham, MD: Rowman and Littlefield, 1995), p. 109, and, for an indication of Elshtain's own perspective, pp. 111–12. A number of the essays in this volume also bear on the problem. Christopher Wolfe's "Subsidiarity: The 'Other' Ground of Limited Government" and Michelle Watkins and Ralph McInerny's "Jacques Maritain and the Rapprochement of Liberalism and Communitarianism" may be especially pertinent to the problem and to this chapter in general.
16. Nothing less than the holism-individualism issue lurks here, the problem of whether wholes such as social groups are more than the individuals composing them and their interrelations. For our purposes an individualistic reading of the principle is best, but the normative issues could be similarly treated if one plausibly formulated the principle as applying directly to institutions as such.
17. If the obligation is moral, it is presumably not contingent on churches' being committed to good institutional citizenship: that commitment itself would presumably be a prima facie institutional moral obligation. Moreover, at least if the obligation is moral I would take its prima facie character to imply not just that there is a reason for the conduct in question and that when that reason is overridden there should be an appropriate explanation, say in terms of one relevant value's outweighing another in the context, as illustrated by the case in which resisting tyranny justifies direct political action by a church.
18. I exclude those laws and policies essential for the existence of civil society of any kind, say the prohibitions of murder, rape, and theft. Details of these laws, say of the schedule of punishments, may be political issues in the relevant narrow sense, but the need for such laws is not an issue in that sense.

19. The constraints proposed here, though strong, are not rigid and are compatible with Michael Perry's thesis that "religiously based moral arguments" be presented in political debate in order to test them in that context. See, e.g., "Liberal Democracy and Religious Morality" (forthcoming). It is important that the kind of argument in question is *moral,* and it is essential to take account of the kind of political debate in question.
20. Stephen Carter nicely expresses part of my point: of a young minister he heard preaching in detail about El Salvador, he says, "For her, politics should lead faith, rather than the other way around – a proposition that is by no means the special reserve of the left. Her sermon, like many that were preached in support of Ronald Reagan's presidential candidacy, exemplified the problem of the political tail wagging the scriptural dog." *The Culture of Disbelief* (New York: Anchor Books, 1994), p. 69. I differ with Carter, however, on how religious motivation should enter politics: the religious dog should be joined by a secular dog, sufficient for the task even if less important to the citizen and less vociferous than its religious companion. Given what in Chapter 4 I call theo-ethical equilibrium, the two will pull together.
21. For valuable discussion of the general problem here see David Hollenbach, S.J., "The Political Role of Religion: Civil Society and Culture," *San Diego Law Review* 30, 4 (1993), pp. 877–901. At one point he says,

    > [S]ome fundamentalist Christians draw policy conclusions about the rights of homosexuals or about prayer in the public schools directly from the *Bible* . . . Some more conservative Catholics regard the legal banning of abortion as similarly entailed by the moral teachings of the pope and the Catholic bishops. From what has been said above about the need for believers to enter into dialogue with others in society as they develop their vision of the larger meaning of the social good and its consequences for policy, it is evident that I do not accept this understanding of the relation between religious belief and policy conclusions as immediate and direct. Roman Catholic thought, like much Protestant thought as well, maintains that religious belief must be complemented by the careful use of human reasoning, both philosophical and social-scientific, in the effort to reach decisions about policy that are both religiously and humanly adequate. (p. 898)

22. It is noteworthy to what extent some churches have articulated standards consistent with the principle of ecclesiastical political neutrality. See, e.g., *Political Responsibility: Proclaiming the Gospel of Life, Protecting the Least Among Us, and Pursuing the Common Good* (Washington, DC: U.S. Catholic Conference, 1995). A fundamental point is that "A key to a renewal of public life is reorienting politics to reflect better the search for the common good (i.e., reconciling diverse interests for the whole human family) and a clear commitment to the dignity of every person" (p. 3).

23. Essentially this objection has been posed by Paul Weithman, and in responding to it I draw on my "Religious Commitment and Secular Reason: A Reply to Professor Weithman," *Philosophy & Public Affairs* 20, 1 (1991), pp. 66–76. For a more detailed statement of his view see his "Taking Rites Seriously," *Pacific Philosophical Quarterly* 73, 3–4 (1994), pp. 272–94.
24. For discussion of the Burger Court's treatment of the prayer issue up to 1984, see Leo Pfeffer, *Religion, State, and the Burger Court* (Buffalo: Prometheus Books, 1984), esp. Ch. 3. For a useful recent survey see David M. Ackerman, "Church and State in the Supreme Court: The Non-Revolution of the '80s," *Federal Bar News and Journal* 33, 7 (1986).
25. That the establishment clause can be violated by non-compulsory activity seems to have been recognized in a number of Supreme Court decisions. In *Illinois ex rel. McCollum* 333 US 203 (1948), e.g., Justice Black, writing for the majority, said of a program of (voluntary) released time for religious education,

    > This is beyond all question a utilization of the tax-established and tax-supported public school system to aid religious groups to spread their faith. And it falls squarely under the ban of the First Amendment (made applicable to the states by the Fourteenth) as we interpreted it in Everson v. Board of Education [330 US 1, 1937]. There we said: "Neither a state nor the Federal Government can set up a church. Neither can pass laws which aid one religion, *aid all religions*, or prefer one religion over another . . . No person can be punished for entertaining or professing religious beliefs *or disbeliefs*, for church attendance or nonattendance . . . (italics added)

    There is, however, a quite different body of opinion on non-establishment. Michael J. Perry, e.g., says (approvingly) that "in the United States, government is free to affirm – but only noncoercively – the belief that there is a God,who created us and both loves us and judges us, and the belief that because God created us and loves us, we are sacred (inviolable)." See "Freedom of Religion in the United States: *Fin de Siècle* Sketches," *Indiana Law Journal* 75 (2000).
26. For a detailed treatment of government aid to sectarian schools in the United States with discussion of numerous court cases, see Martha M. McCarthy, "Religion and Education: Whither the Establishment Clause?," *Indiana Law Journal* 75 (2000).
27. I am assuming that a condition of aid would be its educational adequacy. For an interesting recent discussion of the related question of teacher competence in religious schools, see *State of Nebraska ex rel. Paul L. Douglas et al., Appellees, v. Faith Baptist Church of Louisville, Nebraska, A Corporation, et al., Appellants, Nebraska Reports* 207 (January 1981).
28. I have already suggested that the best course may be a multiple-criterion approach like Alston's (in *Philosophy of Language*). For a different defini-

tional discussion see Philip E. Devine, "On the Definition of Religion," *Faith and Philosophy* 3, 3 (1986). While he holds that "A value-free definition of 'religion' is . . . impossible" (p. 271), he also offers two central criteria, which (he maintains) together yield a sufficient condition, and singly yield one depending on non-central factors. One is "doctrinal: a religion affirms the existence of one or more superhuman agents, on whose favor the welfare of human agents depends. . . The second is psychosocial or functional. A religion by the second criterion unifies . . . the framework by which an individual or group regulates its thought and its life . . ." (p. 272). I assume that Christianity, Judaism, and Islam are paradigms of religion and this book should be read with them in mind as examples; there is no need to endorse a specific notion of religion here.

29. On one view, "Civil religion is *a generalized faith that binds together the nation and links the national purpose to a higher or deeper reality* . . . Jimmy Carter, for instance, maintained that his human rights policy was consistent with the U.S. role as moral leader of the world." See Robert D. Holsworth and J. Harry Wray, *American Politics and Everyday Life,* 2d ed. (New York: Macmillan, 1987), p. 141. For critical discussion of civil religion see John T. Noonan, *The Lustre of Our Country: The American Experience of Religious Freedom* (Berkeley: University of California Press, 1998).
30. For a discussion of civil religion in which its kinship, or perhaps implicit commitment, to theism is noted, see Robert Booth Fowler and Allen D. Hertzke, *Religion and Politics in America* (Boulder: Westview, 1995), pp. 243–5. They cite the frequency of "God bless America" in political contexts and Ronald Reagan's use of the Puritan expression 'shining city on the hill' as indications both of the existence of a civil religion and of its being a religion in a fairly rich sense.

3. Church-State Separation and the Justification of Governmental Power

1. John Rawls, "The Idea of Public Reason Revisited," *University of Chicago Law Review* 64 (1997), p. 775.
2. For a plausible defense of this negative conception of morality see Bernard Gert, *Morality* (Oxford: Oxford University Press, 1998); and for some critical discussion of the view (including a case that his theory is not as negative as he makes it sound), see my "Rationality and Reasons in the Moral Philosophy of Bernard Gert," forthcoming.
3. See John Rawls, *A Theory of Justice* (Cambridge, MA: Harvard University Press, 1971).
4. I am of course implicitly rejecting an instrumentalist conception of rational action and of practical reason in general. Detailed arguments to this effect, taking account of qualified versions of that conception, are given in my *A Theory of Rationality,* in progress.
5. For a brief account of the notion of harm and its importance for liberal democracy see Gerald F. Gaus, *Social Philosophy* (Armonk, NY: M. E. Sharpe,

1999), esp. Ch. 8. Here Gaus defends a conception of harm as setting back a person's interest, understood in a way that does not presuppose the person's moral view.

6. These are "(1) the idea of goodness as rationality, (2) the idea of primary goods, (3) the idea of permissible comprehensive conceptions of the good, (4) the idea of political virtues, and (5) the idea of the good of a well-ordered (political) society." See John Rawls, "The Priority of Right and Ideas of the Good," *Philosophy & Public Affairs* 17, 4 (1988), p. 251. For related discussions see Thomas Nagel, *Equality and Partiality* (New York: Oxford University Press, 1991); Michael J. Perry, *Morality, Politics, and Law* (New York: Oxford University Press, 1988); Richard A. Flathman's essays in *Toward a Liberalism* (Ithaca: Cornell University Press, 1989); and Richard W. Miller, *Moral Differences* (Princeton: Princeton University Press, 1992). Perry is a critic of at least Rawlsian liberalism, Flathman a defender of liberalism. For wide-ranging studies of Perry's views quite relevant to this chapter, see Theodore Y. Blumoff, "Disdain for the Lessons of History: Comments on *Love and Power*," *Capital University Law Review*, 20, 1 (1991); and Edward B. Foley's review essay, "Tillich and Camus, Talking Politics," *Columbia Law Review* 92, 4 (1992).
7. The reason must be essentially related because otherwise the agent's hypothetical attitude will not be sufficiently connected with the coercive reason to warrant the coercion. A typical case would be this: where *r* is the state's reason, e.g. to protect other citizens, the related reason would be, say, to fulfill my duty not to harm others. Roughly, if the agent's reason is not *r*, it is something like a first-person version of *r*. It should also be noted that this approach does not imply that *all* moral obligation is discernible by reflection of this kind. It does seem appropriate, however, that the obligations grounding state rights of coercion should be thus discernible; and this is one reason to think that such obligations correspond to rights of citizens. Conditions (a)–(c) might be extensionally equivalent to conditions under which, on T. M. Scanlon's view, no one can "reasonably reject" the provision in question; there is at least an interesting resemblance. See his *What We Owe to Each Other* (Cambridge, MA: Harvard University Press, 1998).
8. I assume here that a *fully* rational person with certain information about others has certain altruistic desires; if rationality is understood more narrowly, my formulation must be revised (unless we may assume, as I do not, that for fully rational persons motivation to do something is entailed simply by a realization that it is one's moral obligation). The basic idea could, however, be largely preserved. I make a case for such desires in *Theory of Rationality.*
9. This is not to deny the possibility of weakness of will or to suggest a motivational internalist view on which self-addressed moral judgments or other self-addressed action-guiding judgments are intrinsically motivating. For an account of motivational internalism and many references to literature on the topic see Ch. 10 of my *Moral Knowledge and Ethical Character* (Oxford: Oxford University Press, 1997).

10. This is so, at least, on the plausible assumption that fully rational persons can see their moral obligations. A further qualification is this: if purely rational considerations would convince a fully rational and adequately informed person to do certain religious deeds, such as worship God and follow certain religious principles as such, they are still not an appropriate basis of coercion in a liberal democracy. This is one reason the condition stated here is only necessary and not sufficient for justified coercion. Similar restrictions would apply to other possible domains in which a liberal society protects one's freedom to decline even what reason, when rightly employed, commends or requires. Morality, I take it, is not such a domain, and some of its principles seem essential to fully justifying liberal democracy itself.
11. See, e.g., John Rawls, *Political Liberalism* (New York: Columbia University Press, 1993). Kent Greenawalt's preferred term (which I also consider preferable), in *Private Consciences and Public Reasons* (Oxford: Oxford University Press, 1995), is 'accessible'. I take up some of the relevant differences below.
12. This suggestion was put to me by David Alan Johnson.
13. Indeed, my position is (as the next two chapters will confirm) compatible with a quite far-reaching use of religious ideas and standards in liberal-democratic politics; e.g., with some version of all of the roles indicated in a wide-ranging essay calling for church involvement in public policy: it should (1) play a vital role in defining the ethical norms basic for public policy, (2) demonstrate the values it urges on government, (3) be a source of "responsible information for individuals," (4) apply ethical norms to real political situations, (5) speak to the tactics of political behavior, and (6) bring a perspective of hope. See Phil D. Stricklund, "The Involvement of the Churches in Community and State Affairs," in *Religion and Politics* (Waco: J. M. Dawson Institute of Church-State Studies, Baylor University, 1983), pp. 92–4.
14. A sociological argument may be religious in content in the sense of having premises attributing religious beliefs to people; but here the attribution itself carries no religious commitment, and so it is not relevant to the notion we need here.
15. If the premise does not warrant the conclusion, it cannot be known to; presumably, in this example religious considerations also could not justify attributing a warranting relation, but that is not quite self-evident. Still, it would not be expected in a case like this, where the premise is largely irrelevant to the conclusion.
16. Here is a different example. Imagine an island society's discovering, on the beach, the inscription "Circumcise!" Someone might argue: This writing cannot be an accident; hence we should (prima facie) practice circumcision. Now arguably this conclusion cannot be known or justifiedly believed on ethical or medical grounds (at least for an adequately hygienic society); if it can be, it would perhaps be on grounds of just the sort of authority which only a deity could have. One might reply that the argument is en-

thymematic and has a suppressed religious premise, in which case it is religious in *content;* but to insist on that seems to me to import the likeliest *defense* of the argument into its content. One obvious candidate for a presupposed defense is something like this: we ought (prima facie) to heed a directive non-accidentally found in nature. That, in turn, might be argued to be plausible only on theological grounds.

17. For a detailed philosophical account of a notion of proper function see Alvin Plantinga, *Warrant and Proper Function* (Oxford: Oxford University Press, 1993).
18. Two further points may help, both readily understood in relation to the apparent historical dependence (in some contexts) of the anti-suicide argument on the life-as-a-divine-gift argument. First, call argument (or proposition) *a, implicit* in the background of another argument, *b,* on an occasion of the presentation of *b,* when *a* is not articulated, but *b* as presented is based on at least one of the premises of *a* (or on *a* itself if *a* is a single proposition) as a ground, or would at least be taken to be so based by a reasonable interpreter in the context. Second, the genetic line need not go through the *speaker's* mind: it is enough if the argument as presented has a history that meets the condition of traceability to religious considerations. The relevant causal chain, moreover, can branch: a single argument offered on one occasion can trace back historically, as it can motivationally, to two or more sources that are causally or evidentially independent.
19. This point underlies my stress, in this and later chapters, on my principles' setting out prima facie oughts (and even then only for advocacy in certain contexts) and not restrictions of rights.

4. Religious Convictions and Secular Reasons

1. A good case for a view of this sort is made by Nicholas Wolterstorff in his contributions to Robert Audi and Nicholas Wolterstorff, *Religion and the Public Square: The Place of Religious Convictions in Political Debate* (Lanham, MD: Rowman and Littlefield, 1997). Kent Greenawalt's position is less permissive, but is a good foil for both mine and Wolterstorff's. Greenawalt's *Private Consciences and Public Reasons* (Oxford: Oxford University Press, 1995) contains much explication of the rationale for a range of positions on this issue before us.
2. Calling the kinds of obligations in question *religious* is not meant to presuppose the truth of theism. If it is objected that apart from God's existence there are no religious obligations (at least for those who conceive them as ordained by God), we could simply speak of *presumptively religious* obligations, referring to the kind reasonably taken to be incumbent on votaries of a particular religion as such, and proceed: the kinds of church-state issues under discussion would be largely unaffected.
3. It is interesting to note that Paul J. Weithman, in discussing John Courtney Murray, suggests that Murray may have held a view implying that one *cannot* violate an obligation so long as one is acting within one's rights: "If

someone has a moral right to do something, then she violates no obligation by doing it." See "The Privatization of Religion," *Journal of Religious Ethics* 22 (1994), p. 15. Weithman does not himself note the possibility that concerns me here – a possibility illustrated by, say, a case in which an instructor has a right to criticize a student for certain errors but ought not to do so because under the circumstances it is better to leave the matter to a colleague closer to the student.

4. I do not say '*an* adequate secular reason'; we should leave open the possibility of a set of reasons for a position or action that are each short of adequacy but that might together give one overall reason. In some cases they might be drawn together into a single reason, but doing this is not strictly necessary for having adequate reason – a point that applies in non-normative matters as well as here. Requiring such unification of one's several grounds would make my principle more restrictive.
5. See Robert Audi, "The Separation of Church and State and the Obligations of Citizenship," *Philosophy & Public Affairs* 18, 3 (1989), pp. 259–96. The principle applies with different degrees of force in different contexts. Moreover, the adequacy requirement rules out some *non*-religious reasons, e.g. those that are ill grounded; but my concern is with the specifically religious in relation to the political. I might add that the principle is not meant to require that an adequate reason be objectively correct in a sense implying that it is equivalent to a true proposition. A false proposition that is sufficiently well justified can count as an adequate reason. My paper just cited spoke of an adequate reason for something as one "whose truth is sufficient to justify" that, and at least one careful commentator on the paper has read this conjunctively rather than conditionally; i.e., as implying both truth and justificatory sufficiency, rather than (as intended) on the model of, e.g., "You need a witness whose testimony for your side is sufficient to sway those in doubt," which does not imply that either the witness or the testimony is actual. An alternative wording is 'a reason which, if it should be true, justifies . . .'. See Philip L. Quinn, "Political Liberalisms and Their Exclusions of the Religious," *Proceedings and Addresses of the American Philosophical Association* 69, 2 (1995), pp. 35–56, esp. 38–9.
6. It does not, e.g., imply the possibility of existing apart from divine creation. In case taking a reason to be evidentially independent of God seems somehow irreverent, note that the most famous arguments for the existence of God are supposed to have premises with just this status: if they did not, they would fail of their purpose, which is roughly to provide evidential ground for believing God exists, on the basis of considerations not dependent on one's already having that ground.
7. Moral skepticism is not easily refuted, but I have attacked some of its most plausible forms in "Skepticism in Theory and Practice: Justification and Truth, Rationality and Goodness," Ch. 3 of my *Moral Knowledge and Ethical Character* (Oxford: Oxford University Press, 1997). (A positive non-skeptical moral epistemology is developed in Chs. 2, 4, 5, and 11.)
8. For a recent treatment of public reason in contrast to what I call secular

reason, see John Rawls, "The Idea of Public Reason Revisited," *University of Chicago Law Review* 64 (1967). In commenting on my characterization of a secular reason he says, "This definition is ambiguous between secular reasons in the sense of a nonreligious comprehensive doctrine and in the sense of a purely political conception within the content of public reason" (n. 40). In fact my characterization cannot *mean* either of these but is broad enough to encompass both. Rawls is perhaps influenced here by his own neutralist determination to contrast the purely political with what would normally be called secular, even if it does embody a comprehensive concept of the good, and to argue that the latter kind of secular reason cannot in general be an adequate basis of coercion (he allows a major exception in a proviso which will be discussed in some detail in Chapter 6).

9. To be sure, probabilities and other complexities may enter in, as with fluoridation of water. But even here a poorly educated person might be able to see that, e.g., we are better off with fluoridation than without it. This point, in any case, is neutral with respect to differences between my view and alternative positions on the adequacy of sociopolitical reasons.
10. I offer a detailed account of the nature of testimony and the conditions under which it confers justification in "The Place of Testimony in the Fabric of Justification and Knowledge," *American Philosophical Quarterly* 34, 4 (1997), pp. 404–22.
11. Perhaps the most influential treatment of prima facie reasons is W. D. Ross's in *The Right and the Good* (Oxford: Oxford University Press, 1930). I discuss his conception in detail, clarify it, and bring out how knowledge of major moral principles can have a basis in secular reason in "Intuitionism, Pluralism, and the Foundations of Ethics," in my *Moral Knowledge*.
12. Kent Greenawalt has written instructively on this general topic, particularly the appropriate range of considerations for judges. See *Private Consciences and Public Reasons*, esp. pp. 141–50.
13. See Greenawalt's *Private Consciences and Public Reasons*, p. 67.
14. This objection is made by (among others) Jeff Jordan in attacking the principle of secular rationale. He says, e.g., "Despite the initial appeal of the idea that one should *couch public discourse* in terms of public reasons, there are at least two reasons to think that adopting the PSR [principle of secular rationale] is ill-advised . . . the PSR carries an unpalatable epistemic consequence . . . [and] would hinder political participation." See Jeff Jordan, "Religious Reasons and Public Reasons," *Public Affairs Quarterly* 11, 3 (1997), p. 248 (italics added). As noted in the text, the principle says nothing about the vocabulary in which public discourse is to be couched; it allows prudence to settle that. As to the epistemic consequence, Jordan claims "the PSR could mandate that one assert a secular and weak reason for a policy and ignore a religious, yet evidentiary [*sic*] stronger, reason for an incompatible policy" (p. 248). First, the requirement that one have and be willing to offer *adequate* secular reason should *not* lead one to assert a reason one takes to conflict with one that is evidentially stronger – nor does the principle even preclude there *being* religious reasons that are eviden-

tially cogent and indeed evidentially stronger than some secular reasons (Jordan's note 15 on p. 254 suggests he has not noticed this point in work of mine he cites). One should regard a reason as *inadequate* if it conflicts with what one considers an evidentially stronger one. Second, the objection again assumes the issue is what to say, as opposed to what kind of reason one should have for advocacy or support of laws and public policies.

15. This case is presented by Peter Smith, in "Civility as a Christian Virtue, Part One: Robert Audi's Rules of Secular Rationale and Motivation" (in preparation). He suggests that my view requires her "to vote against her conscience" since she should "vote yes or abstain" (p. 11).
16. Indeed, it is by no means self-evident, and I do not assume, that rationality always requires us even to fulfill a moral obligation on balance, in which case we would *not* have a moral right to do otherwise. This is too large an issue to pursue here.
17. It has been claimed otherwise, e.g., by Vern Sima, in a letter to the *Lincoln Journal-Star* (23 October 1993): "I belong to a church that teaches abortion is murder. I am open-minded enough to accept the church's unbounded wisdom. But what ultimately convinced me was scientific evidence and observation. What we have here is science confirming religious truths, not religious truths standing alone, even though that would be enough." I doubt this claim because, for one thing, I cannot see why one must be open-minded to accept what one conceives as "unbounded wisdom" or why, if one thinks that the church's view manifests it, one would not be convinced *before* discovering the scientific evidence. The question is especially urgent given that the writer says the religious truth "would be enough," apparently meaning that the church's view would be acceptable *without* scientific confirmation.

    Compare the claim that "There is no longer any serious scientific dispute that the unborn child is a human creature who dies violently in the act of abortion. This brute fact is the root of our national distress over the abortion license." See "The America We Seek: A Statement of Pro-Life Principle and Concern," signed by Michael Novak and Ralph Reed among dozens of others, *First Things* 63 (May 1996), p. 40. This statement treats the claim following 'dispute' as scientific. But if being a child entails, as it ordinarily does, being a person, or if being a creature entails being created by God, then the claim is apparently not scientific but theological or philosophical or both. If, on the other hand, a creature is just a living thing, and a child is a genetically human entity in *any* stage of development from that of zygote on, then the supposed brute fact does not appear to sustain the anti-abortion conclusions it is used to support (a matter discussed in Chapter 7). We might ponder the question whether so many conscientious people would let this kind of ambiguity go unremarked apart from religious motivation to establish their conclusion regarding abortion. And might the attempt to establish that conclusion scientifically bespeak a sense that a secular rationale is needed for justified coercion and perhaps that secular motivation is needed for the conscientious imposition of that coercion?

18. Not just any anti-religious motivation would fail to count as secular, e.g. where the desire is simply to weaken a religious group enough to prevent its dominating a society. But for purposes of taking the motivation principle to be an element in civic virtue, it is reasonable to construe a desire to destroy a religion or to discredit its deity as non-secular.
19. The accrediting may take account of certain factors that are not purely academic. It is one thing to give vouchers to support free parental choice, including religious choice; it is another to allow them where racial discrimination is practiced. It is a difficult question when criteria of admission are objectionable in a way that warrants differential governmental treatment.
20. The government in the Netherlands funds both public and sectarian schools, compensating, in part, for any advantages this gives to the latter over the former by requiring national examinations keyed to a core curriculum constituting 80 percent of what students study in the secondary school years. For a brief description of the system see the article by Laurel Shaper Walters in the *Christian Science Monitor* for 12 December 1992.
21. One may wonder how a religious person who seeks to do everything in fulfillment of God's will can abide by the principle of secular motivation. It would seem that such a person can without irreverence be motivated by the sense of just conduct as dictated by the dignity of persons, at least if the property of being thus dictated is equivalent to the property of being commanded by God. The same point surely holds where the person justifiedly *believes* this equivalence to hold (and perhaps even in certain cases in which the belief is not justified). Even if, in addition, such a person is not sufficiently motivated by any secular consideration *without* thinking of it as religiously acceptable, on a liberal reading of the principle of secular motivation – more liberal than I gave it in "Separation of Church and State" – the person can still be sufficiently motivated by that consideration. If the person is motivated by the consideration and not just by the thought that God commands the action it supports, this would be a case of being motivated *by a secular consideration,* without being (purely) *secularly motivated.* It would not be a pure instance of *civic* virtue (a notion explored in Chapter 6), since the motivation in question depends on the belief that the consideration in question is religiously acceptable, but this consideration would at least not be a mere rationalization and would, in addition, be a candidate to satisfy the principle of secular rationale. I am not here endorsing the suggested liberal reading of the principle of secular motivation, but as stated the principle can bear that reading.
22. Accessibility in the relevant sense is no simple matter: ordinary sensory data of the kind needed to use a ruler or a gauge are clearly accessible, and a clairvoyant sense of the future is clearly not. But it might be argued that anyone who is open-minded, considers natural theology, and attends certain religious services in a good-faith effort to find God thereby has access to good theistic reasons for a certain view of the world. Many people who reluctantly or ambivalently leave their faith would claim to be counterex-

amples to this; but even if that judgment is accepted, the notion of accessibility is not precise and will remain controversial.

23. Such a position does not imply that these propositions are necessarily true simpliciter but that it is impossible that they be *both* endorsed or accepted by God and false. Thus, one may presumably be as certain of their truth as one is that they are divinely endorsed or accepted. For many people this is a very high degree of certainty.
24. Stephen Carter vividly voices a related point: "I have always been deeply offended by politicians, whether on the left or on the right, who are ready to seize on the language and symbols of religion in order to grub for votes." *The Culture of Disbelief* (New York: Anchor Books, 1994), p. 47.
25. I should add that to Unitarianism – particularly the more common nontheistic forms – my points concerning what is special about religious reasons apply far less than to many other religions. There may indeed be forms of Unitarianism and other broadly religious outlooks that are not plausibly considered religions – though they would be *religious,* in the sense John Dewey noted, in which appropriate attitudes, e.g. of reverence, can mark a perspective as religious even if it is not part of *a religion.* Dewey's distinctions among the notions of religion, the religious, and *a* religion is a major topic of definition that I cannot address directly in this book.
26. In "Acting from Virtue," in *Moral Knowledge,* I provide an account of such action which supports the conception of it employed here.
27. The determination of evidential adequacy is also a difficult matter, but is not peculiar to my position on religion and politics: any plausible political philosophy must employ some such notion. It is perhaps some help to say that standard deductive and inductive logic are highly relevant, as is whatever logic of moral discourse there may be that goes beyond them.
28. A number of recent writers have commented on this, including Carter, *Culture of Disbelief;* and Quinn, "Political Liberalisms." For discussion of the putative "marginalization" and "privatization" of religion in the United States, see Theodore Y. Blumoff, "The New Religionists' Social Gospel: On the Rhetoric and Reality of Religions' 'Marginalization' in Public Life," forthcoming.
29. Here one can be conscientiously mistaken: one can falsely but excusably believe a reason to be secular.
30. Paul J. Weithman, in "The Separation of Church and State: Some Questions for Professor Audi," *Philosophy & Public Affairs* 20, 1 (1991), pp. 62–5, and others have questioned how feasible it is to try to follow the principle of secular rationale. See also Lawrence B. Solum, "Faith and Justice," *DePaul Law Review* 39, 4 (1990), pp. 1083–1106, esp. 1089–92. Also relevant is Weithman's "Rawlsian Liberalism and the Privatization of Religion: Three Theological Objections Considered," *Journal of Religious Ethics* 22, 1 (1994), pp. 3–28. The above is only the beginning of a reply to such worries. For another pertinent discussion see Jonathan Jacobs, "Theism and Moral Objectivity," *American Catholic Philosophical Quarterly* 66, 4 (1992); and for more recent discussion of related issues by Weithman see his valu-

able collection, *Religion and Contemporary Liberalism* (Notre Dame: University of Notre Dame Press, 1997). Some of the authors represented are discussed or cited elsewhere in this book. Regarding the others, the papers by John A. Coleman, S.J. (pp. 264–90), J. L. A. Garcia (pp. 218–53), and Sanford Levinson (pp. 76–92) are pertinent to this chapter, and Martha Nussbaum's "Religion and Women's Human Rights" (pp. 93–137) is particularly relevant to Chapter 7.

31. One might think that a person must have *some* motivating reason for any belief or action. But this is not so, if we distinguish reasons from causes or, more subtly, *reasons for which* one believes or acts from mere (explanatory) *reasons why* one does: wishful thinking is a non-rational source of beliefs, and actions not performed intentionally need not be done for a reason, as where one quite unwittingly offends someone.
32. This result is suggested to be implicit in my view in Quinn's "Political Liberalisms," p. 36.
33. Cf. Wolterstorff's remark that "there is an eminently honorable reason for discrepancy between the reason one offers in public discussion for a certain policy, and one's own reason for accepting that policy; namely, one wants to persuade one's discussion partner to accept the policy, and one knows or suspects that different reasons will attract her," though "if I say or suggest that my reason was such-and-such, when in fact it was not, that would be dissembling." *Religion in the Public Square,* pp. 106–7.
34. A reason offered in leveraging may *be* evidentially good; but in leveraging one is not offering it as such, but *relative* to the point of view one is in a sense taking. Detailed discussion of leveraging and of the question of the need for sincerity in giving reasons is found in my "The Ethics of Advocacy," *Legal Theory* 1 (1995).
35. I have defended this point about manipulation in "Ethics of Advocacy" and in "Separation of Church and State."
36. Wolterstorff, *Religion in the Public Square,* p. 109.
37. There are many issues here. Some are discussed above, and Kent Greenawalt discusses the issues in both *Religious Convictions and Political Choice* (Oxford: Oxford University Press, 1988) and *Private Consciences and Public Reasons.*
38. The notion of neutrality is also informatively discussed by Rawls, "Idea of Public Reasons," and Carter, *Culture of Disbelief.* See also Robert van Wyk, "Liberalism, Religion, and Politics," *Public Affairs Quarterly* 1, 3 (1987), pp. 59–76, and "Liberalism, Religion, and Politics Again: A Reply to Gordon Graham," *Journal of Social Philosophy* 25, 3 (1994), pp. 153–64. (Some of van Wyk's criticism of my view is at least implicitly answered in this chapter.)
39. The Declaration of Independence is one famous document supporting liberal democracy that seems to imply otherwise; but I am not certain that it must be so read, nor do I take it to be as authoritative on this matter as the work of, say, John Stuart Mill.
40. This point (among many others relevant to this chapter) is brought out by Greenawalt in *Private Consciences and Public Reasons.*

5. Religion and Ethics: Toward Integration

1. Perhaps those with resources giving all they have to the poor is an example pertinent in this context, though the force of Jesus's directive is open to more than one interpretation.
2. This formulation applies both to *types* of conduct (the more problematic case) and their *tokenings,* the specific performances of those types by an agent at a time. A particular person's obligation to *A* – say to give money to a particular church-supported cause – could, at a specific moment, be grounded in secular considerations, such as the effectiveness of its famine relief, even if the primary grounds of *the* obligation to *A* (for virtually all who have it) are religious. Then, the specific act token – donating a sum in writing a particular check – might be at least in part secularly grounded even though the same person might have written a similar check a week earlier entirely for a religious reason. Deeds of the same action type, such as donations to a church or synagogue, may be performed (tokened) at different times for different reasons, or different combinations of reasons, among the reasons there are for deeds of that type. When agent, time, and circumstance are fixed, there may, for a token of a religiously obligatory deed, be only a secular reason or only a religious reason or a happy marriage of the two.
3. Such an entailment may hold for some propositions, but apparently not for *every* proposition supported by a source. This is by no means beyond controversy; certainly scripture, religious authority, and tradition tend to overlap in regard to the obligations that they imply are incumbent on believers. But my purposes here are compatible with the existence of exceptions to the independence claim.
4. Jesus says, e.g., that the *greatest* commandments are to love one's God with all one's heart and to love one's neighbor as oneself; and given how the Ten Commandments are ordered and expressed by Moses, together with their role in the Hebrew Bible in general, there is some reason to think the order of their presentation may indicate a kind of relative importance.
5. For a detailed and authoritative case for the relevance of the sciences to theological understanding, see James M. Gustafson, *Ethics from a Theocentric Perspective,* Vol. 1 (Chicago: University of Chicago Press, 1981).
6. It is useful to compare John Rawls's notion of public reason in this context. The notion seems narrower than that of a secular reason, but usable for some of the same purposes. See his *Political Liberalism* (New York: Columbia University Press, 1993), esp. pp. 212–54. Some of my case for constraints on the use of religious reasons applies also to certain secular reasons, especially those that (like certain esoteric reasons) cannot play a proper role in public policy debate in a liberal democracy. They might, e.g., fail to be (justificationally) adequate.
7. The notion of fallibilism here may raise the question of the appropriate attitude for those who believe in papal infallibility. It should be noted that this doctrine is restricted both as to content, covering above all moral mat-

ters, and as to manner of expression: it applies only to pronouncements *ex cathedra*. Since there can be vagueness on both counts, a measure of fallibilism may be appropriate concerning any *interpretation* of just what is regarded as infallible. My concern here is also with quite specific sociopolitical matters; and on these even people who give authority an enormous role in their lives may wish to be fallibilistic regarding their own judgments of what they should do *as citizens*. Consider a statement by Mario M. Cuomo, then governor of New York: "My church and my conscience require me to believe certain things about divorce, birth control and abortion. My church does not order me . . . to pursue my Salvific Mission according to a precisely defined political plan." See "Religious Belief and Public Morality," *Notre Dame Journal of Ethics and Public Policy*, Vol. 1 (1984), p. 21.

8. A weaker condition would require only the capacity to understand the grounds, but I doubt that this condition is sufficiently strong. Actual identification, however, is not required; since we are not talking about ideally rational citizens, such things as confusion or prejudice can interfere.
9. This is a partial reply to Michael J. Perry's contention against John Rawls and me (and implicitly against the liberal tradition in political philosophy as expressed in, e.g., John Stuart Mill's *On Liberty*) that it is not clear why we fail to show the respect due to other people as free and equal citizens when we offer them, in explaining a coercive law, what we take to be our best reasons for it (so long as we do not imply their inferior humanity). Michael J. Perry, *Religion in Politics: Constitutional and Moral Perspectives* (Oxford: Oxford University Press, 1997), Ch. 2. My suggestion is that even one's best reasons can be unsound or partisan or even bigoted. Cf. T. M. Scanlon's contractarian approach to understanding this issue in "Contractarianism and Utilitarianism," in Amartya Sen and Bernard Williams, eds., *Utilitarianism and Beyond* (Cambridge University Press, 1982).
10. I use 'standard Western theism' with some hesitation. The idea may be in part a philosophers' construction, but there is a recognizable set of assumptions here. What follows will clarify the idea.
11. It would not be unqualifiedly impossible, since one might be moral from good fortune rather than from application of one's moral knowledge. I assume, what all but a few radical theists grant, that even if rejection of God can be a moral wrong, it is not the only kind of moral wrong, nor does it make all the others insignificant.
12. More than one philosopher has raised the question how these points might square with an Augustinian theology for which, without grace, our reason is too corrupt to discover basic moral truths. This question is treated in some detail later in this chapter. For a perspective on evil, divine grace, and the fall that provides some contrast to the corruptedness view, see Marilyn M. Adams, "The Problem of Hell: A Problem of Evil for Christians," in Eleonore Stump, ed., *Reasoned Faith* (Ithaca: Cornell University Press, 1993).
13. In Chapter 1 I referred to the intuitionism of W. D. Ross and to some detailed development and defense of it in my *Moral Knowledge and Ethical*

Character (Oxford: Oxford University Press, 1997). There are many other ethical positions one might take to deserve rational assent on reflection, or together with empirical information, and I believe that there is considerable concurrence among the most plausible of them.

14. For noncognitivists, who reject the view that moral principles are properly considered true or false, the considerations in this paragraph, like other considerations in this book that I take to support the truth of normative principles, can be considered to provide a kind of rational support for approval of the relevant principles as opposed to their truth.
15. If natural properties include theological ones, e.g. being commanded by God, then the case for the existence of secular grounds for moral truths becomes more problematic. But the relevant properties of God (as opposed to, say, divine power) are not usually considered natural. Moreover, if they are natural, it may be that moral properties could supervene on them *by virtue of* supervening more basically on other, "earthly" natural ones: God might, e.g., command honesty because of what it is to be honest as opposed to deceitful, i.e., because of the (ontically) constitutive natural properties of honesty. Thus the obligatoriness of honesty would supervene directly on its divine requiredness, which would in turn supervene on its divinely judged appropriateness to relations among persons. Call this the *embeddedness* of natural base properties in theological properties (it can take various forms, which I cannot distinguish here). Alternatively, one might say simply that God commands honesty because it is necessarily right (or good or both). On this view, God infallibly sees the rightness of honesty, presumably through comprehending its natural basis (a basis itself created by God, to be sure), as opposed to determining what that basis is by sheer will, in a sense implying that, e.g., lying and murder could have been right. This alternative line of thought may be the more plausible conception of divine moral commands and would be consistent with honesty's supervening on natural properties apart from embeddedness.
16. What does commonly happen is that we cannot be sure what our obligations *on balance* are even when we know, from natural facts, what our prima facie obligations are. The secularly based moral map is thus limited – a point crucial for Kent Greenawalt, who argues that (as I would put it) where there is an appropriate kind of secular indeterminacy on certain moral issues individuals may properly rely, even in the political domain, on religious considerations to decide their conduct, including voting. See *Religious Convictions and Political Choice* (Oxford: Oxford University Press, 1988) (to be discussed on this point in the next chapter). I would stress that there may be similar problems in the religious domain, e.g. where two prima facie commandments in the Decalogue conflict. For critical discussion of Greenawalt's view in this book see my "Religion and the Ethics of Political Participation," *Ethics* 100, 2 (1990), pp. 386–97.
17. I do not consider here the possibility that there *are* no moral truths. This seems neither plausible nor accepted by the religious traditions of main concern in this book. As suggested in an earlier note, the noncognitivist

view of what I call moral truths could be accommodated by my perspective by taking what I consider grounds for true principles to be instead grounds for adopting the *attitudes* those principles require. The details of this accommodation would take us too far afield.

18. It would be only one aspect of the divine nature one would thus come to understand, but such understanding could be incalculably important and might facilitate understanding other dimensions of God. Cf. Lenn Goodman's view that "for monotheism goodness is constitutive in the idea of God" and that "Ethics is constitutive in framing our idea of God but does not exhaust its content, and theism is a source of moral resolve and sublimity of principle but far from being the sole source at which such values can be tapped. All human beings know a good deal about their obligations without turning to God." See *God of Abraham* (Oxford: Oxford University Press, 1996), pp. 81 and 83.
19. Depending on one's theology, this might apply to a secular ground for which there is no religious counterpart ground that supports the same normative conclusion, as well as to a religious ground that seems isolated from supporting secular considerations. On common theistic assumptions, however, if there is a cogent truth-entailing secular reason for a normative conclusion, then God believes that conclusion (like any other truth), and the absence of any specifically theological ground should not prevent one's acting on the conclusion. Note, too, that disequilibrium between theistic and secular elements is a stronger reason for reluctance than is mere lack of integration; my suggestion, however, is that a positive integration should, in major moral matters, be expected to be achievable. If, e.g., those who think on religious grounds (and perhaps other grounds) that abortion in the first trimester is killing a person cannot convince conscientious people whose morality they otherwise fully respect to accept the point, they should consider this a datum in disequilibrium with their theo-ethical view.
20. Stephen L. Carter criticizes Kent Greenawalt, Bruce Ackerman, John Rawls, and me on this score, suggesting that "religious citizens are forced to split off vital components of their personalities." See *The Culture of Disbelief* (New York: Anchor Books, 1994), p. 230. Here I reply from my point of view, but some of what I say might apply to the other positions, especially Greenawalt's in, e.g., *Private Consciences and Public Reasons* (Oxford: Oxford University Press, 1995), esp. Chs. 2–8. Cf. Cuomo, "Religious Belief and Public Morality."
21. A possible example is Timothy P. Jackson's agapistic liberalism (as I would call it). Holding that Christianity puts charity first as a reason for action, he says, "The Christian is enjoined to 'make love *your* aim' (1 Corinthians 14:1), not merely to make love *an* aim." See "Love in a Liberal Society: A Response to Paul J. Weithman," *Journal of Religious Ethics* 22, 1 (1994), pp. 29–38.
22. See, e.g., the two chapters on divine command ethics in R. M. Adams, *The Virtue of Faith* (Oxford: Oxford University Press, 1987). Adams notes the important difference between (in my terms) a *semantic* divine command

theory, which implausibly takes our everyday moral terms to have a theological meaning, and an *ontic* version, such as the one noted in the text, in which despite semantic difference the theological property of being divinely enjoined on us is identical with the moral property of being obligatory for us.

23. Jeff Jordan poses a similar objection: "there is a strong theistic tradition which holds that human reason, because of sin, is, thereby, an unreliable guide to the Good. Think of the Calvinistic doctrine of Total Depravity . . ." "Religious Reasons and Public Reasons," *Public Affairs Quarterly* 11, p. 254, n. 17.
24. Thus, Jordan claims that "Audi's contention [concerning the likelihood, on certain theological assumptions, of finding secular grounds for religiously grounded true moral principles] would have the effect of favoring some theologies over others if one is to participate in political matters" (ibid.). If so, this kind of different effect is compatible with a reasonable neutrality with respect to theological questions. A theology can make moral and even "scientific" (factual) claims, and there is no good ground for claiming that unreasonable positions in these matters have no bearing on assessing it, particularly in its bearing on sociopolitical life.
25. For an informative discussion of Thomistic natural law theory that confirms this (e.g. by countenancing self-evident moral principles), see Germain Griset, Joseph Boyle, and John Finnis, "Practical Principles, Moral Truth, and Ultimate Ends," *American Journal of Jurisprudence* (1987), pp. 99–151. For a contrasting perspective see Steven D. Smith, "Nonsense and Natural Law," *Southern California Interdisciplinary Law Journal* 4, 3 (1996), and "Natural Law and Contemporary Moral Thought," *American Journal of Jurisprudence* 42 (1999), pp. 299–330, a critical study of Robert P. George, ed., *Natural Law, Liberalism, and Morality* (1996).
26. Given the value of reflective equilibrium in general as a way to formulate, refine, and test normative standards, analogous equilibrium principles might be found that apply to non-religious people who have more than one source of presumptive obligation, such as a secular authority or extrasensory perception; but those cases do not carry the same presumption that equilibrium is achievable or confirmatory, and need not be explored here.
27. It is conceivable that abiding by the principle would be theologically impermissible for some churches. I would hope there are in fact few if any such cases; and given that the theo-ethical equilibrium can be properly sought even if theological considerations are given significant priority, the likelihood that a church must reject the principle is much reduced.
28. This point responds to an insightful remark of Jean Bethke Elshtain's, suggesting that I should do justice to the merits of disequilibrium.
29. These, among other points in this chapter, bear on the case made by Lawrence Alexander in "Liberalism, Religion, and the Unity of Epistemology," *San Diego Law Review* 30, 4 (1993), pp. 677–702, to the effect that liberalism tends to assume that the epistemic credentials of religious claims

are inferior to those of, say, scientific claims. Granted, many *liberals* do tend to assume this.

30. I do not take consentingly playing to entail *having consented* to play; and the analogy to the consent of the governed is intended. I am not even implying "tacit consent" if that entails some act of consent, as opposed to having certain dispositions and behaving in certain ways.
31. This holds even for a noncognitivist version of the autonomy view. Here one would speak of, e.g., justified moral attitudes rather than of moral knowledge or warranted moral belief. One might even think that ethics is autonomous in a sense and still be a skeptic: ethics has arguments independent of theology; they simply are not good enough, and hence there is no moral knowledge (or, for a stronger skeptic, even moral justification).
32. It might be objected that the same should hold for the evils themselves, or at least moral evils constituted by wrongdoing: that there must be a secular route to their elimination. Even if there is some plausibility in this conclusion, notice that it apparently *presupposes* that there is a secular route to moral principles or at least some kind of moral justification. Otherwise free agents would not be *overcoming* evil or responsibly *abstaining* from it, but at best luckily avoiding its commission.
33. Of course, on one traditional theistic outlook there is a weak sense in which every (contingent) truth is divine, since God is responsible for (at least) the truth of all contingent propositions, by virtue of knowingly realizing the possible world in which they hold. But we may still distinguish – and must to understand the problem of evil aright – between those truths God willingly ordains and those God merely permits, e.g. those describing evils that are necessary for a greater good.

6. Civic Virtue

1. I use 'citizen' to apply to both permanent legal aliens and citizens. I do not include illegal aliens, but take it that conscientious citizens, even if they favor deporting the former, should be at least humanely concerned with their well-being.
2. This may be controversial. It might be rejected, e.g., by G. E. M. Anscombe, at least in her celebrated "Modern Moral Philosophy," *Philosophy* 33 (1958), reprinted in Roger Crisp and Michael Slote, eds., *Virtue Ethics* (Oxford: Oxford University Press, 1997), pp. 26–44, which Crisp and Slote, in their introductory essay, describe as "having inaugurated the present revival of virtue ethics" (p. 3).
3. This section will draw on, but also extend, my "Acting from Virtue," in *Moral Knowledge and Ethical Character* (Oxford: Oxford University Press, 1997).
4. Cf. Philippa Foot's point about the virtue of practical wisdom: "the man who is wise does not merely know *how* to do good things such as looking after his children well, or strengthening someone in trouble, but must also want to do them." See "Virtues and Vices," in Crisp and Slote, *Virtue Ethics,*

p. 167. For discussions of many other pertinent aspects of virtue ethics see *Midwest Studies in Philosophy* 13 (1988), devoted to the topic of character and virtue. The studies by Robert C. Solomon, on love, and Gabriele Taylor, on envy and jealousy, are helpful investigations of specific virtues; the papers by Marcia Baron ("Remorse and Agent-Regret"), Amélie Rorty ("Virtues and Their Vicissitudes"), Nancy Sherman ("Common-Sense and Uncommon Virtue"), and James D. Wallace ("Ethics and the Craft Analogy") are among the helpful studies of more general aspects of virtue ethics.

5. My interest here is mainly in moral virtues, but much of what is said applies to intellectual and other virtues.
6. There are alternative views about how to determine targets, e.g. the functionalist position of Edmund L. Pincoffs in *Quandaries and Virtues* (Lawrence: University Press of Kansas, 1986). For critical discussion of this view see Alasdair MacIntyre, "*Sophrosune:* How a Virtue Can Become Socially Disruptive," *Midwest Studies in Philosophy* 13 (1988), pp. 1–11. MacIntyre argues that "Pincoffs' thesis about the virtues denies their teleological character. But on an Aristotelian account the only way in which a virtue such as *sophrosune* can be characterized adequately . . . is by relating it to the *telos,* both directly and through its relationship to *phronesis*" (p. 7). The sixfold scheme presented here is an effort to give a partial explication of this relation. For further discussion of virtue ethics in general and in particular of the teleological aspects of virtue, see William J. Prior, *Virtue and Knowledge* (London: Routledge, 1991).
7. Special problems are created by such groups as inwardly focused religious communities and certain military units, particularly in times of crisis or war. Here there may be explicit promises of obedience that make fidelity more far-reaching than it would otherwise be, and in extreme cases, such as war service, conduct that would ordinarily be required by one virtue, such as beneficence or compassion, may be prohibited by another, say fidelity to the war effort. The latter, however, should not be understood so as to license atrocities.
8. Two points are in order here. First, this formulation is intentionally vague, but should serve our purposes. Second, I do not think beliefs can carry all the motivation required; but for this chapter, as opposed to a full-scale analysis of traits, what is essential to the point is only that traits require both a cognitive and a motivational dimension. It is at least more perspicuous to separate these as I do in the text.
9. For helpful discussion pertinent to the bearing of virtue ethics on liberal democracy see Richard Flathman, *Reflections of a Would-Be Anarchist* (Minneapolis: University of Minnesota Press, 1998), esp. the section on "virtue liberalism," pp. 8–11.
10. There could be an appeal to an overarching principle, but it is unlikely to be thought to apply to action except via intuitive first-order principles. An account of this development of intuitionism is given in my *Intuition and Intrinsic Value,* in progress.

11. See W. D. Ross, *The Right and the Good* (Oxford: Oxford University Press: 1930), p. 21.
12. Ross himself thought that there is a prima facie duty to obey the law grounded partly in the duty of gratitude (to one's country), partly in the implicit promise to obey that goes with permanent residence, and, for countries with laws that are "instruments for the general good," partly in that fact. Ibid., pp. 27–8. For discussion of Ross's view and of the case for the duty to obey the law being a basic one, see M. B. E. Smith, "The Duty to Obey the Law," in D. Patterson, ed., *Companion to the Philosophy of Law* (Oxford: Basil Blackwell, 1996). A different perspective on the duty to obey the law is explored in relation to jury nullification (roughly, a jury's acquitting a defendant despite legal guilt) in Robert Schopp, "Verdicts of Conscience," *Southern California Law Review* 69 (1996), pp. 2039–2116. For more detailed discussion of this and related issues see Schopp's *Justification Defenses and Just Convictions* (Cambridge University Press, 1996).
13. For the main presentation of the two principles of justice see John Rawls, *A Theory of Justice* (Cambridge, MA: Harvard University Press, 1971); and for an account of public reason and its place in a liberal democracy see his *Political Liberalism* (New York: Columbia University Press, 1993), esp. Lecture VI.
14. Robert Nozick's *Anarchy, State, and Utopia* (New York: Basic Books, 1974), develops a partly historical conception of the basis of the state that is instructive in this context. It derives much from John Locke's *Two Treatises of Civil Government* (1689), especially the second. The influence of this work on the liberal-democratic tradition in Britain, the United States, and indeed at least the English-speaking world, is enormous, and some of its provisions are taken into account in the theory defended in this book.
15. I have defended it in, e.g., "Intrinsic Value and the Dignity of Persons," Ch. 11 in my *Moral Knowledge*. The approach of the latter has elements in common with both the universal standards and the pragmatic approaches.
16. In "Acting from Virtue," in *Moral Knowledge*, I present a detailed account of acting for one or more reasons that are connected in the relevant way with a virtue.
17. The notion in question is significantly similar to what Rawls, in *Political Liberalism*, describes under the heading of *public reason* and Greenawalt calls accessibility. See Kent Greenawalt, *Private Consciences and Public Reasons* (New York: Oxford University Press, 1995), esp. Ch. 3. For a proposal of some definite rules of civic virtue for public officials see Michael Davis, "Civic Virtue, Corruption, and the Structure of Moral Theories," *Midwest Studies in Philosophy* 13 (1988), esp. pp. 355–7.
18. On the value and appropriate character of such discussion and deliberation, see Amy Gutmann and Dennis Thompson, *Democracy and Disagreement* (Cambridge, MA: Harvard University Press, 1996); and Fred D'Agostino, *Free Public Reason* (Oxford: Oxford University Press, 1996). Cf. the discourse ethics of Jürgen Habermas; see, e.g., "Discourse Ethics: Notes on a Program of Philosophical Justification," in his *Moral Consciousness and Communicative*

Action, trans. Christian Lenhardt and Sheirry Weber Nicholsen (Cambridge, MA: MIT Press, 1990) (first published in Frankfurt, 1983).

19. Even where an act is excusable, the agent may be blameworthy for a related *previous* act. This seems clear where someone knowingly gets drunk and then stumbles unknowingly into the path of a car. But suppose I reject opportunities to consider the overall merits of a proposed law and for that reason cannot find or be motivated by any secular reason for it (though there are some); then, even if my supporting it for religious reasons alone may be excusable, I am criticizable on a related ground. Alternatively, we might say that I am not excusable for supporting it as I do, owing to the kind of reason for my inability to find an appropriate reason.
20. On accessibility and public reason see Rawls, *Political Liberalism;* Greenawalt, *Private Consciences and Public Reasons;* Thomas Nagel, *Equality and Partiality* (New York: Oxford University Press, 1991), and Charles Larmore, "Beyond Religion and Enlightenment," *San Diego Law Review* 30 (1993), pp. 799–815.
21. Rawls, *Political Liberalism*, p. 247.
22. There may be cases in which a reason is grounded in a comprehensive view *as a whole*, so that every proposition belonging to it is important for the adequacy of the reason. Such reasons are less likely to be of a kind that meets my standards of comprehensibility and secularity, but I do not think it impossible that one should do so.
23. See the Preface to the paperback edition of *Political Liberalism* (1996), pp. li–lii. Some further discussion of this proviso is given by Rawls in "The Idea of Public Reason Revisited," *University of Chicago Law Review* 64 (1967), esp. sec. 4. I do not believe it adequately treats the problems I raise here.
24. If we count as religious the significant number of theological noncognitivists who identify themselves as such, e.g. as Christian, there is further difficulty in understanding the normative force of religiously grounded reasons: since religious language is (roughly speaking) expressive, and not assertive of propositions, the authority of normative claims supposed to be grounded in divine command is at best problematic.
25. Our voice is, however, likely to be also determined *in part* by what we say, and other things equal a civic voice is not fully achieved if one is proposing religious reasons as grounds for public policy decisions. It may be possible, however, to present such reasons in a context that preserves a certain balance, e.g. by noting that, in addition to sufficient secular reasons for a piece of legislation such as permitting state aid to handicapped children in religious schools, many religious citizens will feel better able to provide for their children services they believe God requires. Thus, the emphasis on achieving a proper civic voice as part of civic virtue leads to no simple rule about the admissible content of advocacy of laws or public policies.
26. For a representative position on standards for coercion, see Richard S. Regan, S.J., who suggests "that legislation to enforce public morals, as a matter of prudence, should satisfy two principal conditions. First, such legisla-

tion should concern activities which cause serious harm to citizens and the community. Second, the legislation should enjoy broad support from citizens of different religious and ethical persuasions." See *Midwest Studies in Philosophy* 13 (1988), p. 346. The results of adopting this proposal would very often be the same as those of adopting mine; but the principles are very different. His embody weaker safeguards against a domination of the non-religious by the religious and even of some subset of religious groups by others. This is particularly so if the relevant notion of harm is not secular (in his paper, it seems not).

27. There are theoretical problems in the way of grounding a general prima facie obligation to obey the law of the kind associated with political obligation. For a detailed treatment of some of the major problems see A. John Simmons, *Moral Principles and Political Obligations* (Princeton: Princeton University Press, 1979).
28. There are kinds and degrees of alignment, and even cooperating motives can, in some cases, support divergent conduct; but these complexities need not be pursued here.
29. This phrase comes from the title of a book by Richard John Neuhaus, *The Naked Public Square* (Grand Rapids, MI: Eerdmans, 1986), which explores the relation between religion and democracy in contemporary America. Deeply concerned about the naked public square in the United States, he says, "When recognizable religion is excluded, the vacuum will be filled by *ersatz* religion, by religion bootlegged into public space under other names" (2d ed., p. 80).
30. Richard Rorty is an example. See the quotations and discussion in Philip Quinn, "Political Liberalisms and Their Exclusions of the Religious," *Proceedings and Addresses of the American Philosophical Association* 69, 2 (1995), esp. pp. 38–39.
31. See, e.g., Quinn, "Political Liberalisms"; and Jeff Jordan, "Religious Reasons and Public Reasons," *Public Affairs Quarterly* 11, 3 (1997). As Quinn notes in the paper cited, there are liberal positions that do call for this. He cites Richard Rorty as advocating the view Rorty called a Jeffersonian compromise: that religion be privatized and kept out of the public square. See Richard Rorty, "Religion as Conversation-Stopper" (a review of Stephen Carter's *The Culture of Disbelief), Common Knowledge* 3,1 (1994), p. 2.
32. See Rawls, *Political Liberalism* (1996), pp. li–lii. This passage is discussed in some detail in the previous section.
33. I hope that the points made in this paragraph, as well as others in this chapter, can be useful in reflection on how best to formulate ideals and recommendations in such official church publications as some published by the American Catholic Bishops.
34. A special exception regarding neutral behavior is advocacy, especially the *representative* kind appropriate to someone like an attorney officially taking the point of view of another, as opposed to the *subscriptive* kind of advocacy appropriate to individuals speaking for themselves in a letter to a newspaper. In such individual statements, clergy and others should not be uncrit-

ically taken to represent their respective institutions, nor should individuals playing the role of advocate for someone else be taken to be representing their own views. In "The Ethics of Advocacy," *Legal Theory* 1 (1995), pp. 1–31, I offer a theory of advocacy that supports the general position of this book on the nature of civic virtue.

7. Religious Conviction and Political Activism

1. Both rationales are dealt with in just war theory. A different and in many ways wider approach to justifying violence is given in my "On the Meaning and Justification of Violence," in Jerome A. Shaffer, ed., *Violence* (New York: David McKay, 1971), and "Violence, Legal Sanctions, and Law Enforcement," in Sherman M. Stanage, ed., *Reason and Violence: Philosophical Investigations* (Totowa, NJ: Littlefield, Adams, 1974).
2. There are some unclarities about what, biologically, constitutes the point (e.g. conception) at which a human life as such begins. Moreover, if pregnancy is understood technically, it occurs only at implantation of the fertilized egg and thus later than conception, taken to occur upon fertilization of the ovum. A large proportion of fertilized ova never reach implantation. For a minimally technical discussion of some of the details concerning the sequence here and the term 'conception', see the National Institutes of Health Report of the Human Embryo Research Panel, chaired by Steven Muller (27 September 1994).
3. Much literature and ordinary parlance concerning abortion is remarkably insensitive to (or at least free of critical consideration of) the presuppositions of the term 'unborn child'. An interesting case in point is John Finnis, "Abortion, Natural Law, and Public Reason," delivered to the American Political Science Association in a panel on Natural Law, Liberalism, and Public Reason (Washington, DC, August 1997).
4. An important reason for noting that the physician need not disbelieve this, and may even believe it, is that under the doctrine of double effect even Roman Catholic physicians may sometimes abort a pregnancy. If, e.g., an appendectomy is needed to save the pregnant woman's life, then if the physician does it in order to save her life, but with the belief that doing the procedure will have the unfortunate effect of killing an innocent child, the physician may still do the surgery. From the perspective of double effect, the killing is done consentingly but not intentionally (and is certainly not intended).
5. There is more to be said here than I can take time to discuss. Suppose Nazis or slave owners claim to believe their victims or slaves are not persons. One possibility is rationalization or self-deception or both – and in either case such people can be so lacking in moral decency in the matter that violent resistance may be warranted. The point that an action is not murder is not meant to imply that it is not an outrage. We should also consider, however, what positive criteria Nazis and slave owners of the kind in question used for identifying people in general. Would not a slave owner, e.g., have

thought one lied or spoke falsely if, in answer to "How many people were in the wagon you just passed through the check point?" one said "Two" when there were two non-slaves and two escaping slaves?

6. John T. Noonan appeals to a version of this argument in "An Almost Absolute Value in History," in John T. Noonan, ed., *The Morality of Abortion: Legal and Historical Perspectives* (Cambridge, MA: Harvard University Press, 1970).
7. This is suggested by elements in Noonan, "Almost Absolute Value," but, in implicit forms, is pervasive in the English-language media. The common phrase 'in the womb' is not essential here; proponents of the argument might also be happy to say, e.g., 'in the mother's body' (which would allow for personhood before implantation).
8. This argument is more often criticized than defended, but it is surely influential. It is apparently operative whenever people say, in giving a premise for fetal personhood, such things as "I don't see how you can draw a line." This wedge argument is of course not equivalent to the wedge argument to the effect that once we countenance abortions we will start practicing infanticide, since there is no clear line at which we must stop. Birth could more easily be taken to create a clear line in that case.
9. The ensoulment argument is one to which Roman Catholic theology has apparently long been committed (Aquinas posited ensoulment, though interestingly he placed it much later than at conception).
10. This is not to say there *cannot* be a plausible philosophical basis for an atheistic ensoulment view of persons, but there is no need here to explore its prospects.
11. The priority does not imply that just any right of a person is stronger than *every* right of a potential person, such as its right not to be killed. The relative strengths are a complicated matter.
12. It may be objected that it is an oak tree in an early stage of its development. If this is so, however, then to be an *F* in an early stage of its development apparently does not imply being an *F* – for surely the implanted germinating acorn is not a tree. It may naturally *grow into a tree*, and a tree may come from it; but it is not one now. It would be wrong to say one has an oak tree in the garden when one has only that acorn; even saying one has *planted* one is at best misleading, since it indicates planting a sapling or other actual tree. One can insist that the implanted, germinating acorn is an early-stage oak tree; but if this view can be sustained, the sense of 'oak tree' in question is surely insufficient to imply the importance of oak trees in the normal sense. The analogue in the case of conception – the early-stage person – would then not have to be taken to have all the rights of a person, or at least rights of the same strength. It will have some, but the matter is eminently contestable – in a way that supports my conclusion about the capacity of the genetic argument to sustain the charge that rejecting it implies a kind of moral guilt.
13. Don Marquis, e.g., talks as though (despite long-standing legal practices to this effect) there is not even a prima facie case to be made for birth as nor-

mally a dividing line: "Personhood, theories . . . cannot straightforwardly account for the wrongness of killing infants and young children." See Don Marquis, "Why Abortion Is Immoral," *Journal of Philosophy* 86, 4 (1989), p. 192 (his point is not that birth is not a straightforward notion). I do not ignore the possibility of rejecting *both* conception and birth as points at which personhood is first instantiated. One might argue for some intermediate criterion, such as quickening or some point of strong resemblance in form or function or both between fetus and normal newborn. Such intermediate criteria might or might not be theological, as with taking quickening as a sign that ensoulment has just occurred. These intermediate criteria are scarcely less controversial than conception. I cannot discuss them here, but some of the points to be made on the moral status of abortion will hold both for them and for, say, the conception criterion.

14. For a list of some different proposed times of ensoulment, see H. Tristram Engelhardt, "The Ontology of Abortion," *Ethics* 84 (1974), pp. 217–34, reprinted in Samuel Gorovitz et al., eds., *Moral Problems in Medicine* (Englewood Cliffs, NJ: Prentice-Hall, 1976). In this context one might ponder Genesis 2:7, where God "breathed into his nostrils the breath of life; and man became a living being." This is sometimes read as suggesting that life begins with our initial (independent) breathing, in which case live birth would normally be the crucial point (and a period before breathing is possible would not even be a candidate).
15. I thus find puzzling J. Budziszewski's stark alternatives: "if abortion kills a baby then it ought to be banned to everyone; why allow it? But if it doesn't kill a baby it is hard to see why we should be uneasy about it at all; why restrict it?" See "The Revenge of Conscience," *First Things* 84 (June/July, 1998), p. 23.
16. It would be claimed by many to be inadmissible because the abortion is a means to protecting the woman's mental health. It surely is so intended here; but the issue seems to be when one *does* something as a means rather than producing it as an effect consented to, since the underlying moral point is apparently that one must not aim at evil. Some might argue that just as the appendectomy causes the abortion, the adoption of the plan to protect one's patient's health is what causes it (via one's agency, to be sure).
17. I have of course not considered all the plausible arguments against the moral permissibility of abortion and do not mean to suggest that all of them imply, or must depend on assuming, personhood of the fetus or conceptus. For valuable discussion of much literature on the problem and a case for the immorality of abortion, see Marquis, "Why Abortion Is Immoral." He holds that "what makes killing *any* adult human being prima facie seriously wrong is the loss of his or her future" (p. 190), and that "the primary wrong-making feature of killing is the loss to the victim of the value of its future . . . The future of a standard fetus includes a series of experiences, projects, activities, and such which are identical with the futures of adult human beings" (p. 192). We may wonder whether this argument really is independent of personhood: if a future experience is *mine,* I am (identical

with) the person whose experience it is, and I can look back to a time when *I* had not had it, even into (at least) early childhood. If the sense in which a future experience is *a fetus's* (is "its experience") is appropriate to give it moral status, it appears that continuity of personal identity is similarly presupposed; i.e., there seems to be a presupposition of the existence of the same person at the fetus stage of the person's history and at the time when the future experiences of the fetus are uncontroversially those of a person. A quite different question concerns the plausibility of the moral principle even assuming personhood is not presupposed: why isn't it worse to kill a younger than an older person in proportion to the (often vast) differences in the values of their futures? Given these and other difficulties for Marquis's account, we may at least conclude that it leaves room for reasonable disagreement on the main question of moral permissibility. For developments of Marquis's position and further discussion of abortion, see his "Why Most Abortions Are Immoral," *Advances in Bioethics* 5 (JAI Press, 1999), pp. 215–44.

18. I mention a tendency to believe because the closer one comes to believing a thing one intends to kill is a person the closer one can come to intending to murder. In the typical cases, of course, the physician strongly *dis*believes the conceptus or fetus is a person.
19. This is how Kent Greenawalt tends to see the issue in *Religious Convictions and Political Choice* (Oxford: Oxford University Press, 1988). For a sketch of his positive theory in that book and some critical discussion of its approach, see my "Religion and the Ethics of Political Participation," *Ethics* 100 (1990), pp. 386–97. I leave aside the difficult question of exactly how to characterize the relevant kind of accessibility.
20. Kent Greenawalt and John Rawls emphasize the special responsibility of the judiciary to use accessible secular standards. A contrasting view is defended by Michael J. Perry in *Religion in Politics: Constitutional and Moral Perspectives* (Oxford: Oxford University Press, 1997). My position does not require construing the need for an appropriate secular basis to be any greater in the case of judges than in that of juries.
21. For some key elements in the case for neutrality see Thomas Nagel, *Equality and Partiality* (Oxford: Oxford University Press, 1991), and Charles Larmore's contribution to the *San Diego Law Review* 30 (1993). The right, within a free democracy, to be judged by one's peers is at least political, but it may be a moral right as well depending on the extent to which this aspect of a free democracy is morally grounded. A contrasting view of neutrality is developed by Nicholas Wolterstorff in his contribution to Robert Audi and Nicholas Wolterstorff, *Religion in the Public Square* (Lanham, MD: Rowan and Littlefield, 1997). For an attack on the very idea of state neutrality, see J. Budziszewski, *True Tolerance: Liberalism and the Necessity of Judgment* (New Brunswick, NJ: Transaction Publishers, 1992), and (for a shorter statement) "The Illusion of Moral Neutrality," *First Things* 35 (August/September 1993), pp. 32–7. Insofar as Budziszewski is arguing that a liberal state is not

morally neutral, I agree; but I do not take the kind of neutrality I call for in Chapter 1 to be beyond its reach, as he apparently believes.

22. One might think that if there is such a right, then the obligation expressed in the principle of secular rationale cannot be only prima facie. That is not so; for one thing, the right would not be absolute. For another, we are talking here not just about law and public policy but about laws whose violation is a crime.
23. See Greenawalt, *Religious Convictions and Political Choice,* p. 12. This view is refined and defended in Greenawalt's later work, especially *Private Consciences and Public Reasons* (Oxford: Oxford University Press, 1995), but the kinds of comments I make here should not be substantially affected by his further work on the topic. Some of the points I make below are extended or given a wider context in "Religion and the Ethics of Political Participation," *Ethics* 100, 2 (1990).
24. I leave aside violence to property, such as homes and libraries, but for important property a similar principle apparently applies.
25. In case it seems that all violence is prima facie wrong, recall certain athletic and affectional cases. If these are viewed as involving a prima facie wrong that is obviously outweighed, they are at least not normally cases in which issues of religious versus secular reasons are pertinent.

Conclusion: Ethics, Reason, and Democracy

1. Richard John Neuhaus, *The Naked Public Square* (Grand Rapids, MI: Eerdmans, 1986); and J. Budziszewski, *True Tolerance* (New Brunswick, NJ: Transaction Publishers, 1992) are good sources for such criticism, especially as focused on the United States.
2. The normative position I favor for this purpose is a Kantian intuitionism, a view developed in my *Intuition and Intrinsic Value,* in progress.
3. That there can be such a theory is argued in my *A Theory of Rationality,* in progress.
4. In Ch. 11 of *Moral Knowledge and Ethical Character* (Oxford: Oxford University Press, 1997) I have argued that intrinsic value is basically realized in individuals, and that this has profound implications for the nature and content of moral obligation. I do not presuppose that in this book, but if it is true it strongly supports my (moderate) version of individualism.

INDEX